# THE SEARCH FOR
# HISTORICAL MEANING

# THE SEARCH FOR HISTORICAL MEANING

*Hegel and the Postwar American Right*

PAUL
EDWARD
GOTTFRIED

NORTHERN ILLINOIS UNIVERSITY PRESS

DEKALB, ILLINOIS

1986

Copyright © 1986 by the
Northern Illinois University Press
Published by the
Northern Illinois University Press,
DeKalb, Illinois 60115–2854
Manufactured in the
United States of America
All rights reserved
Designed by Jo Aerne

Library of Congress
Cataloging in Publication Data
Gottfried, Paul.
The search for historical meaning.
Bibliography: p.
Includes index.
1. Conservatism—United States—
History—20th century.
2. United States—Intellectual life—20th century.
3. Hegel, Georg Wilhelm Friedrich, 1770–1831.
4. United States—Politics and government—1945–
I. Title. E743.G66 1986 148 86–5279
ISBN 0-87580-114-5

# CONTENTS

# PREFACE

THANKS ARE DUE, FIRST TO MY WIFE, DANA, WHO KEPT THE YOUNGER kids from ransacking my drawers. Her attentive eye and shrewd application of discipline prevented this book from being lost to me as well as to posterity. I would like to acknowledge Professor Claes Ryn of Catholic University, Professor Lee Congdon of James Madison University, and, above all, Aileen Kraditor, Professor Emerita, Boston University, for critically reading the entire manuscript. Through my exchanges with these able scholars, I was forced to reconsider and, in some cases, led to qualify controversial findings. Needless to say, ultimate responsibility for the views here expressed are mine.

Of those who commented on different parts of the first draft, mention should be made of Professors Peter Stanlis, John Lukacs, John Diggins, Clyde N. Wilson, Reney Myers, and the late Dr. David Collier. I am also grateful to both the Guggenheim and Earhart Foundations, which funded the respite needed to write this work. To Rockford College, particularly Dean Gordon Wesner, I wish to express thanks for the thoughtful grants that paid for the preparation of my manuscript. Money from these grants went to a superlative typist, Miss Jean Avery, who is also responsible for most of the bibliography and index. Miss Avery and the Northern Illinois University Press managed to turn what began as chicken scrawl into a legible and attractive book.

Last, I am expressing my debt to a young midwestern publisher who, in responding to an inquiry about the marketability of my projected study on Hegel and the American Right, judged the undertaking to be worthless. According to this publisher, treating Hegel as a serious or significant thinker for the twentieth century would put me "outside the mainstream of modern philosophy." Even more to the point: "It does not help to simply ignore the fact that most philosophers consider Hegel wrong, silly, or even dangerous." Although the publisher claimed to have the resources necessary to publish the book I intended to write, he felt morally bound to discourage my project. Part of my study would deal with a bogus philosopher whom Karl Popper, in *The Open Society and Its Enemies,* had considered both a progenitor of Communism and Nazism and the enemy of true scientific method. The rest of my study would be devoted to tracing Hegel's putative influence on thinkers the publisher professed to admire—and whom he did not want to associate with the wicked Hegel.

I decided to continue my research, struck by the dogmatic, vehement tone of these remarks. If my hunches were correct, as I believed they were, the revisionist scholarship that I was undertaking was bound to be noticed. It would also serve a therapeutic function, even if it placed me outside someone's mainstream. This book developed at least partly as the unintended result of a tirade for which I am now actually grateful. Although I do not consider myself a Hegelian, I have tried to demonstrate that Hegel was a significant thinker who influenced serious modern intellectuals.

# INTRODUCTION

THE FOLLOWING BOOK CONSISTS MOSTLY BUT NOT ENTIRELY OF reflections on a single theme: the influence of Hegelian thinking on intellectuals who played recognized and critical roles in the postwar conservative movement in the United States. The developmental and dialectical models that Will Herberg, Karl Wittfogel, Eric Voegelin, Frank Meyer, and James Burnham all used in studying cultures suggest their debt to nineteenth-century historical thought. The application of such models also indicates in varying degrees the continuing appeal of Georg Wilhelm Friedrich Hegel, who aside from Karl Marx was the most famous nineteenth-century historical theorist. Postwar conservatives, however, placed Hegel in the unsavory company of Marx, for despite their own ties to Hegelian philosophy, they saw Hegel increasingly through the eyes of Marxist-Hegelians: that is to say, as a proto-Marxist. It has thus fallen to a later generation to examine the Hegelian aspect of postwar conservative thinking.

I shall argue that Hegelian concepts shaped the historical attitudes and cultural judgements of prominent postwar conservatives, who because of their concern with personal freedom as a political and ontological value denounced Hegel and ascribed their own Hegelian ideas to less offensive sources. I have tried to trace the mostly residual Hegelianism of my major subjects to certain shared experiences. Herberg, Wittfogel, Meyer, and Burnham moved to the Right after they had disavowed a Marxist-Leninist ideology that included Hegelian assumptions about history. As I attempt to show, their historical thinking was never entirely Marxist, even while they were Communists. There was an explicitly Hegelian component in their outlook that survived their break with revolutionary socialism. It is also significant that almost all of my subjects studied philosophy extensively. Herberg was a student of John Dewey's at Columbia University and was exposed to Dewey's organic view of nature and to other academic formulations of Hegelian thinking. Both Voegelin and Wittfogel studied philosophy in Central Europe at a time when Hegel and other idealist philosophers were considered giants of Western thought. Although both reacted against some parts of the Hegelian tradition, they also absorbed other parts into their historical views.

At the outset I should state that much of my thesis rests on guesswork. Because most of my subjects made strenuous efforts to distance themselves from Hegelian philosophy, particularly after their turning to the Right, it is necessary to probe beyond their stated beliefs to uncover the Hegelian source of their thinking. An experience that led me to this investigation was my friendship in the early 1970s with two of my subjects: Will Herberg and Karl Wittfogel. Neither, when I knew him, expressed publicly favorable views of Hegel. Herberg had inveighed against Hegel in a paper delivered at Princeton University in fall 1969, blaming him for modern attacks on the facticity of the Bible. Yet, both men in private extolled Hegel as a teacher with deep historical insight from whom they had never ceased to learn. I perceive a similar ambivalence in Eric Voegelin's writings. Voegelin and his American disciples portray Hegel as a blasphemous megalomaniac who claimed to fashion reality within his own consciousness. Voegelin's German interpreters, particularly Helmut Kuhn, however, stress the Hegelian roots of his dialectical understanding of history, as the history of consciousness. Moreover, despite Voegelin's many blasts at Hegel, philosophically divergent commentators such as Thomas Altizer and Jeffrey Hart describe his thought as "neo-Hegelian."

The attempt by Voegelin, Herberg, and other eminent American conservatives to dissociate themselves from Hegelian thought was often no more than a ritualistic gesture. Hegelianism was a permanent aspect of their historical thinking, whether they picked it up originally at the University of Vienna, in the classes of John Dewey at Columbia University, or as Communist catechumens who studied the ancestry of the Marxist-Leninist dialectic.

In preparing this book, I have accepted two limitations up until the last chapter. First, I have avoided dealing with contemporary conservative Hegelians who exerted no significant influence on postwar conservatism. One such Hegelian has published extensively on philosophy and has even founded a study group at St. John's University in New York in order to explore the continued relevance of Hegel's *Philosophy of Right*. Although I personally find such activities exciting, I recognize that they have not generated much interest or enthusiasm on the intellectual Right and have therefore relegated them to a few sentences in my final chapter. Conversely, other figures who have had considerable impact on postwar conservatism (e.g., William F. Buckley, Jr.; Milton Friedman; and Richard Weaver) have not been influenced at all by Hegelian thinking and are therefore not among the subjects of this study. My choices of whom to include in this analysis are dictated by the theme, not by personal affinity or by the extent of someone's literary fame.

The final chapter puts the Hegelian strain in conservative thought into its larger context. In the process of doing my research, I discovered that the unacknowledged Hegelianism of my subjects was only a subcategory of a more widespread tendency among postwar conservative intellectuals. This larger tendency, historicism, has recently, like Hegelianism, become anathema to much of the intellectual Right. According to one thoughtful European traditionalist and an ardent neo-Thomist, David Levy, "At its heart the Right is anti-historicist, and where the influence of historicism pervades an apparently Rightist political theory, like the conservatism of Hegel, the Left will have little difficulty in reversing the conclusions at which the theory arrives, as Marx's young Hegelian comrades discovered to their glee."[1] Levy warns his readers specifically against "the metaphysical historicism" of Hegel, which "sees history as the process by which Reason, the solvent of fixed appearances, becomes incarnate in the world through dissolving everything stable in the torrent of its own becoming."[2] Contrary to Levy's assertion, historicism not only is compatible with conservative thought but contributed decisively to postwar conservatism in the United States. Furthermore, Levy's interpretation of Hegel betrays his implicit faith in the way Marxist-Hegelians read the thinker he attacks. Levy's frequent references to Alexandre Kojève and Herbert Marcuse as experts on Hegel indicate how limited are the foundations of his analysis.

A similar criticism applies to his reduction of historicism to moral relativism, to a process by which values are allowed to dissolve in the solvent of onrushing time. Although such a tendency may sometimes be found in Hegel as well as in other non-Marxist historicists, what we should be seeking is a dispassionate understanding of historicism, and certainly one that incorporates sources other than Marxist-Hegelians. By *historicism* is meant an ethical and epistemological perspective that makes the awareness, and ultimately the validity, of values dependent upon historical experience. The historicist, by this definition, does not deny the ontological status of values that are unrelated to historical practice but simply treats them as irrelevant, like the unnoticed leaf in the forest over whose existence, or nonexistence, philosophers once disputed. A historicist outlook similar to the one presented previously influenced my subjects. They arrived at this outlook, at least partly, through their exposure to Hegel, who expressed it emphatically in almost all of his writings. For the historicist, man is knowable and definable through his historical situation and cultural upbringing, but never as the object of purely abstract predicates. The charge raised by Levy, however, does not go away completely, even if we present historicism in its most favorable light. Historicists, and among them Hegel, have sometimes treated moral and intellectual truths as being relative to particular epochs and cultures and thus fated to vanish in a changing world. Yet, this exaggerated emphasis on historical change does not represent the whole of historicist thinking. Many historicists, including Hegel, have stressed historical continuity more than change. They have also presented history as a vehicle for teaching and testing values without ascribing the origin of morality to a changing historical process.

It must, of course, be stated that not all historicists have been Hegelians. Edmund Burke, who had a keen sense of the historical and evolutionary aspects of human society, preceded Hegel by almost two generations. And though Hegel was the most systematic and influential historicist of the nineteenth century, he was but one among many who tried to relate human activity and values to changing historical situations. In the modern age, and within postwar conservatism, one finds historical conservatives who had only minimal contact with Hegel's work or with Hegelians. Russell Kirk, the conservative theorist and exponent of Burke, is one case in point.

Among our subjects there were different types of historicists, who studied historical particularities from differing perspectives. Burnham and Meyer had prolonged, bitter disagreements over the place of theological and ethical considerations in the formulation of political policy. Burnham, now a man in his eighties, may speak about the divine Logos that illuminates the human mind, but to his critics on the Right as well as on the Left he remains, justly or unjustly, a "positivist" who disparages moral absolutes.[3] By contrast, Voegelin, Meyer, and Herberg were seen even by their critics as concerned defenders of the religious consciousness of their civilization; their choice of this role is apparent from their writings. Despite these differences, the subjects of this book adapted historicist thinking to what they perceived as the crisis of the postwar age. Like the founding generations of other movements, postwar conservatives had a shared sense of the uniqueness of their time. They appealed as critics of their age to overlapping ideas and themes, marked in varying degrees by historicist and quite often by Hegelian-historicist features. They thought that a dialectic of ideas was an essential part of the present age of global struggle, which had its origins first, in the Great War and then, in the Bolshevik Revolution. Burnham was perhaps the most explicit in depicting the world since 1914 as a steadily boiling cauldron. The self-destruction of European civilization that had occurred between 1914 and 1945 was only a preliminary stage in the accelerating conflict. It had simply cleared the way for the struggle for world empire between an expansive Soviet Union and its reluctant American rival.

All our subjects believed passionately that the postwar "struggle for the world" (to borrow from the title of one of Burnham's most controversial writings) contained a spiritual dimension. The cold war had to do with principles and values that were necessarily and irreconcilably opposed. Herberg, Meyer, and Voegelin saw this conflict as pitting the defenders of Western spirituality against godless collectivists. Burnham, Wittfogel, and the Central European founders of *Review of Politics* conceived of the same struggle as one between Western freedom and its enemies. Although other struggles over principle had transpired in the past, the present one stood out by virtue of its awesome magnitude and the unprecedented tyranny that the enemies of the West now exercised. Wittfogel, in his remarks on Communist China, distinguished Maoist totalitarianism from the forms of Oriental despotism he had treated in his books. The Communists, Wittfogel maintained, were destroying the social space and traditional bonds of community that remained present in China under the older imperial bureaucratic rule. Wittfogel denied any real continuity between the pre- and postrevolutionary regimes in Russia and China. He tried to prove that the Communist had imposed on non-Western societies far greater controls than those to which they had been accustomed.[4]

Burnham made a similar distinction between the lack of freedom in some traditional societies and the assault on liberty that the Soviets had unleashed. Addressing the Indian Congress for Cultural Freedom in March 1951, he states that "[i]n our day the threat to cultural freedom has in reality no precedent: none at least since the ideal of freedom first entered into the hearts and minds of men. Heretofore the threat has always been negative and limited. But today's tyranny is absolute." Burnham goes on to explain, "Totalitarianism wears many masks. . . . Communism is the worst form of totalitarianism, since it is absolute and there is nothing worse. Today as the past six years have daily proved, Communism is also the most powerful and immediate totalitarian threat, the present danger."[5]

Burnham's interpretation of the Communist threat to free societies was historicist and dialectical. In both respects it was related to Herberg's and Meyer's views of history as a confrontational process operating through polarities. Burnham, Meyer, and Herberg all saw the making of ethical decisions as the result of historical confrontation. Western society would have to reaffirm its values through conscious choice in a long twilight war that had resulted from differences in principle. Herberg made this point clearly in 1952, in speaking to a gathering of clergy about "the conflict that admits of no compromise because it is a conflict of ultimates." In this struggle Western society can prevail only by acting through "the faith underlying American democracy."[6]

Burnham emphasized the problem of ethical will in the fight against Communism when he spoke to the Indian Congress for Cultural Freedom. "The internal danger of Communism is greatest," he observes, wherever there is a "failure in will, in resolution, a failure to make up one's mind." The Russian provisional government's leader in 1917, Alexander Kerensky, illustrated the danger of irresolution when he took no action against his enemies on the Left. Although Kerensky and his government fell, others resisted the Soviet Communists with greater determination: "Confronted with its question [Stalin's attempted annexation of its southern lands], in 1939 Finland decided and fought; and for twelve years she has sustained the defence of freedom."[7]

Conservatives who have viewed history as shaping ethical choice have usually cautioned against the danger of moralizing. The most brilliant, and most unapologetic, representative of conservative historicism, James Burnham, defined *conservatism*, in a letter to William F. Buckley, Jr., as the "integral incorporation of history" into a political worldview.[8] Later, in response to the sociologist Peter Berger's proposal for the construction of a "conservative humanism" in 1972, Burnham observed:

> Conservatism can be considered humanist only if humanism is interpreted to mean a concern with the interests and well-being not of abstract Man or Mankind but of existential man, historical man, or actual men as they actually exist in space and time. Existential man is not a bare identity, a featureless constant, but a node of particularities, distinctive relationships, differences, qualities, peculiarities.[9]

Burnham's remarks give proof of his commitment to a historically defined form of conservatism that prevailed among conservative Hegelians and disciples of Edmund Burke from the early nineteenth century on. This commitment in Burnham's case was even more noteworthy because it came from someone whom William F. Buckley called "the dominant intellectual influence" upon *National Review*, the leading conservative journal of the postwar era. Curiously, however, Burnham did not acquire this "Right-Hegelian" perspective by studying Hegel firsthand. According to his biographer, Samuel T. Francis, Burnham learned Hegel by studying Marx and Italian political thinkers of the nineteenth and twentieth centuries.[10] His "Hegel" was thus different from the real Hegel. Because I agree with Francis, I devote little space in this analysis to discussing Burnham as a Hegelian.

The Hegelianism found in other conservative thinkers, however, reveals some of the same historicist attitudes that Francis notes in Burnham, although not necessarily Burnham's contrast between a "historical and pragmatic" outlook and "a theologically or metaphysically based conservatism."[11] The common ground of all historically minded conservatives of the fifties and sixties was a rejection of abstract universalism. This rejection was linked to the recognition of the particularities and distinctions with which actual human beings were required to exist in order to live fully. The disguised Hegelianism of postwar conservatism was often an attempt to justify Western civilization as a historical legacy. This Hegelianism was more a set of attitudes and perceptions than a systematic philosophy. It aimed at placing the American phase of the modern era into a framework of traditions that had weathered conflict. In opposing the dominant liberal view that the American Founders tried to create a new regime based on individual reason and rationalist values, Hegelian and other historicist conservatives stressed the synthetic character of the American founding. They called attention to the living roots of the American regime, which they found in the ancient and medieval worlds, as well as in the eighteenth century. Meyer and Herberg repeatedly depicted the Founding Fathers as bringing together established though sometimes conflicting Western values into a higher union of old truths than previously had been possible.

I believe that Burnham's differences with Berger adumbrate the tensions that eventually split the American intellectual Right. Although Berger speaks well of Edmund Burke and has written sympathetically of traditional religion, his "conservative humanism" indicates his willingness to move in a direction uncongenial to historically minded traditionalists. Unlike Burnham, who would find such a concept philosophically questionable though strategically useful, Berger has appealed to the ideal of human rights. He has also exhorted the United States government to work more actively to "convert" the Third World to liberal democracy.[12] By contrast, the historicist conservatives of the postwar years always rejected ideals that were not grounded in historical reality. Both Herberg and Meyer, although they sympathized with oppressed blacks, distrusted the civil rights movement for what they considered its vague and utopian aspirations. Although they certainly noted the indignity produced by segregated institutions, they warned against attempts to legislate a color-blind, and later unisex, society. Herberg, Meyer, and Burnham thundered against social engineers who wished to change actual human beings in accordance with their personal visions.

The concluding chapter outlines the split on the American intellectual Right between historical conservatives and antihistorical conservatives. My own sympathies are clearly with the former. Despite their philosophically and morally shaky positions, those who stand on what now passes for the intellectual Right are mostly indifferent, if not hostile, to a historical-evolutionary understanding of society. The reasons for this development, as I try to show, may have less to do with the intellectual prowess of the victors than with a combination of cultural changes and the antitheoretical bias of most conservative research foundations.

It is the other side for whom I try to speak. "Conservatives" who glorify abstract individuals and abstract ideals finally become their own opposite: not the defenders of a living and experienced tradition, but the inventors of ideal societies and of gossamer dreamworlds. My remarks about the late Leo Strauss and his disciples are an attempt to illustrate the folly of trying to renew civilization by appealing to abstract rationalism. I hold no brief for this project, and for its implicit denial of historical experience as a necessary yardstick of 'the good'.

These polemics relate to my central theme, which is the Hegelian ideas in postwar conservatism. I move beyond this original theme because of what I think was the integral relationship between Hegelianism and historical conservatism in the postwar period. The Hegelianism of postwar conservatives was sometimes derived from an otherwise outworn Marxist identity; yet it often served to express the sense of a living past. My last chapter treats the paradox of a self-defined conservatism that has lost its interest in "historical man."

# THE SEARCH FOR
# HISTORICAL MEANING

# 1

---

# THE HEGELIAN LEGACY

EDMUND WILSON, IN *TO THE FINLAND STATION*, CONSTRUCTS AN INTEL-lectual genealogy for Marxist-Leninism intended to explain the Russian Revolution. Fixing first upon Lenin's arrival at Petrograd's Finland Station in October 1917 to take command of the Bolsheviks, Wilson turns next to those thinkers who inspired Communist revolutionary doctrines. Wilson reserves his most lavish praise for Marx and Lenin, but he also writes about Vico, Saint-Simon, Fourier, and other historical theorists and prophets of socialism. He predictably discusses Georg Wilhelm Hegel (1770–1831), philosopher of the dialectic, whom Marx claimed to have stood "right side up" when he ascribed historical change to material rather than spiritual conflict. Marx rehabilitated Hegel by rendering his ideas usable for Lenin and for other modern revolutionaries. Cleansing his historical analysis of inappropriate references to the "Absolute" and "World Spirit," Marx "extracted the rational kernel of the Hegelian dialectic from the mystical wrapping."[1]

Needless to say, there was little reason for Marx, Lenin, or even Wilson, an embattled socialist, to study Hegelians who clung to the mystical wrapping. Neither the Hegelian Right nor anti-Marxist Hegelians have generally enjoyed the kind of adulation that has gone to Marx and his disciples. In some intellectual histories it is difficult even to pinpoint the Hegelian Right's defining characteristics. The label is sometimes attached to innocuous antiquarians who labored over Hegel's unedited texts in the decades following his death. Such scholars were dedicated to passing down unchanged a body of teachings on logic, epistemology, and law. Elsewhere we learn of socially conservative German nationalists, such as Constantin Rössler and Adolf Lasson, who placed Hegel's theory in the service of Bismarck's Germany. Marxist writers have bestowed a more sinister reputation on the Hegelian Right. Georg Lukács and Herbert Marcuse, for example, have depicted its members as the wayward defenders of a partly decayed but still destructive European capitalism. Lukács and Marcuse place "Hegelian" advocates of "irrationalism," that is, anti-Marxism, into the line of fascism's intellectual predecessors.[2] Isaiah Berlin, who wrote a popular biography of Marx, describes thus the emerging Hegelian Right in the Germany of the 1830s: "Patriotism and political and social reaction lifted their heads again." According to Berlin, the Right-Hegelians denied that "all men were brothers" and proclaimed the "idealist counter-thesis, according to which such [national, racial, and social] differences, for all their apparent irrationality, express the peculiar role of a given race or nation, and are grounded in some metaphysical necessity."[3]

Were the Right-Hegelians, as Berlin describes them, defenders of anti-rational forces or of politically inflexible institutions? Were they primarily the uncritical admirers of the Prussian monarchy, the government that had given Hegel a prestigious chair at the University of Berlin and whose administration he had repeatedly praised? A common means of dividing Hegelians into right and left is to attribute to each side an opposing interpretation of Hegel's dictum: "What is real is rational." Whereas the Marxists and other radical Hegelians identified rationality with revolutionary change, the Hegelian Right defended the inherent rationality of their own society.

Henning Ottmann has treated these questions of definition by producing his own taxonomy of political Hegelianisms. As Karl Löwith before him, Ottmann underlines the difficulty of associating Hegelian political movements with two polarized interpretive camps. Despite his warnings about strict categorization, he finally replaces the now challenged view of two Hegelian traditions with his own scheme of three: Right, Left, and center-liberal. He defines each of these schools in terms of a cohesive outlook and a favored reading of particular texts taken from Hegel.[4] The present chapter will treat thinkers and political personalities whom Ottmann identifies as center-liberal– and Right-Hegelians. These figures opposed the Hegelian Left from two related but distinct perspectives. Both the center and Right rejected the view of history as materially caused and considered historical change the work of Spirit, or of cosmic consciousness, as It operated on finite human minds. They both interpreted history *dialectically,* as moving through a series of contradictory but interrelated principles. Opposing principles, such as freedom, order, being, and nothingness, shaped the evolution of human knowledge and world history and were most conspicuously at work in Spirit's highest achievements: art, religion, philosophy and the state.

The centrists took their bearings from the early sections of Hegel's *Philosophy of Right,* his most comprehensive political statement, together with the addenda produced by his liberal *Assistenten.* They viewed individual freedom and property rights as an indispensable stage in Spirit's formation of the state. They defined their ideal government as the state under law (*Rechtsstaat*) and aimed at harmonizing individual moral imperatives (*Moralität*) with public ethics (*Sittlichkeit*). Karl Rosenkranz, Hegel's most famous nineteenth-century biographer, cited his writings in defense of these positions.[5] More recently, Joachim Ritter, a European classical liberal, has tried to find further support for the view of a "centrist Hegel." He depicts the philosopher as steering between two apparently irreconcilable ways of thinking: the French Revolution's appeal to the "rights of mankind" and the Aristotelian practice (that Edmund Burke also embraced) of justifying rights and duties within the context of experienced political traditions.[6]

Rejecting this liberal emphasis on liberty, the Hegelian Right in the nineteenth century defended established authority and programs of national expansion. Almost all Right-Hegelians, from Rössler and Lasson in the 1850s to Giovanni Gentile in Mussolini's Italy, have looked to *The Philosophy of Right* for a defense of a powerful state. They have paid special attention to Section 261, which places "the spheres of private right and private well-being" under the state as "the immanent purpose" of individual and family relations.[7] Although center-Hegelians quoted the same section's explicit affirmation of the state's duty to protect individual and corporate rights, Right-Hegelians hailed its endorsement of political authority. Right-Hegelians also focused selectively on Sections 337 through 340, which contain Hegel's observations on war and international relations. Among these passages they singled out the repeated warnings against judging the conduct of states from an individual moral perspective.[8]

Although further distinctions between the two schools can certainly be drawn, they may for our purposes be somewhat irrelevant. Ottmann states that Right-Hegelians living in the nineteenth century often produced center-liberal interpretations of Hegel's texts. Liberals, on the other hand, embraced the Right's perspective when they came to defend German unification. Ottmann's main contribution, however, is not having created a new system for classifying Hegelians so much as having underlined the dynamic and creative aspects of the Hegelian Right and center. He has helped to discredit the popular historical stereotype that would reduce all nonleftist Hegelians (save perhaps for Benedetto Croce, the Italian classical liberal who allegedly did not consider himself a Hegelian) to either counterrevolutionaries or antiquarian pedants. Nonleftist Hegelians exercised a far-reaching influence on Western culture that extended beyond politics to art, religion, and philosophy. Cataloging these achievements would carry us beyond the compass of this study; yet such a task might reveal that there were substantial areas of agreement among nonleftist Hegelians: for example, a common understanding of the dialectic as operating through moral and conceptual polarities, and a belief that political and cultural history contained an immanent design arising from a universal mind.

The Hegelian Right and the Hegelian center shared common views of modernity that differed dramatically from the Hegelian Left's belief in an atheistic and egalitarian future. Modern society for nonleftist Hegelians was capable of reconciling individual liberty and political authority, intellectual creativity and respect for traditional religious values. Hegel and his disciples believed that the synthetic nature of their civilization created the possibility for integrating seemingly opposed principles. This Hegelian picture of the modern age acquired its contours in the nineteenth century, and it seems to have been revived by American conservatives since 1945, as they looked for visions of order. Will Herberg's politically and morally united but confessionally pluralistic America and Frank Meyer's description of the American regime can both be cited as cases in point. These and other conservative visions were related to a view of modernity as a combination of order and liberty that nineteenth-century Hegelians ultimately derived from Hegel's philosophy of history.

Hegel himself was an ambivalent teacher of historical progress. His *Lectures on the Philosophy of History,* delivered first in Berlin in 1822, presented political and cultural change as the activities of the Absolute. The Absolute, as World Spirit, aspired to perfect self-knowledge, and the self-illumination by which it exercised its freedom led mankind into growing self-awareness and increasing self-determination. The *Lectures,* which continue to be Hegel's most widely read work, keyed their philosophical argument to a survey of four distinct civilizations: Oriental, Greek, Roman, and Christian-Germanic. All these civilizations were vehicles for an unfolding World Spirit and, through their art, religion, and politics, embodied the successive stages in the expanding freedom of both Spirit and mankind. The modern Germanic world, for Hegel, was the most fully free, having benefited from the Protestant Reformation and the French Revolution. Christianity from the beginning had affirmed man's inner freedom, but only fifteen hundred years later did the Protestant reformers remove "the unspeakable injustice of having ecclesiastical authorities meddle into temporal affairs."[9] The Reformation restored to Christianity its true role as a spiritual force, while asserting its value as a moral power within society.

The modern Germanic world, according to Hegel, was inwardly pious, though mostly free of outward ecclesiastical control. It upheld the rights of property and person that the French Revolution had proclaimed. The Germanic world shunned, however, the social leveling that radical revolutionaries had undertaken at great human cost. Hegel ascribed the Revolution's excesses partly to the non-Protestant religion of the French people. Since the French were unable to find moral constraint in "religion or [in] some inner disposition," they appealed to "the abstract principle of freedom," even in humiliating their social enemies.[10] Only the Protestant nations of northern Europe properly understood liberty as the willingness to obey authority through the assent of conscience rather than as the right to pursue personal interests. These nations identified religion not with coercive political power, but with the reformation of the individual human spirit.

Certainly Hegel, as he uttered this judgment, was aware that state churches existed in Protestant lands. There too, people were taxed in order to support a politically favored clergy. In the *Lectures* he attempted to anticipate this type of objection when he insisted that national churches must enjoy popular backing: "It is basic wisdom to separate political laws and constitutions from religion since one fears bigotry and hypocrisy from any state church; but if religion and state are essentially different, they are one at their source so that laws must meet a religious test."[11] State churches represented the institutionalized expressions of the moral sentiments and the piety of particular peoples. No law could be valid and binding that failed to obtain the inner assent of the communicants of a national religion. Nonetheless, churchmen had no business running the state; nor were they entitled to oppress those outside their communion.[12]

More to the point, though not explicitly stated in the *Lectures,* was Hegel's belief that religion in modern Germanic culture was already losing its moral authority to philosophy or, more precisely, to philosophical history. From the high ground of modernity, it was plain, according to Hegel, that philosophy plotted the Absolute's movement more completely than did other forms of knowledge. Standing above religious subjectivity, philosophers apprehended the Absolute in its operation upon history and society.[13] Only philosophers could comprehend rationally and objectively that process of movement for which history had already become the locus classicus. Yet, philosophers perceived this process only retrospectively. Like the owl of Minerva, which took to flight at dusk, philosophy understood Spirit only by means of those tracks that It had imprinted on human consciousness. A philosophical interpretation of the past, Hegel believed, would illuminate the process by which his own culture had arisen through divine necessity. It would recapitulate the way in which Spirit had already produced a modern society that exemplified ordered liberty.

Despite this apparent presentism, Hegel's view of the modern age was more complex than it might first appear. His early religious writings testified to his profound admiration for ancient Greek society. They reflected a pervasive nostalgia for an organic community whose members placed the common good above individual interests. Greco-Roman civic religion instilled public-mindedness, whereas Christianity gained converts only "as all activity and purpose came to center on the individual and no activity any longer would be undertaken for the general good."[14] Hegel's *System of Ethics*, written in 1802, gave further proof of his search for model communities through the study of Classical thought. In this work Hegel constructed an ideal regime that was obviously inspired by Plato's *Republic*. He assigned the highest social honor to a military aristocracy that was willing "to live entirely in the fatherland and for their people."[15] Unlike the custodians and exemplars of public virtues, the merchants and craftsmen whom he described received little praise. Though they were needed to manufacture and exchange vital commodities, Hegel treated them scornfully for their exclusive pursuit of private interest. Their single moral merit was their respect for laws, an attitude that resulted from the desire for material security.[16]

The older Hegel became increasingly sympathetic to both Christianity and modernity, yet certain social attitudes clearly persisted from his early into his later works. Already in *The System of Ethics,* he warned against giving free rein to the commercial class. Such a policy would cause "great wealth to co-exist with abject poverty" and would allow "the absolute ethical bond of a people to vanish and their peoplehood to dissolve."[17] In the late 1790s Hegel had taken notes on Adam Smith's *Wealth of Nations* and summed up its central arguments thus: a system of satisfying individual needs came out of the unhindered exchange of commodities and services; the resulting system, by responding to the forces of supply and demand, brought increasing prosperity despite short-term setbacks.[18] In *The Philosophy of Right* Hegel recognized the creative power of a nascent capitalist economy, but he warned against the attendant danger of depersonalization. Workers had been reduced to cogs in an utterly mechanized society and stripped of whatever pride artisans had once taken in their craft. Hegel advocated workers' corporations and vocational groups in order to provide collective representation for those most vulnerable in civil society. Such corporations, he hoped, would work extensively with a public-spirited bureaucracy and a benevolent monarchy, both of which would preserve an awareness of the common good.[19]

Marxist interpreters have rhapsodized over passages such as these and cite them as proof of Hegel's groping toward socialism. Both Lukács and Marcuse portray a deeply troubled Hegel: having agonized, without seeing beyond capitalist oppression, he turned in desperation away from class conflict, toward the consolations of Greek philosophy and, finally, the celebration of his own state. Such an interpretation, as Joachim Ritter observes, ignores the true substance of Hegel's brief against modernity. When the philosopher castigated a depersonalizing economy and the "quantification of labor," he was writing from a Classical perspective.[20] A Marxist position would have been for him totally unacceptable, precisely because it urged the kind of break with the past that he feared was besetting his age. Hegel certainly did not seek the removal of economic inequality. He wished to remove, as Ritter convincingly argues, "the disjunction between past and present," which he ascribed to the repercussions of the French Revolution.

Consider the part of Hegel's *Lectures on the Philosophy of History* that contains his remarks on the Revolution. His observations indicate his own ambivalence about the event being described. No wonder that the Revolution's admirers and its critics have found in the *Lectures* a profusion of usable passages! In his lectures Herbert Marcuse was fond of quoting Hegel's glowing tribute to the Men of 1789:

> As long as the sun has remained in the firmament and the planets have revolved around it, never had it been seen that man should place himself

on his head—that is, his thoughts—and fashion reality accordingly. Anaxagoras had first said that the *nous* rules the world; now for the first time man has come to recognize that thought controls intellectual reality. It was indeed a divine dawn. All thinking beings joined in celebrating this epoch. An exalted sentiment then ruled; an enthusiasm of the spirit caused the world to vibrate as if a reconciliation were occurring between God and the world.[21]

Several paragraphs later, however, Hegel's nostalgic recollection of the "divine dawn" gives way to condemnation of the Revolution's abstract ideals and violence. The constitutional but weakened French monarchy (created in 1791), we learn, collapsed under the impact of a growing demand for popular liberty. Once having rejected the customary sources of political sovereignty, the revolutionary leaders refused to accept any restraint on liberty in the form of an executive regime. "Abstract principles of freedom" could thereafter be grounded only upon one authority, the individual "subjective will." Individual virtue became the only principle that the Revolution consistently invoked in trying to gain the obedience of French citizens. Hegel pointed out that virtue signifies a subjective disposition as well as an external expression, "a disposition which must be recognized and judged." Therefore states that appeal exclusively to private virtue abet mutual suspicion in their subjects. In the case of the Revolution, subjective morality led to disaster: "Suspicion achieved supremacy and brought to the scaffold the monarch whose subjective will was a Catholic religious conscience. Robespierre proclaimed virtue the highest of all principles, and he took it seriously. Under him there reigned both virtue and terror, for subjective virtue, which comes from one's inner disposition, produced the most frightening tyranny in practice. It exercised power without judicial forms; and its punishment, death, was frighteningly direct."[22]

This mixed judgment of the Revolution has sometimes been attributed to the fact that Hegel, like other conservative liberals of his age, endorsed some revolutionary actions but not others. His *Lectures*, for example, condemn the "unreasonableness" of the aristocratic privilege of the ancien régime. From the text one may conclude that Hegel approved of the moderate revolutionaries who proclaimed the principle of legal equality in 1789 but despised the more radical elements who unleashed the terror afterward. This explanation may wash for Hegel's political statements but does not fully clarify his critical relationship to the Revolution. In the *Lectures* he criticized the divine dawn partly for the reason that he praised it. The attempt of revolutionaries to make society more rational brought forth a blessing and a curse. The bold exercise of intellect that had swept away so many conspicuous anachronisms prepared the way for a "reign of suspicion and terror." The Revolution, which exalted the individual mind and will, excluded the protection of life and property. Political and legal continuity were no longer possible after the subjective will had been allowed to refashion reality. Hegel saw the same problem as characteristic of "modern theory which entrusts everything to the individual will": "There is no guarantee that [subjective] will will produce a disposition that will ensure the state's survival."[23]

Amid these comments about abstract thinking and modern individualism, Hegel contrasted the Protestant appeal to individual conscience with the Catholic stress on external religious-political order. This excursus was not an exercise in self-congratulation. Hegel was searching for an alternative vision of modernity to what the French Revolution had so dramatically but brutally tried to realize. He was pinning his hopes on those Protestant countries of Europe in which people still deferred to established authorities. There reconciliation was still possible between the virtue of public-spiritedness and respect for custom, on the one hand, and individualistic values, on the other. Hegel's disciples would foresee such reconciliations between custom and individualism as taking place in the various societies to which they belonged. Many Hegelians went from lamenting the unresolved problems of modernity to proposing their own syntheses of order and liberty. They invariably grounded such syntheses in the emerging patterns of history and in what they hoped was the "true meaning" of the past.

In 1869, Karl Rosenkranz, one of Germany's leading Hegelians, completed a work originally conceived as an updated edition of his well-received biography *Hegel's Life* (1844). The polemical literature that appeared on his subject during the intervening years forced Rosenkranz to do an entirely new book, which he titled *Hegel as a German National Philosopher.* Appearing on the eve of German unification, his study stresses Hegel's identity as a German and assails the then prevalent notion of him as a Prussophile rather than a German nationalist. The work also scolds various anti-Hegelians: revolutionary socialists, orthodox theologians, and Schopenhauerian pessimists. All are rebuked for either misrepresenting or rejecting Hegel's thought.[24] Rosenkranz sets out to prove that Hegel's historical thinking still speaks to the present age.

The Hegel he depicts overcame politically and philosophically divergent forces and even posthumously might guide moderate nationalists and sober progressives. The same theme dominates a particularly revealing eulogy at the end of Rosenkranz's comments on *The Philosophy of Right:*

> He [Hegel] opposed feudalism, which exalts a patriarchal constitution, by insisting on legality; he opposed abstract democracy, which flatters the masses, by promoting monarchy; he opposed aristocracy by calling for popular representation; the state bureaucracy by calling for freedom of the press, for jury trials, and for the independence of corporations. He offended the hierarchy of all confessions by calling for their submission as

churches to the sovereignty of the state and for the emancipation of science from church authority. He antagonized the industrial state, which seeks to ensnare the people with the promise of riches and material prosperity, by stressing ethics as the state's absolute purpose. He opposed enlightened despotism . . . by demanding a constitution; and he opposed cosmopolitan socialism by subordinating it to the state's historical and national character.[25]

This picture of Hegel as a thoughtful modernist, equally resistant to revolution and reaction, appealed to the Hegelian center and, occasionally, even to the Hegelian Right. The same picture reemerged in lectures on Hegel's politics, delivered by his noted professorial admirers such as Victor Cousin at the Sorbonne and Augusto Vera at the University of Naples.

It may be useful at this point to comment specifically on the political evolution of Vera. His philosophical works blazed a trail in Italian Hegelian studies that Croce and Gentile subsequently followed and widened. Moreover, his later career gave evidence of the pull of the ideas of the Hegelian center upon a thinker long known for his revolutionary ardor. Finally, Vera expressed positions that anticipated those found on the postwar American Right, particularly in the essays of Will Herberg. Settling in France in the 1840s, this self-exiled radical from southern Italy studied Hegel while serving, first, as a government functionary and, later, as a teacher in his adopted land. While in France Vera remained in touch with the democratic Italian nationalist Bertrando Spaventa. At the same time, he assisted the French republican spokesman Jules Simon in editing the periodical *La Liberté de Penser*. His earliest writings on Hegel, which deal with theology, passionately support an evolutionary, scientific interpretation of religious phenomena. When a republican upheaval in France, which started in February 1848, gave way in June to violent rioting and civil war, Vera changed his outlook decisively. An essay Simon commissioned him to write, "The Sovereignty of the People," was never published in Simon's journal. Vera grew suspicious of mass democracy, and he came to advocate the "hegemony of the minority," the formation of regimes by an educationally qualified and stable middle class.[26]

It is apparent that Vera did not consider himself a convert to the Right. Even after 1848 he defended the French Revolution of July 1830, which had led to a constitutional, middle-class monarchy. He appealed to the examples of Hegel and of those Hegelians who tried to chart a middle path between clericalism and atheism, oppression and license, authoritarianism and mob rule. A theoretical and psychological precursor of those former radicals who contributed to the postwar American conservative movement, Vera elicited bitter accusations from his abandoned companions on the Left. His Marxist biographer, Guido Oldrini, calls Vera's Hegelianism "a defense of the material security of bourgeois reactionaries." "From a social perspective his Hegelian system is a massive barrier erected against the sudden rise of Communism and materialism." Vera, said Oldrini, reduced all social-intellectual phenomena to Hegel's "absolute idea," which he conjured up to justify the status quo.[27]

Will Herberg encountered comparable derision when he changed from a Communist to a conservative. Like Vera, Herberg was attacked as a bourgeois reactionary who defended what is as being right. Herberg may indeed have sounded like Vera when he claimed to discover the work of divine reason in political and cultural accretions. Herberg's critics mocked him for combining Hegelianism with Hebraic prophecy to buttress his own historical views.[28] The parallel between Vera and Herberg may be pushed even further. Vera foreshadowed Herberg and other American conservatives when he defended modernity as a concrete historical accomplishment. Vera, like Rosenkranz, gave a concrete point of reference to the abstract and universal elements in Hegel's conceptualization of reality. In lectures on *The Philosophy of Right*, which Vera delivered in Naples during the 1860s, he characterizes the individual "only as a fragment of a single edifice, a product of the epoch to which he belongs and which he reflects under shifting forms and points of view. . . . He who places himself outside his epoch, places himself outside history and wastes himself in struggles and in foolish or sterile desires."[29]

The unabashed historicism in Vera's lectures cropped up again a century later in Herberg's theological and sociological writings. In the essay "Historicism as Touchstone," published in 1960, Herberg offered this self-revelation:

> Much more important, it seems to me, is the conviction I have reached that nothing can be really understood about man and his enterprises unless it is understood historically. I see this as a direct consequence of the biblical teaching about the nature of ultimate reality ("for the Hebrew history is that which is real").[30]

This essay was intended to help confused and rootless individuals to understand the need for "historical stabilities and continuities." Vera's lectures had also emphasized the widespread illusion that individuals determine themselves: "Instead of conceiving of the individual in his concrete and developed condition, we now envisage him in his abstract and potential state. We thereby detach the individual from the authentic life of his people and we imagine him as he might have been at birth." Vera wished to call attention to the already "formed individual attached to a particular epoch and people and to a social environment which claims him from birth, which arouses and guides his activity and which penetrates his life."[31]

Neither Vera nor Rosenkranz believed that an attack on abstract individualism required a denial of individual liberty. Like Hegel they justified property rights and certain personal liberties as essential to modern political life understood in the context of Spirit's quest for freedom. Yet, like Hegel and like nineteenth-century Hegelians who complained about the capricious individualism of their times, Vera and Rosenkranz worried about the sacrifice of authority to unrestrained appetite. But they hoped that by calling attention to the problem, they might help in the search for a solution. Hegel himself had expressed such a hope in his more optimistic remarks on his own age. Modern individualism would lead beyond itself into a re-formation of community along essentially organic lines.

The same hope is apparent in Giovanni Gentile when he composed *Genesis and Structure of Society*. Writing as one of the few surviving intellectual loyalists of the Italian Fascist state in 1943, Gentile, in his last political writing, explored the problem of social obligations. His philosophical investigations, since the publication of *General Theory of the Spirit as Pure Act* in 1916, had examined consciousness, as it emerged from the individual Ego. All thought involved the activity of Spirit, which came to self-consciousness through the individual. Gentile's ontological and epistemological point of departure was strikingly similar to the one that Hegel had adopted in the *Science of Logic*. Yet, Gentile went beyond Hegel when he emphasized Spirit's spontaneity and the irreducibility of Its operations to permanent categories. He defined thinking as pure act and viewed all conceptualization as a continuous "recasting of reality [*rifacimento della realtà*]."[32] The dialectic remained operative each time Spirit, acting through the Ego, assimilated to Itself the objective world through an exercise of volition. Gentile called his philosophy of the dialectic *actualism*, a term by which he sought to convey the fluid, provisional status and creative aspect of all knowing. Because of this interpretation of thought as process, Gentile considered Hegel's system to be a "mere fragment." His own act of intellectual self-assertion both incorporated and went beyond the dialectical perceptions of his predecessor.[33] Like Hegel, Gentile judged Being as something that became conceivable only by being posited. At the same time, he excluded fixed concepts. The thinking subject, conceived as either Ego or Spirit, transcended "what had already been thought." It did this by constantly redefining the world.[34]

Gentile tried to adapt "actualism" to his own nation's need for greater unity. After Austria's defeat of Italy in the Battle of Caporetto in 1917, he wrote pamphlets exhorting his people to renewed military efforts. Both his service to the Fascist regime as Italy's minister of education and his defense of Fascism as a movement to regenerate Italy expressed his intense patriotism. More than almost any other Italian philosopher, including Croce, his frequent collaborator on publications, Gentile deliberately drew his illustrations and arguments from earlier, often neglected Italian thinkers. His cultural nationalism was a persistent aspect of his work, even in his commentaries on Hegel. Significantly, he followed Hegel in giving a more exalted spiritual role to the state than to the nation. In sharp contrast to Nazi ideologues, Gentile considered political authority not a mere reflection of the people, but a tool for educating the entire nation. The state, he believed, was the continuing process whereby Being and Nonbeing were united. It produced self-realization for those associated with it, and it served as the dialectical vehicle through which the Ego linked the other to Itself. Like Hegel's concept of the state, Gentile's was based on the idea of an all-embracing will that through its self-imposed legality expressed an undivided ethical purpose.[35]

Unlike Hegel, however, Gentile glorified a state unrestrained by either cultural tradition or popular consent. His state was the self-actualizing Ego viewed from a philosophical level. Any distinctions between "private" and "public" or "political" and "ethical" questions led to an unwarranted polarization between the state and its people. The "authoritarian state" that Gentile praised functioned as the unified consciousness of its parts. Its members willed the existence of the state through their individual consciousness, while recognizing its origins in themselves. Gentile emphatically rejected the "liberal-empirical state," which prohibited political authority from interfering in civil society. He mocked the defenders of this fictitious state for assuming that society consisted only of isolated individuals.[36]

Despite his consuming political interest, Gentile developed his idea of the state from his philosophical focus on Ego. The state emerged from the individual thinking subject and continued the dialectical encounter with "otherness," which was the essence of "thinking as pure act." Like the Ego, the state produced its own values by willing them; it then created ethics by affirming values in practice. Gentile resorted to "actualist" arguments in order to vindicate the Fascist state. He regarded individual opposition to the state as self-contradictory: the Ego, which engendered political order, had no right afterward to contradict itself. By contrast, revolution, which expressed the *national* will to political renewal, was ethically beneficial. Gentile's critics have asserted that the only revolution that he recognized was Mussolini's seizure of power. In point of fact, Gentile also extolled Garibaldi, Mazzini, and other democratic revolutionaries who had helped unify Italy in the nineteenth century.[37] His view of the state as necessarily in flux justified political and cultural changes.

As a philosopher of movement, Gentile had much in common with Georg Lukács, the Hegelian-Marxist who interpreted the dialectic as endless process. Lukács took over what was supposed to be a Marxist dialectic understood as a struggle between material forces, but he applied this principle of struggle loosely to any situation in which mankind tried to extricate itself from custom and routine. A political utopian and philosophical vitalist, Lukács, ironically, became the court philosopher of the Stalinist regime in postwar Hungary. Leszek Kolakowski accuses him of rationalizing totalitarianism, yet it may be that Lukács, like Gentile, grew tired of the flux and creativity that his thinking honored.[38] Gentile and Lukács were both victims of an endless dialectic of their own devising. In search of spiritual rest, they exalted political societies that would control, even at the cost of stifling, human creativity.

The dialectical thinking of Lukács and Gentile confirms the interpretation of Hegelian philosophy offered by some of its conservative critics. They attack Hegelianism as a source of moral mischief, one that has spawned both personal utopias and crazed social prophecy. The Catholic philosopher Thomas Molnar has chided Hegel and his disciples for seeking to play God in history. Hegelians imagine themselves to be omniscient vehicles of the World Spirit, the favored instruments of the dialectic.[39] Although such strictures may apply to some Hegelians, particularly, if not exclusively, to those of the Left, they tell us little about American conservatives who have been guided by Hegelian thought. Most of these thinkers have tried to defend historical continuities and stabilities within American life and within Western society more generally. Like Rosenkranz and Vera, these American conservatives have stressed the cumulative, inherited character of their civilization and its relationship to a still vital past. The view of Hegel's thought that came out of nineteenth-century America had little in common with the "Marxist-Hegelianism" that arose in Central Europe in the interwar period and subsequently spread to American universities. The "radical Hegel" invoked by Lukács, Marcuse, and, more recently, Alexandre Kojève and Jean Hyppolite in postwar France was not the Hegel whom American scholars encountered in the early twentieth century.[40] A shift of the kind here described did occur in Hegel interpretations, but, as we shall try to demonstrate, it came too late to influence the way our subjects thought about Hegel in their youth.

In 1901 Denton J. Snider, a prominent educator who had spent thirty-five years spreading Hegel's political thought in America, drew a crucial distinction between negative and positive Hegelianism:

> The negative Hegelians, usually called the Hegelian left, developed the dialectical side of Hegel and hurled it remorselessly against all existent reality. From the German universities Russian students coined this negative Hegelianism into Russian, and applied its destructive criticism to the social and political institutions of their fatherland. . . . In Germany, we may add here, this negative Hegelianism ran its course and finally negated itself, as it must, but at the same time it destroyed the Hegelian philosophy, almost extirpating this branch of study from the German universities. Now comes another curious fact: positive Hegelianism has taken refuge in Anglo-Saxon countries, in England and in America, where it is much studied, and is slowly being made the theoretical basis of just that institutional world which it, on its dialectical side, was once invoked to destroy.[41]

It might be well to allow for hyperbole in Snider's view of his age. The left-wing Hegelians did not in fact dominate Hegelian thought in Germany; nor had they made it impossible for other Hegelians to enjoy academic and political respectability in the Old World. A nonradical (i.e., centrist and right) Hegelian influence remained conspicuous in German culture throughout the entire second half of the nineteenth century. Karl Rosenkranz, Rudolf Haym, and Friedrich Überweg in philosophy; Theodor Vischer in aesthetics; Gustav Schmoller and Adolf Wagner in social economics were only a few of the German thinkers who were either outright Hegelians or popularizers of particular aspects of Hegel's work. A charge that has been raised repeatedly by critics of the pre–world War II German academic world is that the widespread acceptance of Hegelian attitudes prevented German educators from criticizing political authority. Although these charges, in my judgment, exaggerate both the danger and power of Hegel's political thinking, they do raise legitimate questions about Snider's picture of a totally radicalized German Hegelianism.[42]

In point of fact, Germany by the end of the nineteenth century was undergoing a neo-Kantian revival inspired by such illustrious professors as Wilhelm Windelband and Heinrich Rickert. Such men and their numerous disciples considered historical and metaphysical justification for social institutions to be less important than the validation of moral values necessary for individual moral decisions. By the beginning of the twentieth century, Rickert, Windelband, the intellectual historian Wilhelm Dilthey, and Max Weber were all turning toward a "philosophy of value [*Wertphilosophie*]" that owed more to Kant's ethical analysis than to Hegelian dialectics. This happened, ironically, while the efforts exerted by such midcentury thinkers as Spaventa and Vera were bringing forth a second great wave of Italian Hegelianism. In 1903 Croce and Gentile founded *Critica*, a journal of aesthetics that would celebrate the Hegelian dialectic. In the United States, immediately after the Civil War, Snider and fifty other charter members organized the St. Louis Philosophical Society. He and his fellow Hegelian William Torrey Harris then launched the *Journal of Speculative Philosophy*, America's most respected philosophical periodical between 1867 and 1893. It was the unwavering belief of the fervent Hegelians who founded both enterprises that America would realize the vision of a free society based on ever-expanding institutional relationships. Cincinnati, Chicago, and Milwaukee all vied with St. Louis to become the center of America's premier Hegelian movement.[43] Karl Rosenkranz, Ralph Waldo Emerson, William Torrey Harris, Joseph Pulitzer, Amos Bronson Alcott, and the Scottish philosopher J. H. Stirling all became contributing members of the St. Louis Philosophical Society, a group that was dedicated to the flowering of Hegel's positive philosophy in the New World.

The leadership inveighed against the Marxist adaptation of the Hegelian dialectic, and it distinguished its members from European "negative Hegelians." In 1901 Snider went so far as to ascribe radical or socialist Hegelianism to a non-Western consciousness present among some Europeans. Marx, for example, had strayed from authentic Hegelian teachings because his Jewish background had given him a prospensity for Oriental collectivism.[44] Indeed all collectivists who sought to substitute an omnipotent state for the web of institutional and historical ties characteristic of modern Western society were truly atavistic. They were attempting to return mankind, in the name of revolution, to primitive Oriental despotism. William Torrey Harris expressed similar ideas on historical evolution when he observed, "Socialism would destroy the precious gain to the sacredness and development of personality that private property had brought, and would cause us to revert to the primitive and Oriental subordination of the individual to the group. It would, in short, turn the hands of the clock backwards."[45] According to Snider and Harris, Marx and his followers had mutilated Hegelian philosophy: "Marx springs intellectually from the idealist Hegel, whose negative dialectic he uses with commanding skill, but whose positive institutional elements he not only ignores but destroys."[46]

Snider and Harris might have been surprised to learn that their idealist reading of Hegel enjoyed as much support in Europe as in America. The materialist revolutionary Lenin tried to cleanse the Russian Left's vision of what he considered the traces of German idealism. Although Lenin preferred to blame the idealist thinking of some Russian socialists on the German neo-Kantians (Lenin, as his widow vividly recalled, had hated Kant for his "abstract" thinking), in *Philosophical Notebooks* (1915–1916) he criticized Hegel, his favorite German thinker after Marx, for assigning ultimate worth to spiritual forces embedded in existing social institutions. Hegel, as Lenin now admitted, had an idealist side that had come from Kant.[47] Intellectually inexperienced socialists were advised to read Hegel only after they had been properly instructed. Indeed it would take nothing short of a "mighty labor" to strip Hegel's thinking of the "mystique of the Idea," which was incompatible with a materialist view of history.[48] The idealist assumption that pervaded Hegel's work and that treated the universal as a specific being seemed to Lenin something "barbaric, incredibly or childishly silly."

Young American and German Marxists, some of whom became conservatives, may have known nothing of this admonition. They may have even recalled that in *Materialism and Empiricocriticism* (1909) Lenin had associated idealist errors with Kant and his disciples, while presenting Hegel as the father of the historical dialectic. Lucio Colletti, the Italian Marxist critic of Hegel, observes that in 1915 Lenin still had praise for Hegel's concept of "becoming" and for the dialectical structure of Hegelian thinking.[49] By reading Hegelian "conceptualism" into Marxist materialism, according to Colletti, Lenin may have unwittingly prepared a Hegelian resurgence at the expense of authentic Marxism.

The Hegel whom American radicals of the early twentieth century studied was not a mere reflection of Marx or a recognized precursor of socialism. Unlike later Marxist Hegelians, American Marxists, and certainly those of them who shifted to the Right, did not read Marx back into Hegel. They would have been astonished by Alexandre Kojève's and Marcuse's attempts to draw from *Phenomenology of the Spirit* anticipations of the Marxist class struggle.[50] The Hegelianism expressed by two of the thinkers about to be analyzed, Herberg and

Wittfogel, developed independently of a Marxist-materialist outlook. Both managed to sound like members of the Hegelian center and Right even when they defended Marx and Lenin. The interpretations of Hegel that were paradigmatic for his nineteenth-century disciples in Europe and America also had appeal for avowed revolutionaries. Marxists such as the young Herberg were drawn to the mystical wrappings that Marx claimed and Lenin hoped to remove from the Hegelian dialectic.

# SIDNEY HOOK AND OTHER
# AMERICAN CRITICS OF HEGEL

ROBERT NISBET, IN RECOUNTING HIS INTELLECTUAL ODYSSEY TO-
ward the traditionalist Right, recalls his first exposure at the University of
California at Berkeley in the 1930s to conservative critics of the European Enlightenment. He mentions his discovery of Hegel, along with Edmund Burke,
Joseph de Maistre, and Alexis de Tocqueville, as critical for the development of
his own social thinking. Through them he came to understand that the West
since the French Revolution has been divided "between two sets of dialectically
opposed values: on the one hand, hierarchy, community, tradition, authority,
and the sacred sense of life; on the other hand, equalitarianism, individualism,
secularism, positive rights, and rationalist modes of organization and power."[1]
Nisbet, who is America's most prominent conservative sociologist, cites Hegel
several times in explaining the origins of his own appreciation for institutional
continuity.[2]

Nisbet's remarks about Hegel call into question a view discussed in the preceding chapter, that Hegelian thought has a necessarily radicalizing effect. For
example, Thomas Molnar calls Hegelianism "speculative acrobatics"; by
identifying "what I think" with "what really is," Hegel furnished the individual ego with an "epistemological, political, and religious *carte blanche*" to
change the world in its own image.[3]

But as the traditionalist Right assigns Hegel to the Left, libertarians and the
non-Communist Left have long identified him with the forces of reaction. Two
former revolutionaries, Max Eastman (1883–1969) and Sidney Hook (b. 1902),
in fact denounced Hegel repeatedly as an authoritarian reactionary. Hegel's dialectic, Eastman believed, did not support individual speculation about either
society or history. Rather, it imposed metaphysical categories on a changing reality and invested the state with a religious mystique. In *Marx and Lenin, the Science of Revolution*, published in 1926 when he was supporting the Soviet Union,

and later, in *Marxism, Is It Science?*, which marked his ultimate break with "the socialist hypothesis" in 1940, Eastman criticized Marxian socialism for its Hegelian core. In *Reflections on the Failure of Socialism* (1955), Eastman condemned Marx for having "concealed from the Left, or at least a major part of it, that he was a man of the Right—a Hegelian state-worshipper in his training, and in his instincts, as Bakunin described him 'a bourgeois through and through.'"[4] Eastman accused Marx of having contributed to Soviet totalitarianism by embracing Hegel's metaphysics of power. Eastman wrote as a libertarian, and his charge has recently found a new resonance in France among the libertarian *philosophes nouveaux*, who blame the Soviet gulag, at least partly, on Hegel's presenting the State as the agent of History. Such *philosophes nouveaux* as André Glucksmann interpret Hegel as a political theologian who transmitted to Marx his preference for established authority over freedom.[5] Despite the oversimplification of this view, its adherents have given a certain credibility to the way in which Hegel was interpreted by the nineteenth-century Hegelian Right. Eastman, Hook, and, most recently, the *philosophes nouveaux* see the essential Hegel as the philosopher of Right and of History who worshipped the established powers of his age.

Hook may have felt a particularly urgent need to explore the real Hegel. Not only had this supposedly dangerous thinker corrupted academic scholarship in the social sciences and philosophy; he had also exercised a continuing influence on Hook's most revered teacher at Columbia, John Dewey (1859–1952), America's premier philosopher and theorist of education for several decades. The evidence of Dewey's Hegelianism, particularly in his early work, was almost as obvious as his social democratic teachings that Hook praised. From the time Dewey had entered Johns Hopkins University as a graduate student in psychology in 1882, he had been interested in Hegelian thought. The philosophy department at Johns Hopkins was then under the theoretical sway of the eminent English Hegelian (and critic of laissez-faire capitalism) T. H. Green. Dewey's professor and later colleague at the University of Michigan, George Sylvester Morris (1840–1889), produced as his major work *Hegel's Philosophy of the State and History: An Exposition.*[6] Dewey characterized Morris's (and his own early) philosophical position thus: "His adherence to Hegel (I feel quite sure) was because Hegel had demonstrated to him in a great variety of fields of experience the supreme reality of this principle of unity maintaining itself through the medium of differences and distinctions."[7]

Dewey's first book, *Psychology,* published in 1887, scandalized experimental psychologists by combining clinical and laboratory data with an organic view of the natural world. No mere scientific naturalist, Dewey evoked a dynamic and interrelated universe reminiscent of the vitalism of Hegel and of other German philosophers.[8] Although the Hegelian elements in his thinking became less pronounced in his later years, two of his principal biographers, Hook and Richard Bernstein, indicate that they did remain.[9] Hook's description of

Dewey's relationship to Hegel is particularly noteworthy because it attempts to explain how someone whom Hook deeply admired could be impressed by someone whom he plainly disliked:

> The immediate appeal of Hegelianism to Dewey lay in Hegel's opposition to dualisms of all sorts, in his historical approach to all cultural life, his mastery of concrete materials, and his extraordinarily acute perception of the continuities between matter and life, life and mind, mind and society. Dewey valued Hegel's method not for its arid pseudo-deduction of one idea from another, nor as a substitute for scientific analysis, but as an approach which put one on guard against introducing into the thick stream of experience facile disfunctions, hard and fast alterations, sharp separations.[10]

Because of Dewey's merits as a thinker, the Hegelian method strengthened rather than destroyed him. According to Hook, Dewey knew how to distinguish the useful parts of Hegelian tradition from the harmful ones without surrendering his critical scientific perspective. Moreover, in applying reason, Dewey took a position irreconcilably opposed to Hegel's:

> Where reason makes a difference it is as intelligence, not as embodied structure and not as a metaphysical trait which all things possess over and above their physical, biological, and racial qualities. For Hegel the world, properly understood, was already an ideal, so that there was no rational way of choosing between different ideals in any concrete situation. The better ideal in their [the Hegelians'] view was not one which proved itself in light of unforeseen consequences, but one which established itself by power of sheer survival.[11]

Hook's discussion of Dewey's Hegelianism tries to put the best face on a bad situatuation, but an essay that Hook wrote in 1939 (the year in which he published the biography), "Dialectic in Social and Historical Inquiry," explicitly condemns the Hegelian method in practice. Hook begins by conceding that in some types of studies it may be useful to apply "the principle of interrelatedness" which lies at the heart of the dialectic method. But since Hegel's time this method has invaded social inquiry to the point of obliterating all distinctions among the fields of law, religion, politics, and economics. According to Hook, the assumption of interrelatedness found in Hegel functioned "not as a heuristic principle subject to the piecemeal verification of scientific method but as a dogma."[12] Hook levels sharp criticism at Hegel and his supposedly numerous followers in the social sciences: he notes their refusal to study a specific phenomenon or event except by reference to an often imaginary whole, and he scolds them for their neglect of real contradictions, which they hide behind theoretical constructs. He concludes that "the term 'dialectic' is so infested with ambiguity that it is not likely to function as a serviceable designation for any concept or intellectual procedure in any inquiry which aims at the achievement of reliable knowledge about ourselves and the world we live in."[13]

Three contributing factors may help explain the unmistakable bluntness of Hook's assault on Hegel and Hegelians. First, we must consider Hook's assumption in the 1930s, and even in the 1940s, that Hegelianism was a powerful force in American academic life. This belief had some basis in fact. At the time that John Dewey began writing as a Hegelian, German idealist thought was being taught in philosophy, theology, and history departments at the best universities in America. In 1930 John Dewey pointed out that in all likelihood he would have become a Hegelian while at Johns Hopkins even without the example of Morris.[14] Interest in German philosophy had soared to such proportions by the 1880s that Dewey believed that he would have been drawn to Kant and Hegel as a result of the general academic environment. That environment was partly created by G. S. Morris, who lectured enthusiastically on Hegel and who also translated Friedrich Überweg's popular *Outline of the History of Philosophy*. The fourth section of Überweg's *Outline* contains a survey of nineteenth-century German philosophy that bestows special attention on Hegel and his disciples.

Undoubtedly the strongest force that worked to spread Hegelian thought in America was the St. Louis Philosophical Society. The three founding fathers of the group organized in 1866, Henry C. Brokmeyer, William Torrey Harris, and Denton J. Snider, were outstanding civic and educational leaders in post–Civil War America. Although Harris achieved perhaps the greatest renown as a U. S. commissioner of higher education, his two colleagues enjoyed public recognition of their own: Brokmeyer as a philosopher-writer and lieutenant governor of Missouri, and Snider as the author of more than forty books, mostly on Hegelian thought, and as the organizer of the kindergarten program in American education. The educators and thinkers who joined the St. Louis Movement (as it came to be called) were numerous and, often, illustrious. They included G. S. Morris at the University of Michigan; George Herbert Palmer, who became chairman of the Philosophy Department at Harvard University; and George Holmes Howison, who carried the study of philosophy and especially Hegel's thought to the University of California.[15]

Two of the movement's critical characteristics were its interest in Hegel as a political theorist and its belief in his special relevance for the American people. While Harris, Brokmeyer, and Snider all wrote on Hegel's theology, logic, and aesthetics, *The Philosophy of Right* provided the conceptual keystone for their entire movement. Its members read Hegel's social thought while keeping in mind the passage from *Lectures on the Philosophy of History* that refers to America as "the land of the future where in all the ages that lie before us, the burden of the world's history shall reveal itself. . . ."[16] A biographer of the St. Louis Hegelians has noted the sense of congruence that Snider in particular claimed to find between their center in the American heartland and America's destiny to represent the future of the World Spirit: "To him [Snider], the bustling city with its overflowing German population and its bourgeois energy signified the working-out of Hegel's destiny for man. James Eads' great iron bridge, the first to cross the Mississippi, was then under construction, and it symbolized for Snider the 'concrete universal' as it applied to America."[17] Significantly, James Eads, the engineer responsible for the bridge that occasioned Snider's thoughts about the "concrete Universal," was himself both a Hegelian and a charter member of the movement.

Anticipating a recurrent theme of the postwar conservative Frank Meyer, the St. Louis Hegelians saw the historical dialectic as culminating in the American nation state. European society had moved beyond the patriarchal states of antiquity by creating a civil order that protected the right of contract and commercial transactions. The European states had begun to incorporate into their laws the Christian understanding of the individual's spiritual worth. Yet, the highest stage of the dialectic could not be attained on the European continent, where nations still struggled for mastery over each other. Hegel's state of Prussia served a "capricious will" rather than morally educating citizens. Thrust into the midst of clashing European powers, Prussia had been forced to transform itself into a military society.[18] Only the Anglo-American world, and preeminently its American part, was realizing the Hegelian ideal of harmonizing individual will and the public good, private activity and communal norms, civil society and political authority.

Snider, in *The State,* undertakes to do for the American Constitution what *The Philosophy of Right* had already done for the regime that Hegel had hoped to see fully implemented in Prussia: to demonstrate its conformity to what the World Spirit was bringing forth as the highest stage of the historical dialectic. Throughout *The State,* Snider admits the derivation of his political thinking from Hegel's conceptualization of the state; both saw the state as the unified ethical will, reflected in civil society.[19] Snider also foreshadowed Frank Meyer when he praised the Founding Fathers for "mediating" the polarity between the will toward national government and an equally strong will present at the time of the founding toward states' rights. Meyer attacked Abraham Lincoln for overpowering the states' rightists and for destroying irrevocably the balance of forces at the heart of the original American system. By contrast, Snider, a biographer of Lincoln, presented his subject as a world historical figure who understood fully the American regime's spirit. Snider's Lincoln wished to reconcile the two founding principles, but History forced him to raise both into a new synthesis. This he did by renewing the sense of nationhood in a society that was freeing itself of the burden of slavery.[20] The St. Louis Hegelians considered the principle of states' rights to be less crucial for freedom than the survival of communal and institutional associations. These associations, they were convinced, had not been impaired by the Union's victory in the Civil War. Harris and Snider identified individual and historical progress with a "process of transition," from the individual through the family and civil society to the nation state. All these relationships were to be viewed as essential and complementary moments in the self-definition of the modern educated citizen. Snider, Brokmeyer, and Harris exalted Lincoln as the figure who had assured the continued existence of a nation state in American life.

The St. Louis Hegelians had ties to an earlier thinker, August Willich, that may have surprised them. A German socialist who immigrated to America, Willich became editor of the Cincinnati *Republikaner*, a local Workingmen's League newspaper, shortly before the American Civil War. An embattled abolitionist who rose to the rank of major general in the Union army, Willich was a man driven by a vision of social justice. He decried "wage slavery" as well as African bondage, and he evoked as his preferred future a socialist economy run by workers' councils. Unquestionably Willich represented the kind of "negative Hegelianism" that the St. Louis Hegelians blamed on the Old World. His dialectical thinking did not admit of syntheses. He imagined that human rights based on a recognition of mankind's equality would triumph over "historical rights" that he thought existed to protect inherited property relations.

Despite such radical thinking, Willich illustrated what from the standpoint of orthodox Marxism were the two most deplorable tendencies of American Hegelians: the insistence on American exceptionalism and the use of idealist methods for interpreting social evolution. Marx, who had known Willich in Germany as a revolutionary zealot, had deep theoretical differences with him. In Europe their personal quarrels had led Willich into challenging Marx to a duel that resulted in the death of Marx's proxy.[21] The editorials for the Cincinnati *Republikaner* substituted a dialectic of principle for the historical materialism that Marx considered necessary for a scientific socialist outlook. Willich maintained that the American regime, unlike European states, was conceptually sound and compatible with the demands of Hegelian Reason. Whereas in Europe historical institutions "were grafted onto human rights and eventually submerged them," in America "these [human] rights alone are rooted in the earth and if the European grafts can be snipped from their stem, then will their own fruit-bearing twigs branch forth."[22] This florid but heartfelt tribute to American exceptionalism reveals the continuity between Willich's politically radical Hegelianism and later publications of the St. Louis movement. A combination of philosophical idealism with American patriotism was a leitmotiv common to both.

In the 1890s American university students and professors discussed the works of T. H. Green and Bernard Bosanquet, the two most famous English exponents of Hegel's political theory. Both interpreters were critical of free-market economics; and they believed, as Hegel had, in the ethical superiority of the state, as a unifying force, to a self-centered civil society.[23] After the turn of the century, Benedetto Croce visited and lectured in America. Unlike Green and

Bosanquet, Croce celebrated individual freedom and creativity, and he tried to bring Hegelianism more into line with a classical liberal perspective. Although Croce's neo-Hegelian approach to ethical questions irritated such Harvard University professors as Irving Babbitt and George Santayana, his books and essays on aesthetics, history, and literature attracted the attention of educated Americans throughout the early twentieth century.[24] Hook may have exaggerated the Hegelian presence in American universities of the late thirties, but one may safely assume that when he and Will Herberg studied philosophy as graduate students at Columbia University in the midtwenties, both were exposed to Hegel's thought. The same no doubt was true of James Burnham, who was a promising undergraduate at Princeton University in the midtwenties and who continued his philosophical studies at Oxford University in 1929. Burnham later specialized in linguistic analysis; yet he remained proud of the "smattering" of Italian Hegelianism that he had acquired during his university years.

Another factor contributing to Hook's critical view of Hegel was the opinion that he shared with many others, that Hegel was a man of the Right. The thinker whom Hook and Eastman denounced was the one Robert Nisbet read and admired as an undergraduate in the 1930s. This Hegel was essentially a romantic organicist. Despite Marx's references to Hegel as a factor in his own education, few if any Anglo-American scholars before the 1940s would have identified the philosopher of the dialectic as a proto-Marxist. Neither the modified (neoidealist) Hegelianism of Bosanquet and Green nor the aesthetic and (in the political sphere) classical-liberal reinterpretation of Hegel by Croce changed the American perception on that point.

One of the strongest indictments of American Hegelianism came from the socially radical historian Merle Curti, who in 1935 assessed the career of "William T. Harris, The Conservator":

> The Hegelian philosophy which Harris made the basis of all his social and educational thinking possessed the virtue of being thoroughly optimistic and idealistic in character. It infused the world with a divine purpose and endowed the individual with a noble and immortal destiny. At the same time it justified the existing order and authorities by declaring that whatever is, is an inevitable stage in the unfolding of objective reason or the world spirit, and is therefore right. . . . At the same time, it subordinated the individual to existing social institutions by maintaining that his true, spiritual self, which was constantly in conflict with his natural or physical self, could be realized only by adjusting himself to the divinely appointed environment and institutions that were in actual existence.[25]

In *Social Ideas of American Education,* Curti treats Hegelianism as a false ideology, a mélange of bromides and half-truths that had retarded social progress in

America. Curti went after the enemy with less subtlety than Hook: "In short, the rightwing Hegelians [sic] to which Harris subscribed . . . subordinated the mass of individuals to existing institutions, which included the corporation, the city, and the machine as well as religion and the national state." Hegelianism in America and elsewhere was seen as an opium administered to the materially deprived who confused ideal institutions with existing ones. The beneficiary of this confusion was supposedly industrial capitalism. Hegel's social theory sought to integrate the individual into an inherited framework of institutional relationships, but it blinded many Americans, educators and others, to the persistence of injustice. In summing up his critical response to Harris, Curti notes with obvious displeasure: "The deep-rooted antagonism which Harris felt toward socialism can be understood only in light of the philosophy of social evolution which he derived from Hegel."[26]

The perception of Hegel as a philosopher of order began to change (erroneously, in my view) only when the Frankfurt School for Social Research moved to America after the Nazi takeover of Germany. By the late thirties, American and English professors were claiming to uncover the Hegelian roots of Fascism.[27] Some of these professors may have drawn the wrong conclusions from Giovanni Gentile's attempted "reform" of Hegelianism in the 1930s. They assumed that Gentile's Italian Fascist reinterpretation of Hegel was an accurate survey of Hegel's thinking, rather than a highly selective adaptation of it for particular political ends. While the attacks against Hegel raged, Max Horkheimer, Theodor Adorno, and, most significantly, Herbert Marcuse sprang to his defense and presented him as a brilliant but misunderstood precursor of Marx. Winning acceptance for a proto-Marxist Hegel involved an uphill struggle, a fact that Marcuse made clear in the introduction to the 1941 edition of *Reason and Revolution*. Before the alternative view could be made to prevail, Marcuse and his fellow émigrés of the Left had to prove "that Hegel's basic conceptions are hostile to the tendencies that have led into Fascist theory and practice."[28] The settled views of Hegel in America before the late thirties were not those of his detractors who linked him to Fascism. They were in fact the pictures of Hegel bequeathed by Morris, Überweg, Green, Harris, Snider, and Croce, which were also the views that the Hegelian center and Hegelian Right had produced in nineteenth-century Germany.

This brings up the matter of the last contributing factor in Hook's war against Hegel: his attempt from the early thirties to save Marx from the residues of Hegelian thought. Because of his current association with the relatively conservative Hoover Institution and his open hostility to the Soviet Union and the imposition of minority hiring quotas on universities, both conservatives and liberals have come to associate Hook with the political Right. Very few take seriously his current expressions of sympathy for Marx and his self-definition as a Socialist. Attempts to trace the genealogy of Hook's ideas more often focus on Dewey's pragmatism than on Marx's materialism.[29] Hook himself is partly responsible for this confusion. In 1927 when he brought out *Metaphysics of Pragmatism*, his first book under the aegis of Dewey, Hook was also preparing an English-language edition of Lenin's collected works for the Communist-affiliated International Publishers.

Hook's work *From Hegel to Marx: Studies in the Intellectual Development of Karl Marx*, first published in 1936 and then periodically updated, makes the case for the "scientific" Marx against the "metaphysical" Hegel. In the course of his analysis, Hook concedes that there were perspectives shared by the two thinkers. Both viewed society in terms of historical process and were properly scornful of attempts to posit "ethical absolutes" without reference to changing historical conditions. Beyond these overlaps, which Hook considers more apparent than real, a vast gulf separated his subjects: "In turning Hegel, to use Marx's own words, 'right side up again,' Marx was definitely returning to the position of one whom Hegel had turned 'wrong side down,' Aristotle. If Marx's philosophical method was Hegelian, his fundamental starting point, as Engels admits, was Aristotelian." Moreover, Marx surpassed even Aristotle as a thinker, by producing "an Aristotelianism saturated with temporalism, freed from the dogma of . . . substantial forms and the piety of the Prime Mover. Dialectical materialism has its basis, but not its fulfillment, in Aristotle's naturalism."[30] Marx wedded "the methodology of science" to "the naturalism of Aristotle."[31]

In comparison to Marx, Hegel was, in Hook's opinion, an utterly pedestrian thinker, who employed organic images in defense of social hierarchy. He depicted organized human activity "not in terms of personal motives or interests but in terms of an objective status in a differentiated social whole." Hegel defined rights as "the natural expression of one's status and duties, not as the result of a contract between independent individuals. Independence is conditional upon a myriad of prior dependencies which flow from one underlying social bond. The ideal community for Hegel is a *Schicksalsgemeinschaft* in which all would find a common, even if differentiated, fulfillment."[32]

In contrast to Hegel, Marx studied social organization from an empirical perspective. He considered "the unity of social consciousness . . . an historical and sociological fact, not a metaphysical assertion." A true scientific empiricist, he traced social consciousness back to its probable point of origin in the concrete needs of social exchange. Hook thought that Marx was right in equating the social structure with the division of labor: "The principle of the division of labor links together the social status and opportunities of man" in such a way that the latter can be understood only through the former. Marx applied his scientific method to the study of ethical questions and recognized that "morality is based upon need, upon what man as a social creature desires."[33] Marx's commitment to socialism flowed from his perception that human needs could not be fully satisfied through a capitalist economy. Capitalism produced goods for profit, rather than for social needs; and it thereby engendered great poverty together with material abundance, a situation that only socialism would remedy through a planned, humane economy. Hook observes that despite their common references to "developmental process," Hegel and Marx used that term differently. Hegel assumed that there was "only one process, one systematic whole in which everything moves and has its being." Marx, by contrast, perceived that "process is purposive only where social categories of the material continuum are involved. . . . It is human need expressed as purpose that split the one Absolute Whole of Hegel into pieces."[34]

The distinctions Hook made between a scholastic Hegel and a scientific Marx tell more about Hook at the time that he wrote his book than they do about his subjects. Like others on the anti-Communist Left, Hook continued to admire Marx, even after he had rejected the political application of Marxist-Leninism in Russia. In the thirties and forties he argued, as did other anti-Soviet admirers of Marx, that the Soviet dictatorship had nothing to do with its alleged spiritual father. Hook followed Karl Korsch and other anti-Soviet Marxists when he blamed Lenin and Stalin for misapplying Marxist theory.

He also anticipated a postwar trend when he traced the derailment of Marxism further back, to a nineteenth-century source: namely, Engels. In one version of this devil theory, which the Frankfurt School for Social Research in its short-lived anti-Soviet phase helped to spread, the theoretical rigidity of Russian Communism resulted from Lenin's having confused Marx with Engels.[35] Unlike Marx, who applied the dialectic flexibly and scientifically, Engels, a crude theorist, bequeathed to Lenin a materialistic and naturalist conception of society that prepared the way for Soviet dogmatism. The work most often cited to prove Engel's theoretical crudity is the *Anti-Dühring*, a book that Marx actually edited and praised.

Hook interpreted Hegel somewhat as the aforementioned theorists interpreted Engels. Although he attacked the Soviets for distorting Marx, he also blamed Hegel as an irresponsible thinker. By using a disfigured dialectic to defend authoritarian institutions and brute force, Hegel had pointed toward the destruction of reason among modern ideologues. Since the 1950s the Italian Socialist Lucio Colletti has presented a thesis similar to Hook's. Colletti has tried to trace Lenin's "vulgar Marxism" to Engels's naturalism and, ultimately, to Hegel's nonempirical dialectic.[36] Hook's attempt, which started earlier than Colletti's, to play off a good Marx against a bad Hegel has remained a permanent part of his thinking. In a review of Michael Harrington's *The Twilight of Capitalism* in 1976, he accuses Harrington of linking "the heuristic fruitfulness of Marx's approach" to Hegel's theory of consciousness: "he [Harrington] performs not a lobotomy on Marx but a brain transplant, substituting for Marx's closely knit grey matter a diffuse Hegelian mess."[37]

It would of course be wrong to deny that Hook has decisively moved away from the revolutionary Marxism of his youth. The anthology of his writings since 1973, *Marxism and Beyond*, testifies to the fact that his profound reverence for Marx the thinker is now mixed with serious doubts about Marx the prophet. What should not be overlooked, however, is that Hook continues to praise Marx as a "scientific" sociologist, who saw as far as his historical condition would permit. And Hook still contrasts Marx with Hegel, the murky metaphysician, the "brutal upshot" of whose view is "that whatever is, is right, or with respect to history, 'Die Weltgeschichte ist das Weltgericht.'"[38] Even in this recent collection of essays, Hook still accuses socialists whom he dislikes of reading Hegel into Marx.

Hook is correct in urging us not to confuse Hegel with Marx; yet there is reason to challenge the highly partisan picture of each man that he provides. Did Hegel entirely ignore empirical facts in constructing his dialectical logic? His *Science of Logic* and *Encyclopedia of Philosophical Sciences* both draw heavily on empirical evidence to illustrate the principle of interrelatedness. For example, Section 82 of the *Encyclopedia* warns against confounding Hegel's "speculative" philosophy with the entirely abstract conceptions found in other thinkers. Hegel tried to ground his speculation in the world of experience: "For philosophy has nothing to do with empty abstractions of [purely] formal thought; what concerns [the philosopher] is concrete thought."[39] As a political thinker Hegel did not justify power for its own sake, contrary to Hook's assertions. He defended, as Carl J. Friedrich has cogently pointed out, a government under law.[40] Although Hegel describes the state in *The Philosophy of Right* as the unified ethical will of its subjects, he defines the regime that fits his characterization as one that permits "personal distinctness and particularity to have full scope within the context of the family and of civil society."[41]

Hook shows bias when in *From Hegel to Marx* he praises Marx's scientific rigor. Marx's "science" was based on a flawed analogy between society and a mechanistically conceived physical world. Marx's view of cultural, moral, and political phenomena as byproducts of social exchange was neither scientific nor empirical. It resulted from a materialist outlook (which seems to be shared by Hook) that traces all human interactions back to the form of production and the accompanying division of labor. Such an outlook as the Marxist one glowingly presented by Hook may typify what the French Orientalist Louis Dumont treats as a peculiarly modern Western superstition: namely, that societies are composed of potentially autonomous individuals. These individuals provisionally operate as an artificially integrated unit because of shared material needs. The theory assumes that at some point in the future these needs will be satisfied without social stratification; thereafter the state will disappear and civil society be radically altered.[42]

But what is most important for this analysis is not Hook's lack of objectivity, but rather his continuing self-identification as an anti-Hegelian admirer of Marx. This identity sets him apart from other former radicals such as Will Herberg, Karl Wittfogel, and James Burnham. They saw history as a process that purified and perfected society; though Hook never denies the historicist aspect in Marx, he has usually downplayed it. Considering it a vestigial "Hegelian terminology," he prefers to stress his hero's scientific diligence and democratic humanitarianism. He pushes the advocate of violent revolution who appealed to historical laws almost completely out of sight. He dwells instead on Marx's righteous indignation over the injustices raging in nineteenth-century Europe.[43]

Hook's fellow radical in the late twenties, Max Eastman, with whom he often debated, marveled at this skill in divorcing Marx intellectually from both Hegel and Lenin. Eastman maintained that all three men had belonged to the ancestry of Stalinist Russia. He also argued that Marx had overcome Hegel only by absorbing him into his own theory of history. Karl Wittfogel, as a Communist admirer of Hegel in the 1930s, took an interpretative position similar to Eastman's. Wittfogel traced Lenin's understanding of cultural particularities back to Hegel by way of Marx. In ever starker contrast to Hook, his classmate at Columbia Will Herberg spent his life in quest of a historically grounded faith. Unlike Hook, a lifelong humanitarian secularist, Herberg went from being a historical materialist to a historical conservative and believing Jew.

Freud once called himself "half a Marxist": whereas he accepted Marx's view of the past as being characterized by violent exploitation, he rejected the hope that socialism would make the future better. In a sense, Hook and Herberg were both partial Marxists, but each embraced a different side of the Marxist Left. In the preface to *Marxism and Beyond*, Hook extols "the first and greatest of all Marxist revisionists, Edward Bernstein, whose stature as man and thinker has grown with the years."[44] Unlike Hook, Bernstein had not decried Hegel while exalting Marx, but he had prepared the way, which Hook eagerly followed, for a social democratic adaptation of Marx.

Perhaps Hook was not quite ready for Bernsteinianism in the 1930s, when he still accepted a materialist sociology, though not historical materialism, as scientific. But if Bernstein was right in comparing orthodox Marxists to Calvinist predestinarians, then Hook from the beginning was a decidedly liberal theologian. In the late twenties and early thirties, he was close to the Communist party but never joined it. Afterward he depicted Marx as both an empirical scientist and a democrat in a hurry, while blaming the social determinism in American scholarship on academic Hegelians.

In a series of polemical exchanges dealing with Hook's *Toward the Understanding of Karl Marx*, which first appeared in 1933, Herberg blasted the author for rejecting Lenin. Hook had, he said, failed to appreciate Lenin's understanding of the critical role of the Party in establishing socialism. He vehemently attacked Hook for reducing the idea of the dictatorship of the proletariat to a "verbal symbol." Mocking Hook for his "philistine worship of the abstract forms of democracy to the exclusion of any appreciation of its concrete social content," Herberg warned his fellow revolutionaries against straying from the path of historical necessity.[45] These remarks, taken from *Workers Age* of 4 May 1935, underscore the permanent difference of outlook between the Hegelian-Marxist Herberg and the social engineer Hook. The difference can be symbolized by their heroes: Hook glorified a contemplative and compassionate if not entirely plausible Marx; and Herberg, a "world-historical" Lenin, who even when he put down mutinying sailors at Kronstadt in 1921, continued to incarnate the spirit of the Revolution. When Hook, in October 1934, criticized Lenin for not having allowed the sailors at Kronstadt their own soviet (council) independent of the Party, Herberg responded by ridiculing him for preferring "the form of [bourgeois] democracy to the substance of the proletarian dictatorship." Unlike the philistine Hook, the true leader Lenin had understood the forces of his time. Lenin had perceived that when the Kronstadt soviet had expelled party officials, "behind them stood the armed counter-revolution."[46]

The terms *historical necessity* and *historically necessary* punctuated Herberg's writings for *Workers Age*, particularly when he defended the implementation of Stalin's first Five Year Plan in November 1934. Both the plan and its unhappy side effects, such as the starving of peasants, were "historically necessary and unavoidable." Herberg went so far as to assert that "it would be mere philistinism to sigh in regret or to whine in despair over those heavy sacrifices and costs."[47] Such remarks, in my view, did not stem merely from callousness, although it may be difficult to exclude that as a factor when trying to understand them. Herberg was expressing his belief in history as the work of monumental figures who grasped historical forces that were incomprehensible to mere "democratic Marxists."

In his arguments with Hook, who inveighed against the danger of hero worship, Herberg affirmed the necessity for world historical figures. He scorned a proposal for a "many-party system under proletarian dictatorship" in Russia that Hook had made, pointing out its inconsistency with the social harmony that was possible as a result of the Bolshevik Revolution. Why bother, except for counter revolutionary ends, to inject differences into a society that was now rising above them? Moreover, it was foolish to believe that workers saw their interests as fully as did the vanguard of the revolution, the Party and its leaders.

These arguments were the standard ones that Marxist-Leninists used against democratic socialists. In Herberg's case, and particularly in his confrontation with Hook, however, such arguments expressed a cultural and aesthetic bias. Herberg was taking the part of the bearers of historical progress against their cavilling, philistine detractors. Thus when Hook compared Lenin to Robespierre at the height of the Terror, Herberg noted his "incredible failure to grasp the historical role of the Jacobin dictatorship." It was precisely "thru [sic] this ruthless dictatorship, in spite of all its abuses, and, curiously enough, at the very height of the reign of terror that the people of France, but particularly of Paris, got the only real bit of democracy they had ever tasted, that is, the practical power collectively to influence their own fate." According to Herberg, Hook was prevented from admiring "the heroic period of the great French Rev-

olution" by his "shabby reactionary attitude." Herberg was here presenting
the kind of Hegelian paradox that he relished and that Hook detested. Out of
private corruption and personal ambition came often genuine human advances, and those who denied these advances because of the accompanying
blemishes revealed truly small minds lacking historical imagination. Indeed
Hook's squeamishness was all the more inappropriate because he applauded
the Bolshevik Revolution and wished to preserve the proletarian dictatorship.

Herberg's critique expressed a mode of historical thinking that was alien to
Hook's reformist mentality. That mode was the recognizably Hegelian views
about history that Herberg held as a Communist. Although it is hard to determine a direct causal relationship, Herberg's polemics may have been in the
back of Hook's mind when he wrote *The Hero in History* in 1943. In this book
more than in any other of his works, Hook combined anti-Leninist positions
with extended attacks on Hegel.[48]

There was another historical view that differed from Herberg's (but was less
Hegelian than his) but was equally opposed to Hook's humanitarian
socialism: the pragmatic historicism of James Burnham. When Burnham
broke formally with the Communist movement, he wrote a letter to Leon
Trotsky on 21 May 1940, in which he cited the defects of Marx's "science of history" as motivating his decision. Lenin had not achieved a true socialist revolution that was later only temporarily derailed by bureaucrats. Historical forces,
which Marx's dialectic could not explain, were changing Soviet Russia and the
West. Thus Burnham concluded:

> I consider that on the basis of the evidence now available to us a new form
> of exploitative society (what I call "managerial society") is not only pos-
> sible as an alternative to capitalism but is a more probable outcome of
> the present period than socialism.[49]

Burnham's relentless analysis of the world-historical significance of "man-
agerialism" culminated in his most famous study, *The Managerial Revolution,* in
1941. In this work he brought forth his own revised Marxist dialectic; he argued
that the current disintegration of Western capitalism was leading not to
socialism but to managerial society.

The historical outlooks of Burnham and of Herberg foreshadowed their later
conservatism in much the same way as Hook's anti-Leninist and anti-Hegelian
Marxism foreshadowed his present social democratic anti-Communism.[50] Establishing connections between these later and earlier loyalties is by no means
an easy task. One explanation would have us believe that extremes here
touched. Those who were embattled and hardened radicals moved ultimately
to the far Right, while the more moderate reformers remained moderate even
after they had become conservatives. This explanation is not entirely
adequate. Neither Herberg nor Burnham ever became a radical rightist.
Moreover, many fervent Communists of the 1930s did not do about-faces after

they had abandoned the Party. For every Whittaker Chambers or Frank Meyer, one can easily cite a Dwight Macdonald or an Irving Howe, both former Communists who stayed on the left.

One possible bridge between Herberg's and Burnham's earlier and later political careers was the historical views they espoused during their radical phases. In contrast to the anti-Hegelian Hook, these men appealed to history as the acid test of truth and source of political values. Both rejected abstract universals, even as radicals, and, unlike Hook, they despised the honoring of forms without reference to historical contexts. Burnham rejected the Soviet model, not because he believed in abstract democratic ideals, but because Soviet society obviously failed to fulfill Marx's historical prediction. That failure, together with the ascendancy of the managerial elite in Western industrial societies, seemed to invalidate Marx's "science of history," which Burnham tried to replace with his own historical interpretation. Herberg invoked History even more enthusiastically than did Burnham. He placed it eventually at the heart of his post-Communist religious faith, a topic that we shall discuss at length in the next chapter.

# TIME AS REDEMPTIVE HISTORY: THE ACHIEVEMENT OF WILL HERBERG

AMONG THE POST-1945 ARCHITECTS OF CONSERVATIVE THEORY, WILL Herberg (1902–1977) was the most openly theological in interpreting his age. In his youth he had joined the American Communist party and by the late twenties was writing profusely on the cultural implications of the "science" of Marxist-Leninism. He believed, like Lenin, that a workers' revolution was possible only if properly led by a party vanguard of theoreticians and social engineers. As he himself would later remark, his background predisposed him to those radical doctrines characteristic of his early years. The mentally agile son of Germanized Russian Jews, he grew up in a polyglot home that taught him reverence for Western rationalism.[1] For the young Herberg participation in the Communist movement conferred the privileged position of working consciously to remake both society and human nature for the better.

His attachment to Communism, no mere affectation, reflected intellectual conviction as well as moral ardor. So earnestly did he embrace Marxist materialism that in 1930 and again in 1931 he labored to reconcile it with Einstein's theory of relativity. Most Communists then still condemned Einstein for rejecting Marx's "scientific materialism" by supposedly denying the objective reality of matter. Herberg, however, insisted that both Marxism and the theory of relativity were "scientifically true." Although Einstein had demonstrated the interchangeability of energy and matter, which he had expressed in the formula $E = mc^2$, he had not denied the existence of matter. Herberg maintained that Einstein's view on the "equivalence of matter and energy" was logically consistent with Marx's dialectical materialism. The Einsteinian position, that at very high velocities relative to a given frame of reference space contracted in the direction of motion while time slowed down, supposedly provided evidence of a dialectic understanding. No longer were there absolute "lines of demarcation" between space and time and between matter and energy: disparate categories were now joined in "dialectical unity."[2]

As a Communist Herberg was relentlessly critical of Leon Trotsky. Trotsky, the first Red army commander and a literary prodigy, was driven from the Soviet government and eventually nto exile by Stalin in the late twenties. From his place of refuge in Mexico, Trotsky called upon Communists to "restore" Lenin's revolution, and he attacked Stalin's "bureaucratic derailment" of the Bolshevik enterprise. His positions elicited the support of many American radicals, most notably James Burnham. Trotsky's American adherents included young Jewish intellectuals, some of whom, like Irving Kristol, would land up years later on the political Right.[3] Although Herberg later moved in the same ultimate direction and expressed admiration for former Trotskyists, he never joined what he considered to be a heretical Marxist group. Stalin's consolidation of his base of support in Soviet Russia did not appear to the young Herberg as a historical accident. While Trotsky had tried to improvise revolutions everywhere without first securing a socialist base in Russia, Stalin had supposedly recognized the necessary connection between Soviet power and international Communism. An industrially productive and militarily formidable Soviet state would offer the best hope for the spread of Marxist socialism outside Russia. Even as a conservative, Herberg viewed the postwar Soviet conquest of Eastern Europe as a belated confirmation of his having made the "right decision" during his Communist phase.[4]

Despite his anti-Trotskyism Herberg did break ranks as a Communist twice. In 1928, during a struggle for power within the American Communist party leadership, he backed Jay Lovestone, an American supporter of the Soviet Marxist theoretician Nicolai Bukharin. Lovestone and Bukharin had both advocated more autonomy from Soviet control for national Communist parties. They had likewise promoted a polycentric approach to Marxist politics instead of an imposed and uniform party structure everywhere under Russian dominance. In 1929 Stalin struck back by demoting Bukharin in the Soviet party and by ousting Lovestone and his followers from leadership of the American movement.[5] Although himself a schismatic anti-Trotskyist, Herberg broke completely with Marxist-Leninist revolutionary movements only in the late thirties, after the Great Purges had begun. By then he had reacted against the way in which the Comintern, the Soviet-controlled agency of international revolution, treated Communists outside Russia. During the purges and particularly after Burkharin's execution in 1937, Herberg began to criticize the "Soviet dictatorship," although even then he defended "the soundness" of "the Stalinist line" against Trotsky's followers.[6]

Herberg's acquaintances sometimes likened his change of heart to St. Paul's conversion on the road to Damascus. The comparison may have pleased him, for, like Paul, whose teachings he would later expound, Herberg stressed the Jews' special role as the bringers of light unto the nations. When Ursula

Niebuhr, the wife of his mentor in the late forties, was once asked how she imagined St. Paul might have looked, she responded, "Like Will Herberg." And yet, his rejection of Communism did not occur under the impact of an alternative faith. Although Herberg moved away from Communism amid abuse and physical threats, he remained on the socialist Left for at least a decade thereafter.[7]

From 1935 until 1948 Herberg served organized labor as a research analyst and pamphleteer for the International Ladies Garment Workers Union. In 1937 he produced a tract, "The C.I.O. and Labor's New Challenge," that advocated a more broadly based and militant American labor movement. He urged that greater power within the movement be shifted to the Congress of Industrial Organizations (CIO), which was then organizing factory workers, and away from its craft-based parent organization, the American Federation of Labor (AFL).[8] Herberg praised industrial unions, particularly the United Mineworkers, the Amalgamated Clothing Workers, and the CIO, for striking in pursuit of higher wages.[9] He chided the AFL's leaders for seeking to revoke the charters of CIO affiliates that had been involved in strikes. He compared the AFL, which then existed in uneasy alliance with the CIO, to a tactically cautious union in nineteenth-century America, the Knights of Labor. Like the AFL, the Knights of Labor had failed the working class by asking for "cooperation (among producers), land, monetary reform, and other such panaceas. In a word, it was not at all a trade union movement in the modern sense of the term."[10]

Long after he broke with the Communist party, Herberg continued to believe in the inescapable confrontation between workers and the owners of the means of production. Moreover, his interest in the "organization of mass production industries" extended from his period of collaboration with Jay Lovestone and his affiliation with the schismatic Communist Party U.S.A. in 1929 until his postwar turn toward the Right. As late as the 1960s, he thought that the Republican party was deplorably insensitive to labor. In the 1960 presidential election, he openly supported John F. Kennedy, to the dismay of other conservative intellectuals, and to the end of his life he viewed the union formed by the merger of the American Federation of Labor with the Congress of Industrial Organizations as a patriotic anticommunist force within American politics.[11]

Other experiences serve as a bridge between Herberg's career as a Communist and his later move toward the Right. A concern with "grasping the historical moment" was a preoccupation that ran through his work. In 1933 while a spokesman for Lovestone's Communist Party U.S.A., Herberg had defended the usefulness of FDR's National Industrial Recovery Act (NIRA) for a then demoralized labor force. Although the newly enacted legislation failed to give workers control over the instruments of production, it recognized genuine workers' grievances. Herberg thought of the NIRA as being an opportunity to mobilize the unemployed not only as a government labor pool but as a dynamic force for change. He did concede that the New Deal legislation, by quelling discontent among workers, might help to salvage the American capitalist economy. Indeed he himself criticized the NIRA for "leaving open shops unchanged" and for "taking over full control of wages and hours and assuming the power to interfere in the concerns of labor organizations."[12] All the same, he focused on what seemed the positive opportunities offered. The American government, by drawing "the forces of mass production industry" into an act of "class collaboration," had at last acknowledged their political significance. Industrial union leadership should join the New Deal and press the demand for a socialist state, while exposing "the complete inadequacy of craft unions." He stressed the need for greater faith in the future "to grasp the manifold aspects of the new situation not only statically but in their dynamic implications."[13]

The appeal to historical process became even more integral to Herberg's defense of industrial unionism in 1937. In his pamphlet on the CIO he denounced the Knights of Labor for opposing strikes and the programmatically revolutionary Industrial Workers of the World for ignoring the American social context. He likewise ridiculed the Communist union movement as one "brought into being simply and solely for political and party reasons." Even more than the timid and tactically unimaginative Knights of Labor, ideologically based unions were, Herberg believed, "inherently artificial creations." Herberg, striking a note that foreshadows his later conservatism, described the revolutionary Left's union activities as "having no connection whatever with the American reality or roots in the American condition. They came into existence and functioned entirely as party auxiliaries, in fact as trade union departments of the political parties in question."[14]

Herberg penned these lines while still proclaiming himself a Marxist activist. His pamphlets extolled Lovestone's Communist Party U.S.A. for "never hesitating to state their position on the present crisis in the labor movement directly and clearly."[15] But his conceptual-historical framework was unmistakably Hegelian. The task that confronted his age, he suggested, was to reconcile a universal vision produced by human reason with the values inherent in his own culture and society. Unlike Marx and Lenin he did not appeal to a dialectic that "overcomes" the past. It was Hegel's concrete-universal that informed Herberg's understanding of the American labor movement. The future he envisaged would realize a universal ideal as part of the Western and, more specifically, American experience. Herberg, in closing, invoked the hope of a better unified union movement suffused by a new spirit of solidarity. By "thinking realistically," by shedding "sentimental illusions and empty phrases," all friends of labor might achieve "the reunification of a divided labor movement on a higher level, on the basis of industrial unionism and democracy."[16]

The appeal for realistic policies should not obscure the philosophical thrust of Herberg's argument. The invocation of a labor movement that reconciles polar positions "on a higher level" while acknowledging "the American condition" betokened the shaping influence of Hegel's historicism. Hegel's view of Reason at work in political and social development and his sensitivity to cultural particularities both left their mark on Herberg's thinking. Until the end of his life, he identified Hegel as a historical realist who had taught him "never to make faces at history."[17] In 1943 while a democratic Socialist, he paid tribute to Hegel together with Marx in an essay, "The Christian Mythology of Socialism." Here he traced Marx's dialectic back to a triadic view of history drawn from Trinitarian Christianity and Hegelian philosophy.

It is obvious that Herberg's interpretive perspective, and particularly his discussion of "energizing myths," owed much to Georges Sorel and Vilfredo Pareto, two analysts of the nonrational sources of social behavior he had by then begun to read. The conclusion would confirm such speculation about the theoretical derivation of his essay: "It is apparently impossible to eliminate the mythological element from the ideology of a social movement without destroying its sources of power. Mythology is the dynamism of a great social movement as it is of great religion."[18] Yet, although Herberg considered social action inseparable from mythic, nonrational beliefs, he also pointed to the generative power of the Western faith in a three-stage history, proceeding from primal innocence through a fallen state toward regained innocence. In his view:

> "The significant philosophies and ideologies of modern Western civilization are in last analysis derived from this source. There is little difficulty in interpreting Spinoza, Descartes (in his metaphysics), Kant (in his ethics), Hegel, Rousseau, and other modern thinkers in this light. Nor is it hard to detect the Christian doctrine of man and society, shorn of its supernaturalism, in the social philosophies of the last three centuries. Socialism reflects another side of this process.[19]

Supposedly Hegel and his disciples, once having taken the "triadic pattern" from Christianity, had then given it a suitable modern form as the dialectic. Hegel's dialectical scheme, with its progression from thesis through antithesis to synthesis, emerged from Christian redemptive history and prepared the ground for the Communist interpretation of social struggle. Herberg, while impressed by Marx's moral enthusiasm, credits Hegel with inventing what became the Marxist dialectic. Marx took over "the familiar triadic pattern of the Hegelian dialectic," which in turn Hegel had adapted from Christianity.

Equally significant, Herberg makes Marx's dialectic resemble Hegel's. Presenting Marx's three-stage history (for Marx there were in point of fact five historical phases, each corresponding to a specific mode of production) as a variation on the Hegelian dialectic, Herberg stresses as basic to Marxian socialism the theme of reintegration. But Marx was hardly emphatic, as Herberg maintains he was, that "Under Communism man is restored to primitive social virtue but on a 'higher level.'"[20] Although Engels, in the *Anti-Dühring*, described a short-lived matriarchal society without private property situated in prehistoric times, the Marxist dialectic presupposed the abolition of the archaic past. Socialist society as conceived by Marx would bear little, if any, resemblance to the patriarchal and collectivist world that Marx identified with the earliest form of production and with predominantly non-Western peoples. Socialist man who would discover his human essence for the first time would be wholly different from a self-alienated, presocialist mankind. All of human society until the advent of socialism belonged to what Marx called *prehistory:* the epoch of man's subjugation to the forces of production and of his generally unhappy social and spiritual condition.

By contrast, Hegel viewed history as the cumulative work of a universal consciousness. Mind, or consciousness, operated not by rescinding the past, but by incorporating it into steadily richer blends of moral and intellectual forces. Each stage of the dialectic reflected the growing self-realization of mind: syntheses were carried forward with those forces that had come to oppose them into new forms of unity. The idea of "restoring," or preserving, values and virtues on a higher plane of consciousness is clearly Hegelian, and Herberg's attribution of this idea to Marx may reveal the Hegelianism present in his Marxist view of history.[21]

Also indicative of Herberg's outlook at the beginning of what he later considered his spiritual odyssey is a study he wrote in fall 1943, "Democracy in Labor Unions." His analysis of bureaucratization and of controlling elites in union organization supports his recollection that he wrote under the influence of Robert Michels and Max Weber. The essay throughout betrays Herberg's keen disappointment with the union movement. In his view, businesslike leaders were keeping unions from acting as a "vehicle—of the submerged laboring masses for social recognition and democratic determination." Moreover:

> The union, as an institution, is in the grip of a contradiction. Each side of this contradiction, each functional aspect, generates its own appropriate habits and attitudes, so that the institutional cleavage is reflected not only in a cleavage between leaders and rank and file but in a cleavage within the bureaucratic personnel, and not infrequently in a sort of psychic cleavage in the leaders themselves. . . .[22]

Herberg deplores the drying up of the old unionism's "quasi-religious spiritual resources" and the transformation of unions into "businesslike service agencies bureaucratically operated, like banks or insurance companies."

The Marxist-Hegelian term *contradiction* appears repeatedly in this study, although its author never holds out the prospect of reconciling polar opposites at a higher level. Herberg's suggestions for union reform—for example, "meetings organized by smaller units of a more organic character" and the protection of workers' rights, if necessary by government, against abusive union leadership—indicate his disgust with corrupt administrators more than any continued faith in the cause. His comments about a despiritualized unionism may have revealed an internal quandary. His faith in a Communist revolution, with or without Soviet support, had vanished forever. His involvement with unionism, which he had considered a moderate variant on the Hegelian-Marxist adaptation of Christian mythology, had led to further disappointment. Having sought redemption through politics, he would now resume his journey of self-discovery by looking specifically to theology for religious answers.

The final leg of this journey would yield Herberg both scholarly recognition and spiritual tranquillity. His achievements are matters of record; the well-earned eulogies to him published in the 5 August 1977 issue of *National Review*, a journal he helped to found, discuss them in reverential detail.[23] Soon after World War II he underwent a profound change of heart. In 1947, in *Commentary*, Herberg announced his intellectual rejection of Marxism and his need for religious explanations in an era tainted by nihilistic thinkers and political totalitarians.[24] His ancestral religion gave him the answers he sought. In his eloquent *Judaism and Modern Man: An Interpretation of Jewish Religion* (1951), one sees the effects on his Jewish theology of his contact with Reinhold Niebuhr both in his historical-existentialist understanding of human sin and in his religious arguments in favor of Western democracy. Here one can also discern the impact of the Jewish existentialist Martin Buber on Herberg's vision of society, one in which human relationships are mediated by each member's sense of the divine presence. In 1955 he published *Protestant, Catholic, Jew*, a study in religious sociology that brought Herberg fame in still another discipline. Here he argued that an American acquired cultural identity in common with other Americans through membership in one of three socially recognized national religions. All three confessions, Protestant, Catholic, and Jewish, preached the same civil religion, and Americans, by joining them, were affirming and even intensifying a shared sense of American allegiance. Despite his support of American interfaith fraternity, Herberg, in his closing chapter, warns against the trivialization of "Judeo-Christian religion." Religion in America no longer forced its participants to confront "the transcendent and absolute"; people went to churches and synagogues to express civil and social obligations but no longer to worship.

In addition to his major writings of the fifties and sixties, Herberg produced anthologies of the works of Buber, Jacques Maritain, and other modern existentialist theologians. He contributed a stream of essays, mostly on religion, to two conservative publications, *National Review* and *Modern Age*, and wrote for at least a dozen other periodicals, including *New Republic* and *Christian Century*. In 1955 he obtained an academic appointment at Drew University in Judaic studies and in social philosophy; in 1963 he received an endowed chair as "graduate professor of philosophy and culture." While in this latter position Herberg lectured at numerous other universities in the United States and Europe on philosophy, theology, and social thought. He also delivered sermons in churches.[25] Both these addresses and his religious writing for *National Review* give evidence of his obvious attraction to St. Paul. Perhaps Paul's daring act of faith prefigured for Herberg his own quest for religious certainty and, above all, the fateful turn he had taken between "Democracy and Labor Unions" and that experience embodied in *Judaism and Modern Man.*

Yet, Herberg continued to change his views even after he had turned toward religion. In the late forties he studied at length the thinking of Reinhold Niebuhr (1892-1971) and of such religious existentialists as Maritain and Buber. His introduction to *Judaism and Modern Man* makes repeated references to the failed secular humanism of the Western rationalist tradition. It affirms the need for faith in the transcendent for allowing modern man to make sense of his social and historical existence. But the religion he defended was both synthetic and culturally bounded; he defined it as "Judeo-Christian" and "Hebraic" as often as specifically Jewish. Herberg, in describing this tradition, drew from Christian authorities as well as from Jewish ones and appealed to the theological views and ethical mission common to Jews and Christians. Although he did assert the universal applicability of his religious tenets, he also identified them with Western civilization and its commitment to social justice. He offered an extended contrast between quietistic Oriental religions and pagan fatalism on the one side, and the West's more socially conscious and ethically sensitive faith on the other.

A sense of apocalyptic urgency is another characteristic of his theologizing in 1951. As he himself later observed about the genesis of *Judaism and Modern Man:* "Ten years ago I was still living in the afterglow of 'the situation of the Kairos,' the time of great expectation. In such a period history is at a discount; all interest is concentrated on the emerging novelty."[26] John Diggins has correctly observed a fusion of biblically based eschatology with Hegelian historicism in Herberg's thinking of the early fifties.[27] The two views, far from being incompatible, both contribute to his understanding of a "time of great expectation." Basic to the Judeo-Christian outlook and helping to set it apart from Greek antiquity and Oriental metaphysics alike is, according to Herberg, the continuing belief in redemptive history. In the Hebraic prophetic religion "time is primarily future; past and present take on significance in terms of that toward which they are directed," In contrast to the Greek cycle of eternal recurrence and to the Hindus' identification of "the whole earthly scene as *maya,* a mist of illusion," Hebraic religion, by accentuating "the full authenticity of time, change and human action, . . . comes much closer to what is best in modern thought."[28]

This exposition of redemptive history is made to bear directly on the problems of Herberg's own time. In his remarks on the final age of the world as foretold by the Hebrew prophets, he sees the vision of humankind's and nature's return to theocentric existence as necessarily resulting in a "vital drive for social action."[29] Jews and Christians must anticipate the "new time" by acting as if it were already part of their lives. Herberg, in searching for an economic model that would conform to the demands of justice in a religiously based society, still expresses admiration for socialism. He castigates the established Christian and Jewish authorities of the nineteenth century for not recognizing this movement's "Hebraic spirit." Condemning the "autocracy" of the industrial magnates in post–Civil War America, Herberg praises Anglo-American trade unionism for helping to realize the biblical tradition of social justice.[30] He also has kind words, as well as criticism, for Marxist socialism. Despite Marx's naturalism and his repudiation of the religious origin of his social ethics, Herberg insisted that the Marxist view of history and vision of the future were rooted in the Hebrew prophets.[31]

Herberg's high regard for socialism in *Judaism and Modern Man* was far more than a lingering legacy of his early radicalism. More than once he focused on what he considered the tragic failure of socialism and Judeo-Christian religion to form a genuine alliance. Their failure to join forces was inevitable, given the institutional narrowness of nineteenth-century churches and the militant secularism of socialist organizations. Herberg did not propose that religionists make up for lost opportunities by supporting Marxist revolutions. He attacked the tyranny of Communist states, which he ascribed partly to Marx's supplanting of religious ethics by science. His preferred regime was an American welfare state infused by a conscious dedication to Hebraic values and an equally conscious opposition to totalitarian politics. In this respect as in others, Herberg followed Reinhold Niebuhr, to whom in the forward he expressed a debt for "the formation of my general theological outlook."[32]

Yet, Herberg did not view the American society of his time as a static perfection. Generalizing from his own experience and the awakened interest in the Catholic Church among cultural conservatives in the postwar period, he spoke of a return to faith among intellectuals in the face of value relativism and dehumanizing politics. This movement toward faith would draw those affected into a quest for synthetic principles needed to transcend the prevailing "polytheism of ultimates." Western society had long been fragmented by a divorce of religious and political values and by the view of education, art, economics, and other pursuits as "distinct and independent spheres of life operating under their own peculiar laws."[33] Although "Hebraic religion" (which was common to Jews and Christians) would help "overcome the spiritual disintegration of contemporary life," this would happen without a retreat into the past. Indeed the precondition for this renewal was a recognition of the theocentric source of historical change. Individuals of faith would pursue "eschatological justice," acting as if the "final age" had already dawned. Drawing on the concepts of Martin Buber and of other religious existentialists, Herberg evokes a godly community in which the "I-Thou" relationship between Creator and creature would be reflected in the social bonds established.

Inherent in this emerging historical pattern are conceptual bridges that unite past and present. For Herberg, as for Hegel, modernity entails a process of fragmentation that will ultimately bring forth new unity of thought. "The polytheism of ultimates" would yield to the pursuit of "eschatological justice." Furthermore, the conflict between revelation and science would vanish once religionists had acknowledged "redemptive history" as the exegetical key to Hebraic revelation. Herberg asserted that the struggle between nineteenth-century religionists and biblical critics was no longer relevant. Both the fundamentalists and those who reject the Bible as an unchanging and factually infallible text confuse revelation as process with revelation as literal word. The truth of Scripture flows from the pledge of redemption made manifest through Hebrew history and prophetic vision.[34] Although Herberg ascribes to Hegel a deterministic, overly intellectual understanding of "history as self-redemption," he employs Hegelian language in his explanation of *Heilsgeschichte*. History was "a process of dialectic interaction between the divine intent in creation and human self-will, or, on the other hand, between the self-transcending creativity of man and the corrupting self-interest that always invades it."[35]

One need not trace all of Herberg's references to a dialectical encounter between the divine and the human to Hegel. Such theological concepts may also be found in Buber and Niebuhr, both of whom Herberg had studied before writing his book. The ideas can likewise be located in the German romantics, and particularly in F. W. J. Schelling. Schelling's dialectical understanding of the Absolute and Its relationship to the universe left its mark not only on such modern theologians as Buber, Niebuhr, and Paul Tillich, but also on Schelling's own contemporary, Hegel. Yet it seems unlikely that Herberg's theological frame of reference came entirely from Niebuhr and Buber. More likely, his early faith in history provided the bedrock of certitude that substantiated his later belief in Hebraic *Heilsgeschichte*. Although Herberg identified the content of redemptive history with biblical narrative and prophecy, he nonetheless embraces the thoroughly Hegelian position of claiming for his age a privileged historical view. Only the modern period could free itself from naive literalism and arrogant scientism by grasping the Bible's essence as process and dialectical encounter. One is reminded here of the historicist reading that Hegel bestows on the Trinity in *Phenomenology of the Spirit* (Section VII).[36]

Yet, although Hegel's view is that of Spirit looking back at religious truth from the high ground of philosophy, Herberg proclaims his process theology at the beginning of an "age of faith." Only ten years later, however, he expressed disappointment at having rashly mistaken a "situation of the void" for a time of great expectation. *Protestant, Catholic, Jew* has sometimes been viewed as reflecting that "disillusionment" that Herberg allegedly experienced during the fifties. In 1952, in addressing the National Conference on the Spiritual Foundations of Our Democracy, he affirmed the need for a spiritually regenerate America to battle against a militantly atheistic Soviet Communism: "Communism and the faith that underlies American democracy confront each other in a conflict that admits of no compromise because it is a conflict of ultimates. Quite literally, it is a struggle for the soul of modern man."[37] In 1955, however, *Protestant, Catholic, Jew* complains of the reduction of religious faith in America to mere church attendance. "The secularism characteristic of the American mind," Herberg notes sardonically, "is implicit in and is not felt to be at all inconsistent with the most sincere attachment to religion."[38]

Herberg's charges about the outward religious conformity of the Eisenhower era have often appealed to critics of the fifties, but what may be described as his idealization of the same period has received insufficient attention. Undoubtedly he was critical of an American religion that reassured its adherents of "the essential rightness of everything American" and is thereby "vitiated by a strong and pervasive idolatrous element."[39] But even this religion, however mingled with a drive toward social conformity, was a possible "force for a new and more viable philosophy of life." And though this American religion had neglected the "crisis of faith," it had helped overcome social and political, if not spiritual, fragmentation. Herberg would appear to have demonstrated Hansen's law, which he himself quoted, and yet in fact he did not show that the grandsons of immigrants remembered what their parents tried to forget. What he associated with third-generation, hyphenated Americans was not an ancestral cultural-religious identity, but membership in one of "three basic subdivisions of the American people." All three subdivisions—Protestant, Catholic, and Jewish—taught the same civic virtues, while providing their members with common points of reference to deal with American society as a whole.[40]

Since the appearance of Herberg's work, a veritable mountain of sociological data, which directly challenges his view of three likeminded religious communities, all socializing and Americanizing their members, has materialized. According to studies by Gerhard Lenski, Edward Laumann, and Daniel Glazer, ethnic and social-educational factors were often far more important in accounting for marital patterns in the fifties and sixties than was religious affiliation. Indeed within religious communities, particularly among Catholics, marriage took place and secondary social contacts were formed largely on the basis of ethnic ties. Poles, Irish, and Italians associated primarily with others of their nationality and social backgrounds rather than with Catholics in general.[41]

One might also question whether Herberg's three religious communities all taught a patriotic civil religion intended to make their members more thoroughly American. Irish Catholic parochial education well into the postwar years instilled a highly negative attitude toward America's Anglo-Saxon Protestant heritage.[42] Although Herberg does note the "strenuous efforts of the Jewish community at self-validation," he fails to see that such concern would lead not to the increasing affirmation of Americanness but to further alienation. Self-defining Jews, that is to say, would define themselves far more often by reference to Israeli nationalism or memories of the Holocaust than by their

membership in a strongly *American* religious community.[43]

Herberg's overemphasis on the social importance and patriotic function of the "three religious subdivisions of American society" may be due to his idealization of American life. Despite their ignoring of the "crisis of faith," he believed America's institutionalized religions were helping to overcome the inherent division that had once separated a culturally heterogeneous immigrant population. The three religious communities supposedly transmitted patriotic values while fitting ethnically distinctive groups into a common national framework. Although obviously dissatisfied with aspects of this arrangement, Herberg depicts what may well have been for him the best of all possible worlds.

He viewed American civil religion not only as a source of national unity, but as a vehicle, however imperfect, to inculcate Judeo-Christian ethical teachings. During the initial legislative successes of the proabortion movement, he lamented the disappearance of the "limits of American pluralism." Confessional diversity, he argued, had posed no threat to American society because of the established value consensus among American churches. By the early seventies, under the impact of the political and theological radicalization of mainline churches and their leaders, the world of *Protestant, Catholic, Jew* had apparently changed.[44] Herberg's reservations about and hopes for civil religion bear some similarity to what the mature Hegel had said on this subject. *The Philosophy of Right* refers to the relative powerlessness of "religious feeling" to find adequate objective expression in the modern world. Theologians must limit their appeal to individuals' "inner disposition," for once churches turn political, they must either supplant the state as the fountainhead of public order or "enter into the state as a means of education and character formation."[45] Herberg's study in the sociology of religion presents American churches of the fifties as embracing this second option. Although not the ideal option from the standpoint of eschatological history and faith, it was nonetheless a modernist solution that Herberg could and did accept—and whose presumed loss he would eventually mourn.

By the sixties he had also abandoned his eschatological perspective for what he proudly called a historicist viewpoint. Contributing to this change were supposedly the Bible, Edmund Burke, and Reinhold Niebuhr, now rediscovered as a historicist. In 1959 Herberg published a thoughtful review of Peter J. Stanlis's *Edmund Burke and the Natural Law*. Stanlis had argued that Burke, an impassioned critic of the French Revolution and the natural right doctrines of the Enlightenment, was an upholder of the Christian Aristotelian tradition of natural law. Burke rejected rationalism and the "political metaphysics" nurtured by both the Enlightenment and the French Revolution, yet this rejection was traceable neither to an aversion to change per se nor to general revulsion for political theory. According to Stanlis, Burke scorned rationalist reformers and revolutionaries not only for being excessively abstract but also for their devia-

tion from timeless truths about human nature.[46] Stanlis takes seriously as the basis for Burke's political practice his repeated appeal to "eternal immutable law." Presumably Burke drew "the moral and legal weapons for his attacks on various eighteenth century radical theories and innovations" from classical and medieval natural law. Having been exposed at Dublin's Trinity College to Aristotle, Cicero, and the Anglican divine Richard Hooker, Burke had supposedly developed his political thought independently of the Enlightenment. Moreover, Burke's rejection of universal rights in favor of evolutionary legal traditions and national legacies resulted from his essentially medieval, Thomistic conception of politics. Right reason and universal moral laws, as understood by Aquinas and Hooker, operated effectively only within an established framework of human relationships.

Herberg praises Stanlis's interpretation for bestowing on Burkean political philosophy "an underlying structure of coherence." Stanlis had made it possible to account for the "surface contradictions": in expounding Burke's understanding of natural law, Stanlis showed how Burke had remained consistent in opposing the "abstract" French declaration of the rights of man even while denouncing revolutionary crimes in the name of "eternal immutable law."[47] Herberg probably sensed the appropriateness of this work for the conservative movement with which he and Stanlis were both then associated. A new appreciation of Burke had developed by the late fifties on the American intellectual Right. Francis Canavan, Russell Kirk, Ross Hoffman, and Stanlis, among others, were then celebrating Burke's wisdom as a political teacher.[48] As a member of parliament and as a political controversialist, Burke had taken stands that would appeal to twentieth-century American opponents of both secularism and social leveling. Burke had been for Catholic and Irish emancipation, more or less for a market economy, and effusively sympathetic toward the American colonies on the eve of their revolution. He had also expressed revulsion for the rationalist, antireligious character of the French Enlightenment. But although he had excoriated the French Revolution for radical institutional change, he had contrasted it with two more modest and defensible alterations of government, the American Revolution and the English Glorious Revolution of 1688. He described the latter event as "a revolution averted." Stanlis's study helped to enhance Burke's position on the American Right, by stressing his essentially Catholic, nonmodernist moral principles.[49] This came at a time when traditionalists were looking to the Church as a bastion of sound ethics and theology, indeed at a time when some of them were converting to Catholicism.

On some points Herberg disagreed with Stanlis. For one thing, Stanlis failed, he believed, to draw adequate distinctions among those thinkers to whom he traced Burke's natural-law theory. "Is Burke's conception of Natural Law," Herberg asks rhetorically, "permeated as it is with the sense of historical experience, really the same as that of Aristotle, Cicero, and Thomas Aquinas, who can hardly be considered historical-minded?"[50] Second, calling attention

to the historicity of all natural law conceptions, Herberg warned against "identifying" Burke's statements with "Mr. Stanlis's collection of brief quotations on Natural Law—taken from thinkers ranging from Aristotle to Thomas Jefferson." Herberg himself read into Burke a moral view that emphasized the historical-existential context of universal justice. Styling this view *historical conservatism,* Herberg defined it thus: "It is in man's historical experience rather than in any abstract metaphysical scheme that we can hope to catch a glimpse of the underlying Natural Law as well as of the modification it must undergo if it is to become operative in social life. The true statesman has a sense of the 'grain of history' which defines both the possibilities and the limits of his statecraft."[51]

Plainly Herberg's avowed Burkeanism stemmed from his attempt to combine historicism with moral universals. In this effort, he was following the path blazed by Rudolf Stammler (1856–1938) and other jurists trained in Hegelian thought but concerned with ethical verities in a time of cultural flux.[52] Herberg had read the English translation of Stammler's *Lehrbuch der Rechtsphilosophie,* yet there is no compelling reason to believe that he had to look there to give natural-law theory a historical framework.[53] Both his Hegelian-Marxist background and his theology of redemptive history had predisposed him toward the interpretation he offered. His mature historicist perspective represented more than one tradition of thought, and it may be idle to pinpoint any one influence in assigning parentage for his "historical conservatism." In a 1961 tribute to Reinhold Niebuhr, Herberg praises his subject for adopting "Burke's view": "A society or nation . . . is an historical community of destiny arising out of the deliberate election of ages and generations. It cannot be made or remade at will, though as an historical structure, it is always remaking itself."[54] Although this citation is at least partly from Niebuhr, it also paraphrases Burke's view of the state in *Reflections on the Revolution in France* and the defense of the organic evolution of societies in section 234 of Hegel's *Philosophy of Right.* Since Herberg had read and taught all three, it may be difficult to determine which thinker had been most crucial in forming his basic conception of the continuity of generations.

Herberg's attraction to Hegel, which persisted down to the end of his life, is illustrated by his treatment of the idea of progress. He attributed to Burke the quintessentially Hegelian belief in historical progress and spoke of that particular conviction as one that had linked Burke, Hegel, and Marx.[55] As a graduate professor at Drew, he introduced a tutorial, "The Concept of Progress in Western History," his outline for which shows how closely he associated the concept of progress with a characteristically Western cosmology.[56] Basic to this view were the "break with Graeco-Oriental eternalism in favor of biblical-Hebraic historicism" and "the conferring of meaning upon history in terms of direction and goal." The outline distinguishes "two types of doctrines of progress" in the nineteenth century: a *gradualist* and a *dialectical-revolutionary.* Although he does not mention Marx, it is obvious which heading includes him.

Equally clear is where Hegel should be discussed: the outline links him to a "developing doctrine of Progress," which seems to anticipate the "gradualist" heading associated with the nineteenth century. Curiously, he mentions Burke not as a historicist or as an exponent of progress, but simply as one who reacted to "the shattering impact of the French Revolution."[57]

Herberg's guarded respect for Hegel and even Marx may have reflected his attitude toward "the concept of progress in Western history." Thinkers and systems who explained the meaning and direction of human change and struggle had given to the West its moral tradition and self-confidence. But in recent times they had also bequeathed a destructive utopianism opposed to both religious transcendence and social stability. Like the aged Hegel, the mature Herberg also agonized over the dilemma of finding continuity and a sense of historical direction amid the discontinuities of a problematic present.

Perhaps he came closest to resolving this question in an essay for *The Christian Scholar* in 1964, "Five Meanings of the Word 'Historical'"[58] Here Herberg first defines *historical* as factual but then advances toward a second level of meaning by designating Judaism and Christianity as two basically "historical religions." Both base their doctrines on the reality of particular events, and each worships God partly by reciting His temporal deeds. *Historical* is also that which shapes a future course of events, and Herberg cites the German theologian Martin Kahler, who contrasted the factually reconstructed Jesus with the "Christ of history." It is Kahler's "Christ of history," Herberg observes, who must be considered the historical one, in the sense of touching countless lives.[59] The last two meanings of *historical* offered are existentially related, and both are attributed to Niebuhr, together with Burke the supposed source of Herberg's historicism. *Historical*, in the fourth sense, is that which defines someone's or something's uniqueness in terms of an ongoing past. To those who hold such a perspective "it is this historicity of man that constitutes his essence—that is, his capacity to transcend indeterminately all fixed structures of being, even of his own being." Out of this view flows the last meaning that Herberg assigns to the term *historical*. It is an openness to time in which one's historicity becomes a springboard for action. The historical participant faces "the future of possibility," affirming both the past and his own individuality. Herberg compares the last two meanings of *historical* to a Janus head, "one aspect looking back and the other forward." Men and societies must reconstitute themselves on a continuing basis, but they can act meaningfully only by reference to their past "doings and sufferings, decisions and actions."

Even though Herberg dealt only briefly with the final two meanings of *historical*, he took profound pride in the essay as a whole. He called it a "useful preliminary" to further discussion. Yet his central ideas were already known to Italian Hegelians since at least the turn of the century. One may be justified in noting the conceptual parallel between the existential historicism of Herberg and the Italian Hegelian focus on continuing self-actualization. Like Bene-

detto Croce and Giovanni Gentile, Herberg identified historicity with man's unfinished self-definition, through which past and future are being repeatedly brought together in discrete moments of decision. According to Croce, such a process occurred through moral, aesthetic, and logical choices. In all three forms of volition the participant, whether by thinking or by acting, became aware of universality as it related to concrete situations.[60]

Like Croce, Gentile, who used the Italian *Spirito* for Hegel's *Geist,* regarded Mind as the driving force in each existential encounter. Gentile's investigation of Mind's self-actualization, particularly in *General Theory of the Mind as Pure Act,* bears remarkable resemblance to Herberg's comments on historicism. For both thinkers man's "essence" was his historicity, and his freedom lay in the process by which he defined his evolving identity. Herberg discussed "existential self-constituting in the face of the future of possibility," whereas Gentile considered successive stages in the self-affirmation of man as acting consciousness. What Herberg viewed as the paradox of man's relationship to the divine—that the divine becomes knowable primarily through the concrete-historical—Gentile treated *mutatis mutandis* as a "historical antinomy": "We are not able to understand man, outside of his history in which he realizes his essence; but in history he reveals nothing of himself but . . . that which contains (preexisting) spiritual value. . . ."[61] According to Gentile, the philosophical explanation for this antinomy lay in the clearly Hegelian notion of a "process of unity which multiplies itself while remaining one, a history both ideal and eternal—inasmuch as eternal time must be considered as Mind's continuing actualization."[62]

Such an explanation would have been unacceptable to Herberg, even if God had been substituted for the Hegelian-Gentilian Mind. He had repeatedly criticized Hegel's (and by implication his diciples') historicism for lacking a doctrine of Creation. Both Hegel and the Hegelians had gone much too far, from Herberg's point of view, in implicating divinity itself in all aspects of the historical process. They had sacrificed God's transcendence to His immanence, and the result was the loss of moral responsibility for man and the Creator. And yet, Herberg's historicism, even when ascribed to Burke and Niebuhr, had a continuing relationship to the Hegelian tradition. His view of time as historical process, his understanding of the dialectical nature of reality, and his replication of Italian Hegelian insights all testify to this relationship. As a professor at Drew University, he was seen as embodying the paradox of being a believing Jew who proclaimed the truth of Christian revelation. He was also a Hebraic critic of Hegelianism who remained under its sway.

A death notice for Herberg, published in *National Review* on 15 April 1977, described him as "the Orthodox Jew who sometimes sounded like a Christian triumphalist" and as someone who had a talent for "explicating abstruse thought."[63] The notice further explained that "on his death, he had bequeathed his post-conversion library—he abandoned Communism in the thirties—to Drew University, thirty thousand volumes fastidiously annotated in his own hand." The announcement failed to mention that among those volumes in Herberg's "post-conversion library" were the well-thumbed works of Marx and Lenin. There may be little justification for dividing Herberg's life into pre- and postconversion stages or, as amply demonstrated, for relegating his Marxism exclusively to the twenties and thirties. Throughout Herberg's adult life divergent beliefs intersected in his mind, a situation that we encounter at every point at which we stop to look at his intellectual development. For example, his writing as a Communist on Einstein's theory of relativity included the romantic understanding of natural phenomena that Hegel had expounded in *The Philosophy of Nature*. Herberg's interpretive approach, precedents for which were both in Engels's *Anti-Dühring* and in Lenin's *Materialism and Empirico Criticism,* linked Marxism to a view of the natural world as the interplay of dynamic and dialectically structured forces.[64] Although Herberg, like Engels, tried to identify romantic naturalism with a materialist dialectic, he often resorted to unmistakably Hegelian (what Marxists derisively call "idealist") language in expressing this idea. Even while invoking Marxist materialism, the earnest young Communist paid unwitting tribute to Hegel's metaphysics by writing thus: "The fixed lines of demarcation disappear, the irreconcilable contradictions (space vs. time, matter vs. energy) are synthesized in the relativity physics into a higher organic unity, the space-time world, the equivalence of matter and energy."[65]

Herberg's characteristic of espousing positions widely viewed as incompatible persisted into his post-Communist phase. As late as the fifties and sixties there is evidence of his simultaneous support of unionism and conservative politics, just as expressions of his admiration for Hegel and Marx continued even after he had become a religious traditionalist. It makes little sense indeed to disregard these overlapping loyalties and sentiments in order to fit his career into a neat but arbitrary evolutionary pattern. Continuing strains of thought accompanied even the cataclysmic shifts that Herberg underwent in his philosophical thinking. Among the persistent traits that frustrate the attempt to reduce his life to pre- and postconversion stages was his lifelong appeal to History. The search for "higher organic unity" in nature and in human affairs led this former Communist into accepting the Bible's promise of historical redemption.

The democratic socialist Sidney Hook, with whom Herberg had argued so furiously in his youth, has recently commented on modern conservatives who "seek to re-enstate the varied traditions of [Karl von] Savigny, Hegel, Burke, and even the Church fathers and philosophers." According to Hook, "they mock with justification the invisible hand of the market but substitute for it the Cunning of Reason, the compensatory rhythm of history, or the Hand of Providence and other obscurantist notions."[66] As in his youth, Hook defines Hegelianism as a conservative ideology that induces resignation before the twists and turns of history, or before the appearance of world-historical heroes. He fails to understand that in the case of men such as Herberg these "obscurantist notions" have been spurs to action and have even provided the test for morally propriate decisions. It should be noted that Hook himself, a few passages further, mentions approvingly the "conservative" prejudice against "ideas of any generality—[being] applied mechanically to any situation regardless of its specificity and history." Although Hook accepts this view as an empiricist and pragmatist, he neglects its obvious relationship to the "obscurantist notions" that he has just attacked. It was Herberg's belief in a value-centered historicism, which combined moral absolutes with faith in the rhythms of history, that allowed him to judge ethical options within changing historical circumstances. Unlike Hook, who still wishes to evaluate circumstances "pragmatically" though in light of the supreme value of preserving a free society, Herberg spoke of moral truths together with the need to find their proper historical application. This historical point of reference, for Herberg, remained constant, although in his youth it was change and in his later years "stabilities and continuities" that he associated with history. Like Goethe, who conceived of the world as an organic whole, the later Herberg looked at change in order to see permanence.

*4*

---

# KARL AUGUST WITTFOGEL AND
# THE UNIQUENESS OF THE WEST

IN DECEMBER 1970, WHILE A PANELIST AT THE AMERICAN HISTORICAL
Association gathering in Boston, I heard a speaker refer contemptuously to
Karl Wittfogel as a "dishonest cold warrior" whose writing still "beclouded"
the popular understanding of Asian revolutions and represented a distortion of
Marx's thoughts on this subject. Since the speaker failed to document his
charge and since I had been invited to be a critical commentator for a session
on Marx predominantly featuring Marxists, it seemed appropriate to take the
offensive. I scolded my colleague for treating Wittfogel's mendacity as self-evi-
dent. This practice, as I subsequently learned from a conversation with
Eugene Genovese, another panelist, prevailed among radical historians. The
reason may be found in the circumstances in which Wittfogel wrote his magnum opus, *Oriental Despotism: A Comparative Study of Total Power* (New Haven,
1957). The author had been imprisoned at Dachau as a Communist opponent
of Hitler. He had fleshed out his thesis on Oriental despotism while writing in
the interwar years as a German Communist. During his Communist phase he
had mistakenly ascribed his ideas on Asia to Lenin, but even as late as 1957 he
continued to praise Marx as an analyst of non-Western societies.

The intellectual far Left scorned Wittfogel (b. 1896) for citing Marx when he
assaulted both Communists and Communist regimes. He himself commented
on his difficulties with the Left when I met him in New York during the spring
of 1972. One of his wife's cousins, whose husband had studied with me in the
graduate school of New York University, arranged for the meeting in her apartment. Since the Wittfogels and I got along at that meeting and discussed,
among other topics, Hegel as an interpreter of the non-Western world, I later
visited them at their apartment on Riverside Drive. I noted a striking difference between his reaction and that of his wife to their professional enemies.
Whereas Esther Wittfogel lamented their social isolation from her former col-

leagues in cultural anthropology at Columbia University, her husband marveled at his writing's effect. "It still sticks in their craws!" he remarked with obvious satisfaction, alluding to his use of Marx's works against Soviet and Third World apologists.

He had cited extensively Marx's observations on the inexorably despotic character of Russian and Asian societies, particularly under "Marxist" regimes. Stalin, Mao, and many of their Western admirers applied to the non-Western world the three-stage developmental scheme since the Middle Ages that Marx had formulated for the West. The feudal-agrarian society and mode of production were seen as falling before the onslaught of the capitalists; they in turn would be overwhelmed by a workers' revolution, which would help establish socialism. It was this scheme that with slight variations non-Western peoples were already supposedly following. Variations, of course, were required to explain how largely illiterate and rural populations might leap all at once into modernity. Thus the great Lenin provided a usable comparison between the prerevolutionary Russian landowners and peasants and the Western industrialists and proletariat. He also implemented a New Economic Program in the early twenties. This plan not only gave Russia the material benefits of a tolerated private sector but was intended to complete retroactively the bourgeois phase of Russian social development.

Drawing upon *Capital*, especially Volume 3, and *Articles on India*, Wittfogel pointed to Marx's own profound doubts about the possibility of Asian societies' developing in the Western manner. Marx associated land tenure and property relations in India and China with what he termed the *Asian system:* this system was neither feudal nor primitive-patriarchal, but involved unchanging state control over peasants and their labor. In *Capital* Marx, following Hegel's *Lectures on the Philosophy of History,* spoke of "the general slavery of the Orient," which he differentiated from both Western feudalism and later bourgeois institutions. Unlike the West, the Orient had shown little social development; the state and its officialdom were the one enduring ruling class.

Wittfogel examined the Soviet and Chinese revolutionary regimes as extreme versions of the "general slavery of the Orient." And though associated by the late sixties with the intellectual Right as an editor of *Modern Age* and contributor to *National Review,* he repeatedly emphasized the Marxist derivation of his critique of both Soviet Russia and Maoist China. He paid tribute to Marxist mavericks, particularly Karl Korsch and George Plekhanov. Korsch had been a contemporary of his in the German Communist Party and an early critic of the Soviet bureaucracy; Plekhanov, a socialist adversary of the young Lenin who had explained Asian societies in terms of geographical conditions. In our conversations, however, Wittfogel never mentioned his indebtedness to Marx or the Marxists. He seemed to show interest in Hegel, whom he styled a "great Hebraic philosopher." Hegel had seen time as filled with Providential meaning; he had recognized that the spiritual personalism implicit in the

Judeo-Christian tradition had definite political implications. "Tell me," he asked, "you have read his *Lectures on the Philosophy of History?*" I nodded, and he continued: "History for him starts with China and other hydraulic civilizations. In them the individual had no real worth. Society lacked structural complexity; the state controlled everything under it." "You do agree with this?" I asked. "Certainly," replied Wittfogel, "as my writing I hope should make obvious. I was impressed by Hegel even back then, when I belonged to the KPD.[1] I wrote an essay about his views on Asia for a party publication in 1931. Naturally I praised Marx and Lenin more than Hegel, yet it was in fact Hegel who had put me on the right track."

Wittfogel's enthusiasm for Hegel evoked my displeasure at the time. "Why," I asked, "did Hegel describe Herodotus and Thucydides as primitive historians? Wasn't it because, having lived long ago, they had produced history instead of his philosophy of a World Mind, which quite conveniently revealed Itself most fully to him?" "But you have to remember," replied Wittfogel, "that Hegel was an Hebraic, not Greek, philosopher of history. His Providential history had little room for pagan chroniclers, or for anyone who did not see as he did a movement toward political liberty and the spiritual ideals that came from the Protestant Reformation."

Our discussions of Hegel were lively but never acrimonious. Occasionally Wittfogel revived Heinrich Heine's distinction between "Hebrews" and "Hellenes," placing Hegel and himself in one group and Schopenhauer and me in the other. Only years later did I try to recall the details of our exchanges. By then, however, what engaged my attention were not my own statements of Hellenic pessimism, but what Wittfogel had said about his favorite Hebraic philosopher of history. His remarks had often coincided with those of Will Herberg, with whom I was discussing the same topics at that time. Both had obviously been influenced by Hegel's historical thinking during their early radical years, and each carried some of the baggage with him on his postwar journey to the Right. There was, however, one manifest difference between them. Whereas Herberg extracted from Hegelianism primarily the historical dialectic, Wittfogel borrowed its contrasting pictures of Oriental and Western civilizations. He took over with some modification the Hegelian sketches of China and India, which he contrasted with "the Western world," his own enlarged equivalent of what Hegel had styled the "Germanic world."[2] Whereas Hegel viewed the Orient as politically unchanging and monolithic, Wittfogel identified the West with historical consciousness, social diversity, and institutional growth.

Wittfogel's early views on this matter are clear from "Hegel on China," an essay he wrote while a Communist in 1931. In this contribution to an issue of the Party publication *Unter dem Banner des Marxismus,* commemorating the centenary of Hegel's death, he explores the ways in which Hegel had anticipated the Marxist-materialist understanding of Chinese society. Wittfogel notes that Hegel had devoted over one hundred pages, in his total writings on world history and the history of philosophy, to discussing Chinese society. He had also glimpsed why since the late seventeenth century, when information on the subject began to accumulate, Europeans had grown increasingly interested in China. The Western bourgeoisie, faced by the ferment that attended their own rise to power, looked eastward for a social model. Imperial China, seen from a conventional Western perspective, had neither a hereditary aristocracy nor a legally privileged class other than educated state servants. Hegel summed up this received assumption as follows: "With this sole exception (the Emperor) all are considered equal and only those possessed of the appropriate skills participate in government. Thus the Chinese state is often presented as an ideal, which might serve as our model."[3]

Despite what Hegel himself considered the absence of hereditary privilege in China, he saw the state as controlling its people impersonally and despotically. Wittfogel lavishly praises Hegel as one of the first Westerners to have uncovered this fact. Although Hegel's "idealistic" standpoint had led him to associate Chinese and other Asian societies with the World Spirit then only vaguely conscious of Its freedom, Hegel drew proper "materialist" conclusions. In fact, according to Wittfogel, Hegel anticipated the Marxist method by grounding his study of China in a "concrete investigation."[4] For example, his analysis of the geographical settings of the various world civilizations improved upon the eighteenth-century anthropologies of Montesquieu and J. G. Herder. Hegel's remarks on the relationship between natural environment and class structure produced "significant results for the history of materialism." Hegel's analysis of China foreshadowed critical aspects of Marx's examination of the non-Western world, particularly the emphasis on a specifically "Asian mode of production."[5]

Wittfogel credits Hegel with having scrupulously studied the primary sources on Chinese history and the reports on Chinese society available in Western languages. These included, *inter alia,* memoirs left by French Jesuits who had visited China, the translated imperial annals *T'ung Kien Kang Mu,* and the ethical precepts of Confucius. His synthetic treatment of Chinese values and customs was done so skillfully that, according to Wittfogel, it assumed an overshadowing importance well into the twentieth century among German and other Western sinologists.

Writing as a nonacademic Marxist contemptuous of both philosophical idealism and "academic groupies [*Zünftler*]," Wittfogel does attack what he considers the mechanically transmitted errors of Hegel's analysis of China. He criticizes Hegel himself for paying insufficient attention to ancient China's evolution from a feudal-warrior society into a bureaucratically managed one.[6] And he scolds the contemporary sinologist Otto Franke for accepting Hegel's view of the Chinese state as "the traditional Confucian family writ large." Unlike Hegel and Franke, Wittfogel presents Chinese Confucian ethics not as the fountainhead of Chinese social practice, but as a Marxian superstructure.[7] The mandarins, as state managers, and the imperial court naturally invoked an ethic of social duty binding upon all Chinese other than slaves. They also exalted the patriarchal family head when they justified the transfer of political and social authority to the emperor and mandarins at the expense of the feudal nobility. On this point Wittfogel is most impatient with Hegel and the sinologists of his own time. He accuses them of belaboring the peculiarities of Chinese ethics while ignoring Marx's materialist understanding of culture.

Nonetheless, he repeatedly ascribes to Hegel ideas that were basic to Marx's and indeed his own thinking about Asia. Hegel's view of Asian societies as the oldest but least developed in political freedom foreshadowed Marx's identification of Asia with a permanent patriarchal society. And though Hegel, from a Marxist perspective, assigned too much weight to Confucian ethics, his conception of a specifically Asian mode of production anticipated one of Marx's perceptions that would become a major theme in Wittfogel's writings. Because of the collective need for irrigation in agrarian societies with either very heavy or exceedingly limited precipitation, the Asian divisions of labor favored despotic and ubiquitous state control. The heads of these societies claimed a patriarchal relationship to their subjects, and in organizing hydraulic societies to maintain their populations, they and their appointed officials exercised virtually unlimited power over their subjects' lives and material possessions.[8] Wittfogel traces back to *The Philosophy of History* not only this geographical-materialist view of Asia, but the implicit contrast between Oriental and Western societies. Marx "split up Hegel's Germanic world (into feudal-agrarian and bourgeois-capitalist phases)," but both thinkers recognized the West's dynamic and creative character in contradistinction to "the general slavery of the Orient."[9]

Wittfogel's admiration for Hegel is even more explicit in his essay published in the August 1929 issue of *Unter dem Banner des Marxismus*, "Geography, Geographical Materialism, and Marxism." This article calls for a further refinement of Marx's materialist method through an intensive study of the force of natural environment. Having already published in the same journal an appreciation of Edward Graf, a geopolitician and socialist, Wittfogel now surveys geographical interpretations of society since the eighteenth century.[10] He tries to demonstrate the compatibility of this line of thought with Marxist materialism and, where possible, to show it as implicit in Marxism. Wittfogel notes with approval the long section at the beginning of *The Philosophy of History* devoted expressly to "the geographical basis of world history." Commenting on Hegel's observation that government and law could develop only with the emergence of an agrarian economy, Wittfogel extols this "serious attempt to present the unity of social phenomena from the standpoint of production and the system of labor."[11] He credits Hegel with far more critical insight into Asian society than the "bourgeois revolutionary thinkers" of the eighteenth century. Voltaire, for example, had preached to the West about China's fortune to be without a hereditary aristocracy. Hegel, however, correctly associated the absence of feudal nobility with a despotic, managerial, and patriarchal state, and he linked both these phenomena, in various places in his writings, to geographical imperatives and an Asian mode of production.[12]

Wittfogel's careful reading of Hegel is abundantly evident from his contributions to *Unter dem Banner des Marxismus.* "Hegel on China," for example, draws not only upon *The Philosophy of History,* but also upon several other works less favored among Hegel's selective Marxist admirers: namely, *The History of Philosophy, The Philosophy of Religion,* and *The Aesthetics.*[13] Wittfogel differed from other Marxist-Leninists, and even from those who eventually became strongly disenchanted with the revolutionary Left such as James Burnham and Frank Meyer, in having learned Hegel from Hegel rather than from Marx or Lenin. During his Communist period he may have studied Hegel, but he never mistook him for the proto-Marxist Hegel whom Herbert Marcuse, Alexandre Kojève and other Marxist-Hegelians have depicted in their writings.

One must account for the scarcity of explicit references to Hegel in Wittfogel's postwar and postcommunist scholarship. His great work on Oriental despotism mentions Hegel only three times; nor do his essays and reviews since the late fifties indicate renewed interest in a philosopher whom he professes to admire. Certainly one cannot ascribe this omission to Wittfogel's continued embarrassment with the ideological follies of his youth. Of all scholars who came to be identified with the postwar American Right, Wittfogel has been perhaps the least uneasy about his past enthusiasms. He cited Marx and Lenin frequently in *Oriental Despotism* and delighted in buttressing his arguments by appealing to the seminal texts of historical materialism.

His autobiographical remarks on the same works are meant to underscore the continuity of his convictions.[14] Thus we are told that the author was imprisoned by the Nazis for his impassioned defense of freedom. One could respond that he suffered this fate for being a Communist partisan and not for defending liberty as he would eventually understand that term. But in terms of the perspective from which he saw his own past, such a distinction would be unwarranted. Wittfogel has defined his life as a process of movement, culminating in his self-recognition as a "Judeo-Christian" devotee of liberty. The early phase of his development was not marked simply by delusion, but represented, to borrow an appropriate Hegelian phrase, part of "the ongoing self-determination of the idea."[15] Even while a Communist, Wittfogel perceived the overriding importance of freedom as a value; by studying the absence of this value in Oriental societies he moved closer to his final moral and philosophical position.

Moreover, there may be no reason to assume that this process occurred at the expense of his admiration for Hegel. His seeming inattention to Hegel since the early thirties may signify less an abandonment of that thinker than the uneventful absorption of his thinking into Wittfogel's own. Wittfogel's view of the West as the civilization of freedom par excellence and his gloomy picture of Asian society both survived his materialist-Marxist phase. He also tried to expand his anthropology by looking beyond geographical conditioning to the role of spiritual factors in history. He has depicted the Hebrews as generally avoiding the Asian mode of production because of their religious-prophetic teachings.[16] The Romans, he argues, sank into despotism because they were insensitive to freedom for themselves and others.[17] One need hardly point out that Wittfogel, by the standards of his own Marxist writings, has lapsed into the "idealist method" that he had once condemned in Hegel.

Equally important, he has come to stress the *consciousness* of freedom as basic to its prospects among various peoples. *Oriental Despotism* offers an extended contrast between the awareness of the self and of the other, which is characteristic of free societies, and the total passivity of those living under hydraulic despotisms. He denies that such discrepancies in attitude simply reflected differing material environments and those specific geographical situations in which various regimes existed. Wittfogel examines the demands for civic responsibility in ancient Greece and the virtues of medieval knighthood, knowing that "in the great agrarian societies of the West obedience is far from being a primary virtue."[18] He repeatedly suggests that resistance to despotism required moral resolution among those peoples living in the shadow of hydraulic societies. Like Hegel, he extols the Greeks for resisting both the role model and imperialist expansion of the Persian state.[19] And he ascribes the Western sense of freedom to something more than favorable natural environment that permits agriculture without collective hydraulic organization. He also associates the West's political liberty with a series of moral choices. The Germanic peoples who came into the decayed Roman Empire rejected imperial absolutism as inconsistent with their tribal values. Despite the incorporation of Roman culture, laws, and ecclesiastical hierarchy into medieval Europe, the idea of "total obedience" to any authority remained foreign to the European mind.[20] Surely views of this type can be found in *The Philosophy of History*.

It is also possible to explain the paucity of references to Hegel (and to others whom Wittfogel admired), in contrast to the frequent appeals to Marx and Lenin, by considering the intent of *Oriental Despotism*. Wittfogel is writing to provide historical reasons for the derailment of the Soviet, Chinese, and other non-Western socialist revolutions. He seeks to demonstrate continuity between the despotic past of those regions examined and those total states created by the revolutionary elites that now govern them. To render his arguments more compelling, he quotes extensively from Marx and Lenin, the revolutionary thinkers most revered in those socialist states he analyzes. He shows that the saints of socialism had doubts about the suitability of Russia, India, and China for a true workers' revolution, or even for more limited forms of Westernization. This obviously is more important for Wittfogel's case than is Hegel's view of history. Marx and Lenin, not Hegel, are the gods of non-Western socialist regimes and of "progressive" circles in the West. Wittfogel cites *their* reservations about those trapped in the Asian mode of production.[21] He tries to show bad faith among self-avowed Marxists not only by exposing the reactionary and modern-totalitarian aspects of the "revolutionary" societies that they defend. He also calls to witness the recognized fathers of revolutionary socialism.

This line of interpretation may explain why *Oriental Despotism* ignores the names of Eduard Graf, Plekhanov, and Herder, all of whom Wittfogel mentioned in his early tracts. It may also explain why Wittfogel, writing for *Modern Age* in 1970, emphasizes Marx's eventual belief in "the ameliorative capacity of capitalism."[22] What more convincing brief can be made against the modern revolutionary Left than Marx's doubts about the legitimacy of Third World revolutions and about an irreversibly crumbling capitalist economy!

There are reasons to question whether that treatment of Hegel found in *Oriental Despotism* stems entirely from tactical considerations. One may argue that Wittfogel's relationship to the Hegelian tradition had grown ambivalent by the late fifties. Thereafter he would try to maintain a critical though respectful distance from a thinker whose judgments about civilizations had once deeply impressed him. In 1945 Karl Popper published a two-volume work that helped earn him a knighthood, *The Open Society and Its Enemies*. His book, in the course of passing through several printings, gained the attention of anticommunist intellectuals, especially in America. The second volume, which conservatives admired mostly for its critique of Marx's historical determinism, contains an impassioned diatribe against Hegel.[23] Denouncing Hegel for his "Platonizing worship of the state" and mystification of history, Popper links Hegel through Marx and Lenin to the despotic Left and through German nationalism to the Nazi regime. Popper's association of historicism with antirationalist and totalitarian forces and his demonic picture of Hegel both left their imprint upon conservatives well into the postwar years.[24] The last section of Friedrich Hayek's *The Counter-Revolution of Science* (1955) recapitulates part of Popper's attack by treating Hegel's "pseudoscientific" theorizing.[25] Ironically, Hayek's classical liberalism puts him much closer to Hegel on political-economic questions than to the democratic socialist Popper. Yet anticommunists, particularly those of a libertarian bent, often accept Popper's judgment (concurred in by Max Eastman and by Sidney Hook), that what was rigidly deterministic in Marx came predominantly from his Hegelian background.

Wittfogel, a libertarian who knew Hook and read Popper and Hayek, also expressed some of their views on Hegel. Evidence for this can certainly be gleaned from those references to Hegel that one finds in *Oriental Despotism*. One such reference identifies Hegel with "nineteenth-century unilinealists" who "disregarded hydraulic society not because they shunned the reality of bureaucratic despotism but because they were inspired by the stupendous con-

sequences of the industrial revolution. Overgeneralizing the experience of a
rapidly changing Western world, they naively postulated a simple, unilinear
and progressive course of societal growth."[26] The examples he gives of such unilinealists include Hegel as a prophet of freedom and Auguste Comte as the
herald of a "just and rational society." Wittfogel also indicates that he had mistakenly "pointed to the geographer Ritter and to Hegel as possibly having influenced Marx" on the Asian mode of production. More recent investigation,
however, had suggested that it was Adam Smith's *Wealth of Nations* and J. S.
Mill's *Principles of Political Economy* that had actually shaped Marx's understanding of this concept. Marx had been reading these works when he first
discussed, in his 1857 introduction to *Capital,* a primitive Asian form of production.[27] Finally, Wittfogel, in commenting on Marx's successive forms of production, compares them to Hegel's worlds, both being "progressive only in a typological way." "Marx's formations recall Hegel's 'worlds' which constitute
advancing stages not historically and in terms of real evolution, but typologi-
cally, i.e., as representatives of a lower or higher degree of freedom. Marx's formations differ according to the degree of private property they represent."[28]

Some of these comments are not only questionable, but incompatible with
that far richer interpretation of Hegel that Wittfogel had produced during his
youth. His lumping together of Hegel with Comte and with early nineteenth-
century French socialists as misguided utopians recalls the final chapter of
Hayek's *The Counter-Revolution of Science,* but without the useful qualifications
made there. Wittfogel's early writings had shown that Hegel did not believe in
a "simple, unlinear, and progressive course of societal growth." And certainly
Hegel, as presented in Wittfogel's writings of 1929 and 1931, had not "disregarded hydraulic societies." However much Hegel identified the progress of
freedom with the Germanic world, and particularly the Protestant nation
state, he saw most of humanity as permanently situated at lower stages in the
World Spirit's march toward freedom. He also viewed the Asian world, the earliest of his four worlds, as the longest-lived. He associated that world, as
Wittfogel himself cogently demonstrates, with a deficient sense of the individual's worth, patriarchal kingship, and a collectivist economy built around
hydraulic and other public projects.

One can also question Wittfogel's expressed doubts in 1957 about Hegel's influence on Marx's view of the Asian mode of production. Marx did read Mill
and Smith in the 1850s, shortly before composing *Grundrisse der Kritik der politischen Ökonomie,* his intended introduction to *Capital* in which he most fully develops his four presocialist forms of production.[29] Yet, this hardly disproves, as
Wittfogel confidently asserts it does, that Marx ceased to be influenced by
Hegel when he wrote about Asia in the 1850s. From 1836 into the mid-1840s,
Marx studied the Hegelian system of thought as a student in Berlin and, later,
as a passionate but respectful critic. It might be useful to observe a certain
parallel with Wittfogel's own relationship to Hegel. This too involved a distanc-

ing from, but never absolute break with, the great philosopher of history.

This process of distancing seems apparent in the denial to Hegel of any role in forming Marx's understanding, which also shaped Wittfogel's, of the Asian mode of production. Considering Marx's years of exposure to Hegel and what Wittfogel had shown to be the foundations of geographical materialism in *The Philosophy of History*, why should we assume that Marx, upon studying Mill and Smith, entirely renounced his earlier teacher? As late as 1957 Wittfogel himself suggested just the opposite when he compared Marx's typological view of economic development with Hegel's succession of "worlds." Hegel and Marx both examined the problem of historical succession in terms of an overarching principle: in one case freedom and in the other private property. Wittfogel intimates that it was Marx's semi-Hegelian typology that caused him to suppress unwelcome truths, for example, the presence of some private property in traditional Asian society. Marx not only absorbed the idea of a developing principle from Hegelian typology but presented four modes of production in place of Hegel's four worlds. Although the last three economic modes did not correspond exactly to the last three Hegelian worlds, Marx did start his analysis with the Asian society and form of production that Hegel had placed at the beginning of *The Philosophy of History*.

Why did Wittfogel deny that Hegel had much influence on Marx and himself? Perhaps the answer lies in his postwar libertarianism. This commitment expressed itself in admiration for Adam Smith and Friedrich Hayek and in a prolonged attempt to enhance the scholarly reputation of William Godwin, Shelley's antistatist, communitarian father-in-law. Both Wittfogel and his wife praised Godwin not only as an active libertarian, but as an early student of the Asian mode of production.[30] Sincere though this discovery undoubtedly was, it nonetheless supports my conjecture about Wittfogel's flight from Hegelianism. One should mention that Wittfogel's strictures on Hegel have never approached in severity those of Karl Popper. Like Hayek he has criticized the deterministic and contrived character of Hegel's historical scheme without linking it to the emergence of totalitarian government. In fact Wittfogel associates the rigidity of the Hegelian scheme (which he almost deliberately exaggerates in *Oriental Despotism*) with Hegel's naive enthusiasm for liberty. Living in a culture marked by substantial freedom for individuals and for civil society, Hegel presented all of past history as a unilinear approach to the modern Western situation. In so doing, he ignored history's true evolutionary aspect and put in its place his own chronologically arranged operation of "the principle of freedom."

It may be Hayek's argument against the Hegelian view of history, published during the writing of *Oriental Despotism*, that seemed most telling to Wittfogel. Hegel's most glaring fault was supposedly not his statism, which Hayek avoids exaggerating, but his claim to scientific omniscience. Hegel foreshadowed the dangerous arrogance of modern social engineers, by believing himself to have created a science of history and, by implication, of society. Through his own "privileged" historical position, he imagined himself able to grasp the laws by which human society progressed and to transmit those laws to others similarly possessed of "Reason." Hayek does not suggest that Hegel was uniquely guilty in either of these pretensions. Both were fully present in the French Enlightenment and far more pronounced in the first self-styled sociologist Comte than in the philosopher Hegel.[31]

But Hegel had a greater impact than the others. The encyclopedic comprehensiveness of his system, his interest in comparative civilizations, and his profound impact on Western learning helped render more respectable the "counterrevolution of science." Comte and Hegel, each in his own way, contributed to the process whereby facts were made hostage to social ideologies. These ideologies, like ancient priestly religions, rested upon closed, esoteric views of history, although in the modern era utopians present their views no longer as insights into divine forces, but as science, while appealing to "laws" often of their own devising.

Hayek's critical observations never lapse into intemperateness. Unlike Popper and later Frank Meyer, he does not condemn historicism unconditionally. Indeed he tries to differentiate the strain of historical determinism that has subverted freedom and science from a proper interest in the shaping role of history. He expresses respect for Burke and for the Historical School in early nineteenth-century Germany; and he warns against exaggerating Hegel's effect upon a process of thinking that would in all likelihood have established itself without him.[32]

This line of criticism is implicit, I believe, in what became Wittfogel's opinion of Hegel. He viewed him as a brilliant but flawed defender of Western freedom: someone whose intellectual and even moral greatness was tainted by historicist delusion. Ironically, the two figures, Smith and Mill, to whom Wittfogel traces Marx's conceptualization of the Asian mode of production have both been libertarian heroes for Hayek.[33] This does not, of course, prove that they could not have contributed to Marx's and Wittfogel's understanding of Asia.[34] Yet, in light of Wittfogel's postwar neglect of Hegel's achievement in this area, which he himself had once documented, one may suspect an intentional distancing at work. As in the case of Herberg, the break with Marx did not prevent Wittfogel from retaining some aspects of his former radical persuasion. The relationship to Hegel was more subterranean and more problematic. It remained what the Germans call *die unbewältigte Vergangenheit*, the disconcerting, unacknowledged past that men often inescapably carry with them.

The attention given in the preceding two chapters to Will Herberg and Karl Wittfogel may be justified on two grounds. For one thing, both figures long identified themselves with the postwar conservative movement. They published articles in its leading theoretical journals, *Modern Age* and *Intercollegiate*

*Review,* and in its most widely read periodical, *National Review.* Both thinkers were associated with the postwar conservative foundation, Intercollegiate Studies Institute. Both spoke often on campuses and before civic organizations and expressed conservative views on spiritual renewal, national defense, and student rebellions. They both received favorable mention in George Nash's magisterial study, *The Conservative Intellectual Movement in America since 1945,* although Nash properly treats Herberg as having exerted a greater influence than Wittfogel on other conservatives.[35] Both are presented as prominent anticommunist intellectuals in John Diggins's *Up From Communism.* From Diggins's radical standpoint, Herberg's career epitomizes the religious zealotry of the anticommunist intellectual.

Yet Diggins astutely observes the presence of a permanent Hegelian element in Herberg's thinking. He also indicates, by linking Wittfogel to a German émigré generation, the kind of heritage that Wittfogel absorbed.[36] Wittfogel's European Marxist background insulated him from the hatred for speculative philosophy characteristic of at least part of the American conservative movement. Having been reared on systematic speculative thought, Wittfogel and Herberg never identified themselves with the antiphilosophic pragmatism that Daniel Boorstin, for example, celebrates as an American strength. Both Wittfogel and Herberg had ties to a European radical tradition that respected Hegel as a creator of the dialectic. Although some European radicals later tried awkwardly to fuse Marxism and Hegelianism or to treat them as identical, we should note that Central European Marxists, unlike Hook and Eastman in America, were critical admirers of German philosophy. The issue of *Unter dem Banner des Marxismus* that contained Wittfogel's "Hegel on China" published other appreciations of Hegel by European Communists. Herberg and Wittfogel exemplify that tendency on the postwar intellectual Right referred to in the Introduction as anti-Hegelian Hegelianism. Both combined their early Marxism with recognizable Hegelian ideas that they expressed even after they had disavowed Hegel as well as Marx. This relationship to Hegelianism was subterranean; it involved less deliberate concealment by Herberg and Wittfogel than the persistence of deeply ingrained views that came from a source that they took pains to reject openly.

Wittfogel's geographically based Hegelianism had antecedents in America among nineteenth-century commentators on American history. The exponents of American exceptionalism plotted the evolution of freedom in doing comparative studies of societies, and, like Wittfogel, they drew their framework of reference from Hegel's *Lectures on the Philosophy of History.* Harris, Snider, and, to some extent, Willich had seen the progress of freedom as moving from east to west, reaching its fullest development in the seemingly boundless territory of the New World.[37] Hegel's land of the future, as understood by American Hegelians, prospered from the expansiveness that Hegel had considered its distinctive mark. For some readers of Hegel, such as the Italian social economist

Achille Loria, American liberties were inextricably tied to the frontier situation. In the 1880s Loria, who made no secret of his debt to Hegel, tried to correlate the course of the American regime to the availability of frontier land, which he held to be the safeguard of American liberty. America could escape the fate of Oriental despotism and the social problems besetting European political institutions only if those frontiers remained open.

Lee Benson, who has translated parts of Loria's magnum opus *Analisi della proprietà capitalista,* has examined the crucial impact of Loria's geographical approach to American politics on Frederick Jackson Turner and on other exponents of the frontier theory of American society.[38] Although Loria's linking of political change to the price and relative scarcity of land owe much to the English economist David Ricardo, his stress on the geographical preconditions of liberty points back to Hegel and forward to Turner. Wittfogel too is among those Hegelians who have identified exceptional societies with the nurturing of freedom and who have studied natural environment as a key to understanding free societies. Unlike Loria and Snider, Wittfogel sees the full evolution of free institutions as the heritage of the entire Western world, not just of the United States. He also chooses to emphasize the moral-voluntaristic component in the histories of societies that establish and preserve liberty both in relation to others and in terms of their own regimes. Certainly it would not be far-fetched to suggest that Wittfogel, unlike Loria, has kept some part of the idealist as well as geographical aspects of Hegel's survey of world history. He has tried to study the idea and consciousness of liberty, together with the natural-environmental factors that have favored free peoples.

Wittfogel's Hegelianism, like that of Herberg and of other postwar conservatives, affected the conservative movement sometimes in terms of values and attitudes more than through a set of systematically constructed ideas. Two examples may demonstrate this point. In the mid-1960s Jeffrey Hart, a Dartmouth professor and frequent contributor to *National Review,* produced the first monograph on the postwar conservative movement, *The American Dissent.* Hart lists among the major currents of thought then present on the intellectual Right a "neo-idealist historical conservatism as found in Hegel and codified by neo-Hegelians and perhaps found in Eric Voegelin's conception of the history of 'order.'"[39] Hart gives no examples of the "neo-Hegelians" on the American Right, save for Eric Voegelin.

His insight, however, was confirmed by the late David Collier, longtime editor of *Modern Age,* who also uncovered a "Hegelian spirit" on the American Right. This spirit, Collier believed, was essential for understanding "the Movement" that he and his journal had helped launch.[40] Despite his stated conviction, Collier could not recall any favorable studies on Hegel published in *Modern Age,* except two written by me. It may be significant that Collier and Hart could not document the Hegelian aspect of American conservative thinking, though they recognized that one existed. Herberg and Wittfogel were both sufficiently schooled in Hegelian thought to express overtly what was only implicit in the writings of their confrères. But the Hegelian strain persisted among conservatives who arrived at Hegelian thinking indirectly: Marxists-turned-conservative who had been drawn to the fragments of Hegel that they thought were embedded in the Marxist system and conservatives of Central European origin who had acquired Hegelian ideas while receiving their education. The "neo-Hegelian" approaches of both groups to a historically grounded conservatism would be recognizable as such to at least some of their political soulmates.

# 5

## POLITICAL REALISM AND ITS HEGELIAN DIMENSION

AN OFT-NOTED CHARACTERISTIC OF AMERICAN INTELLECTUAL LIFE in the 1950s was a widespread sense of national well-being. For example, in a recent popular monograph on this period, Jeffrey Hart stresses the buoyant self-confidence of the Eisenhower era. Hart's title, *When the Going Was Good*, indicates the prevalent attitude of a largely middle-class America toward an age of economic growth, moral certainty, and American military power. Yet Hart finds the seeds of the 1960s counterculture germinating during the 1950s.[1] *Dissent* and *Partisan Review*, the novels of Norman Mailer, and the first stirrings of cold war revisionism (already present in the historiography of William Appleman Williams) all suggest the beginnings of what by the 1960s would become a torrential outcry against "the American way of life." Yet, in the 1950s, most publicists did not applaud David Riesman's rhetorical question: "Were not intellectuals of more use to this country when they had less use for it?" In the fifties, despite the presence of gadfly literary critics such as Dwight Macdonald, Irving Howe, and Edmund Wilson and despite the tirades of social commentators such as Michael Harrington and C. Wright Mills, most American intellectuals professed to admire their country. Indeed even Riesman, though later a New Left sympathizer, defended the American nuclear family in the 1950s.[2]

In the late forties and fifties, the moderate Left both celebrated American democracy and warned against America's enemies. Arthur M. Schlesinger, Jr., in *The Vital Center*, denounced Soviet repression at home and Soviet imperialism abroad; and social democrats like Sidney Hook, Reinhold Niebuhr, and the Americans for Democratic Action called for a vigorous national defense together with expanded social programs.[3] Niebuhr, Hook, and Herberg all tried to demonstrate through their words and their deeds the compatibility of "democratic socialism" with American patriotism. Many thinkers who were still associated in the late forties with the anticommunist moderate Left eventually found their way to the Right, taking some of their ideas with them. James Burnham (b. 1905) and Will Herberg, who joined the editorial staff of *National Review*, continued to believe in a welfare economy. Although some of the older political conservatives, such as Robert A. Taft, clung to their prewar isolationism and sought to revive it during the early phases of the cold war, in the late forties and early fifties the moderate Left favored containing Soviet expansion. The true forerunners of the anticommunist foreign policy formulated by *National Review* were more likely to be found among social democrats such as Melvin Lasky in England and Reinhold Niebuhr and Sidney Hook in the United States than among the stalwart Republican isolationists. Today's neoconservatives of the *Commentary* persuasion may be justified in seeing their ideas as descending from the cold war liberalism of the 1950s. It is also true, however, that as American liberalism veered to the left on questions of foreign policy and social morality, stands that had once been identified with cold war liberalism were transferred to the postwar conservative resurgence. No mere continuation of prewar anti–New Deal, isolationist politics, the conservative movement that George Nash analyzes in *The Conservative Intellectual Movement in America Since 1945* was boldly eclectic and internationalist, both politically and intellectually. Through the publications *National Review*, *Modern Age*, and *Review of Politics*, this movement worked to define its identity. And it did so often by trying to reconcile principles and attitudes that are often considered incompatible, for example, economic liberty and respect for state authority, an activist foreign policy and a distrust of federal government, opposition to ideology and the recurrent demand for a unified conservative Weltanschauung.[4]

The thinking of Reinhold Niebuhr (1892–1971) served as one bridge between the anticommunist, patriotic Left and the rudimentary intellectual Right of the postwar years. Like Georges Sorel, the French anarchist but self-styled reactionary who influenced both the revolutionary Left and Italian Fascism, Niebuhr impressed people of divergent political opinions. According to one established view he strengthened the reformist tendencies in Arthur M. Schlesinger, Jr., while making Herberg into a Burkean conservative.[5] This view may be overstated, since the political differences between Herberg and Schlesinger were not so great during their period of close contact with Niebuhr as they would later become. What may be more relevant to note here is that Niebuhr influenced the American Right without ever joining it. He received the tributes of conservatives and of conservative periodicals even though he identified himself on economic issues with the left wing of the Democratic Party and opposed American involvement in Vietnam. His repeated references to the demonic nature of Communism may have had something to do with his continuing popularity among many American conservatives. In *The Irony of American History* (1952), he declares that Communism, because of "illusory hopes" that it cynically awakens among intellectuals and humanitarians, is a greater threat to Western freedom than Nazism had ever been.[6] In presenting this perception he anticipates the main theme of James Burnham's conservative classic of the 1960s, *Suicide of the West*, without making the sometimes invidious charges against specific journalists and publications that detract from Burnham's arguments. Niebuhr also recommended Edmund Burke as a teacher for the twentieth century, and he offered this judgment in his writings of the early fifties, while conservative writers were making the same discovery.

Finally, Niebuhr was emphatically Christian as well as anticommunist. Although far from being a fundamentalist Protestant, he accentuated the centrality of historical Providence for understanding American history. He devoted one entire book to explaining why a providential Christian perspective was needed to puzzle out the ironies of America's current world situations. His tracts abounded in discussions of original sin, which he interpreted less as a theological tenet than as a point of departure for analyzing society. Niebuhr exemplified Peter Viereck's aphorism that conservatism is the political application of the doctrine of original sin. He expressed grave misgivings about the Enlightenment and warned his fellow Americans that "idealistic liberalism must not obscure the danger of Western democracy becoming unduly dependent upon mild illusions about human nature and the political order. For these illusions obscure the refractory character of man's nature and particularly the collective force of his self-regard."[7]

Niebuhr described his social-moral outlook as "Christian realism," and though his realism allowed him to envisage further redistribution of national wealth, he refused to disparage his country's military security and vital national interest. His book *The Structure of Nations and Empires* (1959) levels the following attack on the advocates of world government:

> The flowering of German culture in a situation of political fragmentation, which was not healed until Bismarck healed it by "blood and iron", was an instructive piece of evidence about the difficulties confronted by a "rational soul" unable to be incarnated in a national body. It is evidence which might well warn the apostles of world government who think it easy to create both an international community and an international government by act of will.[8]

Just before that passage, Niebuhr wrote that Hegel hoped to create a German national state by providing it with a metaphysical foundation."[9] This implicit reproach was unwarranted, since Hegel had produced a detailed critique of German political ineffectiveness in 1802, before he had written most of his philosophical work. Then thirty-two years old, Hegel had proposed the military unification of all German states under the strengthened authority of the Holy Roman Emperor. Hegel felt no nostalgia for the soon-to-vanish Holy Roman Empire whose pageantry and rituals, he believed, concealed inner weakness. He sought to transform the most ceremonial imperial office into a politically powerful position from which one might forge a true nation state. He urged Germans to study the Italian patriot Machiavelli, whom he considered a political thinker with a sense of reality.[10] Hegel had expressed the kind of misgivings about international government that Niebuhr also expressed 140 years later. In *The Philosophy of Right* Hegel notes that "there is no praetor but at most a mediator among states; and even he acts in accordance with particular interests. Immanual Kant's idea of perpetual peace through a union of states that mediates all quarrels . . . and that renders settlements through war impossible, assumes unanimity among states which . . . rest upon particular sovereign wills and are subject to contingencies."[11]

Niebuhr's conceptual affinity with Hegel becomes even more evident when he discovers the ironic side of Christian realism. Although certain aspects of American history seem "obviously ironic" to Niebuhr, he maintains that any consistent understanding of this irony must depend upon "a governing faith or world view."[12] His preferred world view is both Christian and acutely realistic. Unlike the tragic and pathetic outlooks of antiquity, Niebuhr's understanding allows for human limits and the element of surprise in history without being shattered by the seeming twists of fate. Thus he can smile at the foreign policy frustrations of his country, which, despite vast military power, must content itself with only limited influence abroad. He examines the irony of a secularized West representing Christianity in a struggle against an atheist enemy that has turned philosophical materialism into a new religion. Confronting the unexpected and paradoxical, men must have "faith that life has a center and source of meaning beyond the natural and social sequences which may be rationally discerned. This divine source and center must be discerned by faith because it is enveloped in mystery, though being the basis of meaning."[13]

Niebuhr differentiates the Christian sense of irony from two interrelated pagan perspectives: tragedy and pathos. One emphasized the futility of the human condition; the other underscored its desperation. For Niebuhr "the tragic motif is subordinated to the ironic one because evil and destructiveness are not regarded as the inevitable consequence of the exercise of human creativity." Nor could the historical ironist accept pathos since faith allows him to see beyond "meaningless cross-purposes in life, or capricious confusions of fortune and painful frustration."[14] These statements have links to Hegel's conception of history, which also presupposed a rejection of pagan myths about the nature of reality. A substantial part of *Phenomenology of the Spirit* is devoted to studying the evolution of Mind within the context of ancient religion and art. To illustrate the principle of pathos, Hegel chooses Sophocles' *Antigone*, a work that supposedly shows the division in moral consciousness characteristic of Greek tragedy. The world of tragedy did not set evil against good, but rather depicted "the movement of ethical forces against each other." Antigone, by burying her brother, Polyneices, after he had died in rebellion against his native city of Thebes, violated "human law," which prohibited the interment of traitors. From the standpoint of custom, "the government as the pure soul or self of the spirit of a people cannot tolerate the divisiveness of individuality." Antigone took her bearings from the "substance" of an individualized moral conscience. Through this "substance," which is only vaguely glimpsed, Antigone learns what is ethical (*Sittlichkeit*); yet by adhering to the ethical, she comes to grief. Finally, when she utters the lines "because we suffer we recognize that we have erred" she denies entirely the "substance" of her ethics.[15]

Hegel correctly concluded that *Antigone* depicted a conflict of ultimates, for true tragedy involves a struggle of right against right. Quentin Lauer has summed up Hegel's interpretation of *Antigone* thus: "It is the 'pathos' of the individual in a world in which laws are simply given—there is no escape. In one sense Creon [the Theban King] and Antigone are right, in another they are both wrong—and destiny swallows up both of them."[16] *Pathos* stems from the frustrated sense of individual moral worth in a universe of the kind that Niebuhr and Hegel both rejected as inconsistent with providential history. Both attributed the setbacks of nations and leaders to human limits rather than to the tragic character of the universe. The evocations of a thwarted Napoleon brooding in rockbound exile and of lives sacrificed on the "slaughter-bench of history" enhance the dramatic appeal of *The Philosophy of History*. They do not, however, indicate the tragic or pathetic side of history because Hegel, like Niebuhr, identifies human events with a teleological process. Like Niebuhr's depiction of America as a frustrated giant, Hegel's picture of Napoleon is intended to convey the "unconscious weakness" out of which even world historical figures are compelled to act. Men and nations fail not because human existence is intrinsically futile, but because the divine Logos, or the World Spirit, defies human understanding.

Niebuhr himself resisted any comparison between his own interpretation of history and that of Hegel. In *The Structure of Nations and Empires*, he makes one particularly revealing comment about a comparison of this type:

> The loom of history chooses the most disparate and seemingly incompatible ideas and events to weave into pattern of destiny. There is some "logic" in this choice, but not the neat logic which Hegel assumed when he asserted that the "cunning of reason" brought interest and passions under control. The logic of history is steeped in irony.[17]

Niebuhr may be justified in distinguishing between the ultimately transparent rationality of the Hegelian view of history and the Christian sense of wonder before the unfolding of divine Providence. Yet much of what Niebuhr presents under "the irony of history" may serve as fitting illustrations of Hegel's "cunning of reason." Like Hegel, he observes how human weaknesses, like material greed, have been made to serve higher ends. His "loom of history" is broad enough to accommodate a wide range of human types and appetites. It is also one of Hegel's favorite images. *The Philosophy of History* describes the relationship between the idea implicit in the World Spirit and the force of human passion as being a kind of loomwork: "One is the weave and the other the woof of the great carpet of world history."[18] These similarities do not mean that Niebuhr borrowed his "irony of history" or his "Christian realism" directly from Hegelian philosophy. More likely, Niebuhr, a German-American Protestant theologian, had absorbed theological concepts that reflected Hegel's pervasive influence on German Protestant thinking. Niebuhr's most extensive theological study, *The Nature and Destiny of Man*, cites approvingly Benedetto Croce on the need to view moral decisions as "historical choices." Although Niebuhr here dismisses Hegel as a "historical rationalist," he draws freely on the legacy of European Hegelian thought.[19]

It may be useful to note that Niebuhr and his wife, Ursula, had extended contact with German émigré scholars who came to America in the 1930s. Among these refugees could be found not only Marxists and other adherents of the Left but the exponents of a doctrine of political realism. In their bold conceptualizations and in their sarcastic antiutopianism, such thinkers went beyond the more subdued Christian socialist-tinged realism that Niebuhr himself had begun to expound in the 1940s. Joachim Radkau, in a study of the German émigré contribution to American political culture, has called attention to the "conservative tendencies" among some of the refugees from Nazism. Radkau makes the mistake of identifying anti-Soviet view with the extreme Right, and more sympathetic attitudes toward Stalin's regime with a politics of tolerance. Although Radkau has difficulty controlling his political prejudice, his book contains one highly valuable insight. It points to the continuity between the political realism enunciated by some of the Central European refugees during the Second World War and those policies of Soviet containment advocated by James Burnham and other postwar conservatives.[20] Focusing on Waldemar Gurian (1900–1954), the founder of *Review of Politics;* on Gurian's young collaborator, Stefan Possony (b. 1913); on the German evangelist theologian Eugen Rosenstock-Huessy (1888–1973)—and (less convincingly) on the future University of Chicago celebrity Hans Morgenthau (1904–1980)—Radkau examines the distrust of abstract political ideals common to these men. He also points to the Central European, actually Prussian, values that these men brought with them to America, but whose origin they often tried to hide.

Hans Morgenthau, who denounced "moral abstractions" and the spirit of legalism in international relations, warned Americans against imitating the Germans. The Germans had come to ruin because of their fondness for high-sounding phrases and abstractions, but Americans might avoid such a fate by consulting national interest in formulating foreign policy.[21] Needless to say, the prescription that Morgenthau recomended might have originated with Otto von Bismarck and with German nationalists of the 1870s. John Coffey, in analyzing the "political realism" of Morgenthau, emphasizes Morgenthau's conceptual debt to Hegel. Throughout his years in America, this refugee scholar warned against separating political ideals from what was historically feasible. He urged Americans to understand "the specifically human in man's existence and, through it, the divine."[22] Coffey interprets this maxim from Morgenthau's book *Science: Servant or Master?* as representing a Hegelian attempt to ascribe spiritual value to the study and exercise of political power. Coffey notes that Morgenthau attributed his metaphysical realism to his occasional collaborator, Reinhold Niebuhr. Only after the war did he seem willing to recognize the German component in his thinking and, even then, preferred to identify himself with Luther's sober attitude toward the state rather than with the heritage of German historicism beginning with Hegel.

But the attempt that Morgenthau and other émigrés made to dissociate German political values from a German context was certainly understandable. As a refugee Morgenthau wished to associate himself with the country that protected him rather than the one that had expelled him. Two other émigrés, Rosenstock-Huessy and Possony, railed against pacifism during the Second World War; both lamented the absence of a military ethic in an American society that was then fighting Nazi Germany. Rosenstock-Huessy, once in exile, turned furiously against his former nation. After the German surrender he surpassed many leftist émigrés in calling for a punitive peace, although such a move would have probably benefited the Soviet Union, which Rosenstock-Huessy despised as much as Nazi Germany.[23]

The anti-German Germanism represented by Possony, Rosenstock-Huessy, Gurian, and Morgenthau bore some resemblance to the anti-Hegelian Hegelianism discussed in the preceding chapter. In both cases, ideas continued to operate upon the minds of those who outwardly rejected them. The refugees with "conservative tendencies" pleaded their Americanness while internalizing, and occasionally Prussianizing, the American conservative agenda. *Review of Politics*, from the time of its founding in 1939, sought to familiarize educated Americans with the imperatives of international relations. The proponents of political realism grouped around *Review of Politics* were mostly Austrians and Austro-Hungarians (often of Jewish descent), who expounded Prussian Protestant teachings in an avowedly Catholic journal published at Notre Dame. In 1942 Possony used its pages to inveigh against the pacifist mentality as inappropriate for a great power bearing global responsibilities.[24] To measure the distance between this incipient postwar conservative perspective and the older libertarian opposition to Roosevelt, one might consider that most, if not all, congressional opponents of conscription in 1940 came from the American political Right. By the mid-1950s the most vocal supporters of American military power were also conservatives. These were members of a postwar Right that had been influenced by such anti-Communist interventionists as Stefan Possony and his frequent collaborator and fellow Austrian émigré, Robert Strausz-Hupé (b. 1903).[25]

The conservative realism of the 1950s combined dislike for the utopian internationalism symbolized by the United Nations with an even stronger revulsion for Communist totalitarians. Scorning the containment policy practiced by the Truman administration (which Morgenthau and Niebuhr had both defended, though Morgenthau more grudgingly) as a series of halfway measures, conservative realists such as Possony and Burnham called for "destabilizing the Soviet empire." Their view of an expansive and oppressive Soviet state seemed well borne out by Stalin's brutal imposition of Communist regimes on Eastern and Central Europe. The crimes against hapless minorities within the Soviet Union aroused even greater indignation. America's disenchantment with its former ally turned quickly after the war into strong disapproval of the Soviet regime combined with anger at American wartime leaders, especially Roosevelt, for "misrepresenting" Soviet intentions. The conservative realists carried this critique of America's self-deception into a more extensive indictment of democratic moralizing and the crusading spirit of Wilsonian idealism. The most prescient attack of this type may be found in the introduction to James Burnham's *The Machiavellians*. Written during the Second World War, Burnham's book predicts the rift between the Soviet Union and the West. The Americans would discover that the Atlantic Charter and other statements of humanitarian universalism would not turn the Soviet Union from its imperialist aims; nor would the unyielding righteousness with which America fought the Axis prepare it for a flexible response to Soviet aggression once Germany and Japan had ceased to be military threats.[26]

Conservative realists also stressed the "protracted" nature of America's conflict with Soviet Russia. As Possony makes clear in *A Century of Conflict* (1953), the opening salvo in Communist Russia's war against the West came with the Bolshevik Revolution and with the subsequent creation of the Comintern to export Communism to capitalist countries.[27] The struggle once joined was likely to continue well into the future, unless the West yielded its own sovereignty to Communist armies and agents or else subverted the Soviet empire from within. Strausz-Hupé defined the present challenge thus: "In order to survive or win this conflict, strategies must be planned to the scale of decades, not years. An individual conflict should be not viewed as an isolated phenomenon but as a phase of the total struggle, an integral part of a multiple series of interrelated conflicts. One conflict triggers the other; there are no decisive defeats or victories except the last."[28] Strausz-Hupé praises the desire "to rid international society of its oldest scourge," but he warns that "the festering sores on the international body politic cannot be healed by pious homilies on the blessings of peace."[29]

Although conservative realists viewed the Soviet Union as an implacable enemy aided by an international network of spies and fellow-travelers, they never encouraged America, even during its period of nuclear monopoly, to launch a military attack on the Soviets. Burnham, Possony, Strausz-Hupé, and others who called for victory over Communism usually advocated policies that were less fiery than their rhetoric, for example, propaganda offensives in Eastern Europe and a greater military commitment to containing Soviet expansion.[30] It would also be fair to observe that most of the conservative realists, and particularly the Central Europeans among them, hoped to use the cold war to enhance the political virtues of the American people. They warned the American nation against entrusting its fortunes to international bodies and against pursuing idealistic schemes at the cost of national interest.

But this recurrent admonition resulted not merely from the fear that the Soviets and their friends would control international institutions. Conservative realists also despised the thoroughly "utopian" impulse to scorn actual states and living nations in favor of abstract, ahistorical allegiances. The introductory chapter of James Burnham's *The Machiavellians* explores the roots of the modern obsession with an ideal superstate; it traces the lineage of this obsession back to the medieval yearning for a revived Roman Empire. Burnham's line of investigation leads into a curious juxtaposing of Dante's proimperial tract, *De Monarchia*, and the Atlantic Charter of 1941 with its pledge to free mankind from material wants.[31] The émigré Catholic philosopher and political theorist Thomas Molnar (b. 1920) has ascribed internationalism to a misplaced religious need for union with the universal. According to Molnar: "there is good reason why humanity cannot be a political entity: no such formation could be *political* for it would abolish by its very existence, the nation and its national framework, the State."[32] Like Burnham, Molnar sees "political internationalism" as a perennial delusion, and one not always confined to the utopian or imperialist Left. In analyzing the mistaken belief in the presence of uniform values and a single moral purpose in the Third World, Molnar sardonically observes: "All this used to be the dream of the [counterrevolutionary] whites whose system of reductionist classification ultimately allowed for only one class. It was they who had hoped to create a Catholic *oikoumene* for the entire planet; but then came the capitalist empire of the Manchesterian school, and afterwards the democratic ecumenicism of Roosevelt, and finally the Marxist empire supported by the Kremlin and by leftwing intellectuals. One always returns to the same illusion."[33]

The program that conservative realists have most often identified with their counteroffensive against the Communists is the liberation and restoration of captive nations. James Burnham's *Suicide of the West* treats the present struggle against the Soviets and their clients as being largely a confrontation between a wavering party of freedom and the partly insincere champions of equality. The Communist powers are expansionists who appeal to egalitarianism, and the best strategy against them would combine the defense of liberty with the pursuit of American national interest. Supposedly American liberals could no longer fight effectively against Communism. Their utopian universalism and their sacrifice of both freedom and national interest to the collectivist goal of "social justice" rendered them increasingly useless in combating the Communists. Burnham believed that only those who valued concrete (personal and national) liberty could still prevail against an expanding Soviet empire.[34]

The Hungarian émigré Stephen Kertesz, a founder of *Review of Politics*, proposed a spiritual offensive against the Soviets in the 1950s. Such an offensive would involve not only "exposing Communist duplicity," but also appealing to the "national genius in East Central Europe."[35] Such remarks are indicative of the conservative realist understanding of national identity, which stems from the nineteenth-century concept of "historical nations." Although conservative realists have stressed the importance of "national character," what they have usually meant by it are the clusters of characteristics identified with certain Western peoples who have achieved but then in some cases lost their statehood. This point must be kept in mind if we are to understand why self-styled conservative realists have frequently interpreted nationalism as a traditionalist, that is, anti-Communist, force. Their object of study and preferred model has been East Central Europe with its largely Catholic and until recently, rural populations. Molnar, in his French publications, most notably in *Le Socialisme sans Visage,* is perhaps the conservative realist who has worked hardest to expand this frame of reference. Yet he, too, has kept his Central European émigré perspective, which has yielded extended and often provocative comparisons between "Third World" dictatorships and the European Fascist states of the interwar period.[36]

Hegelianism of the Right was another recurrent aspect of the conservative realist outlook. Friedrich Meinecke includes among the intellectual contributions to the movement for German political unification Hegel's "true empirical sense of the relationship of states to each other." Despite the rationalist, deductive character of his philosophizing, Hegel "gave full recognition and free play to empirical and non-rational forces." Meinecke was especially impressed by one particular observation in *The Philosophy of Right:* "In the relationship of states to each other, because they exist as individual units, there is also the most animated interplay of individual passions, interests, aims, talents, virtues, violence, and injustice."[37] Hegel believed that passions and interests found an integrated and constructive expression through the activities of the nation state. Individual concerns acquired "world-historical significance" to whatever degree they became associated with a powerful and widely respected state. Only the state bestowed ethical unity on the otherwise conflicting interests of civil society while enabling nations to survive and prosper within a world of strife. This Hegelianism of the Right was obviously based on a selective reading of Hegel's political-historical writing. Nonetheless, it attracted many scholars throughout the nineteenth and early twentieth centuries, including Italians such as Giovanni Gentile and many German nationalists. The ideas of the Hegelian Right shaped increasingly the classical German historiography of the nineteenth century. For example, the two highly respected historians Leopold von Ranke and Gustav Droysen placed thematic emphasis on international affairs (*die Aussenpolitik*) and on the role of state builders. Both historians and their numerous disciples accepted Hegel's own identification of spiritual reality with political authority. Since the Second World War, the German émigrés of the Left and their American followers have produced a vast literature of indictment against the "German tradition of historiography." These critics have attacked (often with more heat than light) what is seen as the characteristically Hegelian trait among an older generation of German academic historians, the treatment of statecraft as the essence of history.[38]

Although few conservative realists have called themselves Hegelians, most of them nonetheless make complimentary references to Hegel. Possony, who notes Lenin's use of the Hegelian dialectic, himself has extolled Hegel as a political realist sans pareil.[39] Molnar, as a neo-Thomist, has deplored Hegel's impact on modern theology, but he has also praised him as an astute social and political analyst. In his critique of America as a politically fragmented society, *Le Modèle Défiguré*, Molnar calls for a new appreciation of Hegel as a political teacher. The liberal utilitarian view of the state on which most native Americans have been raised is incompatible with both public virtue and political authority. American society, which has become a collection of private interests and organized pressure groups, has lost a sense of cohesion. Rather than the threat of political despotism, America is seen to illustrate the danger of "societal totalitarianism." It was Hegel who tried to anticipate this kind of contingency by "striking a theoretical balance" between the state and civil society. Although Molnar believes that Hegel went too far in defending authority, he praises the Hegelian quest to find a middle ground between despotism and fractious social interests: "We seek in vain the [sense of] equilibrium intuited by Hegel and we commit the error of finding in the United States the ideal model simply because we properly reject its counterpart, the statist totalitarianism inspired by Marx."[40]

James Burnham also gives evidence of being familiar with Hegel's political ideas, which he studied through Italian Hegelians. Burnham, who abandoned his Trotskyist Communism by the late 1930s, came thereafter increasingly under the influence of what he himself styled "Machiavellian realism." Those hard-headed interpreters of irrational social behavior whom Burnham recommended to his age were mostly Italians: for example, Machiavelli, Gaetano Mosca, and Vilfredo Pareto. Burnham acclaimed these thinkers for exposing the illusion of popular sovereignty, for showing that social action has little to do with men's conscious intellectual-moral aspirations.

According to Machiavelli and his alleged disciples, those who speak of political society must assume the existence of elites who can manipulate popular passions. Burnham's beliefs in the inevitability of ruling classes and the enslavement of most individuals to their appetites and emotions predisposed him to accept a strong state. In *The Machiavellians* and in his later works, he castigates Roosevelt not for encroaching on economic freedom by introducing a welfare state, but for exercising power imprudently. Roosevelt had served his nation and the West badly by fighting the Second World War as an idealistic crusade. Never does Burnham challenge either Roosevelt's right to wage war or the right of the American state to pursue its interest through military means. Like Giovanni Gentile, the Italian Hegelian whom he professed to respect, Burnham viewed the state as a necessary source of moral unity in a world otherwise divided by individual appetites and ideological conceits.[41]

John Diggins has stressed the contradiction between Burnham's postwar appeal to freedom during America's contest with Soviet Russia and his earlier reduction of political ideas to mere figments of the popular imagination.[42] In response to Diggins's charge, I have pointed out that Burnham attacked idealistic politics in 1943, whereas his appeal to freedom, in *Containment or Liberation?*, was published ten years later. His thinking on the question of freedom may have changed during the intervening years. He may also have believed that although America's attitude toward the Second World War had been overly emotional, its response to Soviet aggression was insufficiently enthusiastic.[43] I would now add to my argument of 1976 that the continuity between *The Machiavellians* and Burnham's writings during the cold war may be traced to his conservative historicism. Samuel T. Francis finds it running through all his post-Marxist thought.

*Containment or Liberation?* calls for an increase in American economic and military support for anti-Soviet national forces within the Communist bloc and for those refugee groups in the West committed to expelling the Soviets from their countries. Burnham proposed a military strategy for a stalemated struggle in which the other side, because of its united front or the absence of debilitating opposition, may have held the long-term advantage. He called upon the American government not to engage in utopian crusades, but to play a political trump card, to arm the victims of Soviet tyranny and then unleash them against the Soviets. The goal for which the oppressed peoples of Eastern Europe would struggle was fully consistent with Burnham's conservative realism. The revolts against the Soviets would be wars of "national liberation": attempts to restore political independence to the peoples of Central and Eastern Europe.[44]

Burnham, far from changing his values, was remarkably consistent in advocating a statecraft stripped of "utopian" views. He always addressed himself to the ruling class (that he believed existed even in democracies) to provide intelligent direction to the private passions and enthusiasms prevalent in society. He assumed that conflicts inevitably erupted among nation states, but that attempts to establish supranational governments entailed the imposition of tyranny. In both these assumptions, he remained consistent with the historicist attempt to focus on actual men in the context of their necessarily diverse societies and patterns of development. In all Burnham's post-Marxist writings (and even in some of his Marxist ones), he expressed contempt for rhetorical abstraction and for the appeal to universals to justify political actions. The apparent exception that he made by defending freedom had an explanation other than tactical necessity. Burnham believed in freedom as the moral alternative to all universalist creeds that laid claim to people irrespective of their traditions. His defense of freedom did not arise out of an individualistic creed but was grounded in the firm conviction that historical nations and established societies had the right, and even duty, to resist the armed prophets of universal orders.

It is, moreover, possible to find distinctly Right-Hegelian traits in Burnham's thinking. His defense of freedom was more often than not a defense of the sovereignty of nations rather than of the rights of individuals. His youthful reading of Giovanni Gentile may have helped to nurture some of his most long-lived political attitudes. Whereas Burnham mocked the utopian yearnings of many Western intellectuals, he treated the nation state with pronounced respect, as an instrument of power and of a unified national will. How then do we explain Burnham's one apparent denial of the national principle in the postwar period? In 1947, in *Struggle for the World*, he advocated a "universal empire" that would organize Europe under a *pax Americana*. Perhaps it may be useful to state the obvious for those who have read the work. Burnham presented his scheme as a *pis aller:* the only workable plan for keeping the Soviets out of Western Europe. He called his proposed order a *pax Americana* not because of nationalist arrogance, but because of his perception of political reality. The consolidation of Soviet power in Eastern Europe and the large Communist parties in Western countries such as France and Italy left Western Europe highly vulnerable to Soviet intimidation and political penetration. The American monopoly of atomic weapons, however, provided a credible deterrent to Soviet aggression and would strengthen the confidence of anti-Soviet forces everywhere. Despite Burnham's belief in the need for a collective Western response to Soviet imperialism, he saw even that kind of defensive reaction as involving the control of one state by another. However much one might coat the bitter pill, European states would have to yield part of their sovereignty in placing themselves under American protection. The alternative, Soviet control of Western Europe, Burnham believed was sufficiently grim to render non-Communist Europeans receptive to a *pax Americana*.[45]

Burnham distinguished between a world empire and world government. The power vacuum left in Europe by two catastrophic wars would not be filled by the old nation states that had initiated those wars. By 1945, it was the United States and the Soviet Union that controlled the destiny of the West through their armies and political influence. The presence of nuclear weapons increased the possible scope of future wars and rendered obsolete the regional conflicts in which European nation states had once jockeyed for power. Burnham believed that a world empire rather than a unitary world government was most likely to succeed the old European system of regional states. Nation states would continue to function, particularly under the American aegis, since the attempt to remove political and national diversity might prove too costly for future empire builders. Although Burnham denounced the Soviet Union for its brutal, totalitarian government, in 1947 he sensed only vaguely the extent to which Eastern Europe would have Soviet-type states imposed on it. The Soviet world empire that he described was simply a crueler version of his projected American imperium. The new world empire was by definition "a state not necessarily world-wide in literal extent but world-dominating in political power set up at least in part through coercion . . . and in which one group of people (its leaders being one of the existing nations) would have more than an equal share of power."[46] The *Struggle for the World* is the only work in which Burnham argues for the need to move beyond the framework of the nation state. Even there the nation state is not entirely abandoned, but only provisionally sacrificed to what Burnham, drawing upon the rhetoric of the Hegelian Right, calls the demands of "world politics." Faithful to his conservative realist vision, Burnham announced in 1947, "We have entered a period of history in which world politics takes precedence over national and internal politics."[47] In view of the magnitude of the struggle then unfolding, only two world historical nation states would be able to participate in the new age fully.

The analysis of conservative realism offered here rests ultimately on the kind of "ideal type" that Max Weber employed to show the link between Calvinism and capitalism. Weber never found the characteristics that he associated with the moral theology of capitalism fully embodied in any one historical figure. His ideal type was an intellectual construct suggested by his reflection on his data; his illustrations of capitalists who were affected by Calvinist values confirmed the correlation that he proposed without requiring him to identify totally the ideal type with any one particular example. In my study of conservative realism, I have focused on the possible relationship between the understanding of statecraft among anti-Marxist Central European émigrés and the political thought of James Burnham, on the one side, and, on the other, the historical thinking of the European Hegelian Right. No single conservative thinker personifies conservative realism perfectly. Nor is this realism a monopoly of conservatives, as the example of Reinhold Niebuhr's cold war liberalism illustrates. But most of the European émigrés did imbibe the Right-Hegelian tendency to assign foreign affairs primary importance in the existence of nations. Most of them accepted "state authority" as a sacred principle of political life. They believed that Americans, even anti-Communist libertarian ones, were excessively preoccupied with "social issues" and the pursuit of individual gratification.

Certain qualifications must be made to refute the oversimplified view, among critics, of the subjects of this study as "rightwing fanatics." Those whom we have presented as conservative realists preached against the Soviet Union and other

Communist regimes as murderous, aggressive empire builders. Almost all the conservative realists took an equally dim view of Nazi Germany, and they favored military measures against it far more sweeping than those they later urged against the Soviets. It should also be noted that even the most relentlessly anti-Soviet tracts by conservative realists, such as the *Protracted Conflict, Century of Conflict*, and *The Struggle for the World*, defended democratic government while emphatically rejecting a dictatorial alternative. There are of course notable exceptions to the conservative realist defense of democracy, which the writings of both Molnar and Burnham can easily provide. Yet, Thomas Molnar, who more than almost anyone else on the American Right, has mocked both modern civil society and "the erosion of state power [*l'usure de l'état*]" in a world dominated by rampant individualism and timid politicians, heroically opposed the Nazis and, later, the Communists in his native Hungary.[48] Unlike many of their self-righteous critics, the conservative realists have readily opposed totalitarianism on both sides of the political spectrum.

Despite these qualifications, a certain polarity between conservative realism and those libertarian antimilitaristic strains in the American political tradition is perceptible. Such a polarity may be discerned on the postwar Right, where libertarian tendencies have often clashed with authoritarian values. In the fifties and sixties, Frank Meyer railed against the "neo-Hegelians" of the New Conservatism whom he accused of placing the state, as a work of history, on a higher moral plane than the individual members of civil society.[49] Meyer directed this attack at figures who had been only minimally influenced by Hegel's social philosophy, such as Peter Viereck and Russell Kirk, but the attack itself revealed genuine lines of cleavage. By the 1960s it became difficult to define a conservative movement that embraced libertarians like Murray Rothbard, Milton Friedman, and Max Eastman; and political-social traditionalists; and even clericalists. Various attempts were made to bridge this ideological chasm. Conservative periodicals, most notably *Modern Age* and *National Review,* collected editorial staffs and contributors who were broadly representative of the educated Right. Barry Goldwater's presidential platform in 1964 embodied a certain form of fusionism, wedding a defense of private enterprise with an activist foreign policy. The conservative theorist Frank Meyer, undertaking to reconcile traditionalists with libertarians, discovered that the "authentic" American political tradition combined individual freedom with social virtue. Commenting on America's constitutional regime, Meyer maintained that "ours is the most effective effort ever made to articulate in *political* terms the Western understanding of the interrelation of the freedom of the person and the authority of an objective moral order."[50] Meyer's repeated attempt to base virtue on free choice and his attribution of this position to America's Founding Fathers dramatically indicated the search for a middle ground on the postwar Right.

Conservative realism has been very much a part of that dialectic of social

order and individual liberty that has been present in the conservative movement. Conservative realists have justified their defense of the state and their understanding of world politics by appealing to the views of the Hegelian Right.
They have contrasted the unified will of traditional political authority with a
necessarily divided civil society. Unlike the libertarians, who treat the state as
a necessary evil, and the modern liberal, who embraces government in order to
remove social differences, the conservative realists believe political authority is
indispensable for human survival and moral development. Some conservative
realists have also cited Aristotle and St. Thomas Aquinas in arguing that
human beings are naturally political animals. Yet, by asserting the primacy of
the state over what Molnar contemptuously calls "the neo-feudalities" of civil
society and by stressing the imperatives of world politics, conservative realists
have added Hegelian elements to whatever classical and medieval sources they
have cited.

Radkau is right to perceive conservative tendencies at work among certain
Central European refugees from Nazism but is wrong to ascribe those tendencies almost solely to their pro-American or anti-Soviet attitudes. What actually
defined émigré Right was respect for state authority combined with a deep
skepticism about the possibility of supranational agencies' replacing the nation state.[51] These attitudes offended not only the émigré Left with its devotion
to Marxism and Marxist-Freudianism, but also nonleftist refugees of libertarian persuasion such as Friedrich Hayek and Ludwig von Mises. It would
also be wrong, given the writings of James Burnham, to identify the conservative realist outlook exclusively with Central Europeans.

Central European émigrés, however, were conspicuous among those who defended the conservative realist view of the state and of international relations.
Jeffrey Hart has described the righteous anger of Eugen Rosenstock-Huessy, as
he lectured to American university students in the 1950s. Looking with disgust
at a class imbued with pacifist sentiments, the aging theologian scolded its
members as cowards. Because they would not fight for their country, they
proved themselves unworthy of their ancestors' military courage. Those who
renounced war unconditionally had forfeited their right to a history.[52] In 1938
Rosenstock-Huessy had published *Out of Revolution: Autobiography of Western
Man,* a rambling but often insightful study of Western intellectual history as
seen from a Christian millenarian perspective. The author stresses that the history of the West, which is also the history of the most spiritually advanced of all
world civilizations, is approaching its final point in time. The chaos of his own
age was providentially ordained and was intended to be the closing chapter of
what he himself calls *secular history.* Despite his sombre view of the present,
Rosenstock-Huessy engages in the Hegelian practice of pointing with pride to
the "world historical" figures who were responsible for Western political and
moral achievements: Oliver Cromwell, Robespierre, and Pope Gregory VII
were among those who contributed, sometimes unwittingly, to the creative ten-

sion between religious and political institutions. Out of the dialectical relationship between these two powers came political recognition of the right of religious conscience and the moral unity that bound together the Christian West even in times of political strife. Noting that Oliver Cromwell thought himself immortal, Rosenstock-Huessy asserts that "he was right in his vision of a permanent place for himself in the evolution of man." "The evolution of man," the author observes, "is but another term for perpetual victory over death, over the encircling gloom."[53]

Resonating in these words was more than the appeal made by Roman historians such as Livy to ancestral courage and the immorality of fame. Rosenstock-Huessy, who admired Lincoln as a defender of the American Union, believed in the duty of citizens to fight for the preservation of their state. Through nations and states men gained historical identity as living links in the chain of humanity. Supposedly the contempt that Americans felt for their military indicated their decline into a latter-day Chinese society. The Chinese, whom Hegel also placed at the dawn of civilization, lacked respect for military virtue, and it was only natural that a decadent America would want to imitate the alien vices of a stagnant Oriental culture.[54] Rosenstock-Huessy's message came out of a European tradition of thought that brought Hegelian themes by way of refugee scholars into postwar American conservatism.

# DIALECTIC AND CONSCIOUSNESS

ON 20 MARCH 1981 PRESIDENT RONALD REAGAN, ADDRESSING THE CON-
servative Political Action Conference in Washington, D.C., extolled the
achievement of the late Frank Meyer. Having begun his political career as a
Communist, Meyer had subsequently succeded in disentangling himself from
a false faith and "then in his writing fashioned a vigorous new synthesis of traditional and libertarian thought, a synthesis that is recognized today as modern conservatism." "It was Frank Meyer," the president continued, "who reminded us that the robust individualism of the American experience was part
of the deeper current of Western culture and learning."[1] It may be worthy of
note that the synthesis of individual freedom and moral tradition that the president found in Meyer and in postwar conservatism generally was also an overarching theme of Hegel's political and historical writings. Meyer's presenta-
tion of that synthesis incorporated ideas that were already implicit in his early
Marxism. A dialectical frame of reference remained a constant factor in his
thinking, but as he moved away from the radical Left, he associated struggle, as
Hegel had done, with spiritual rather than material forces.

To Meyer, the history of the West from the eighteenth century down to the
twentieth was shaped by two opposing principles, liberty and moral authority.
Both principles stemmed from a combined Christian-Classical heritage but
had come increasingly into conflict throughout the nineteenth century.
Whereas classical liberals rallied to the defense of "limited state power, the free
market economy, and the freedom of the individual person," they scorned the
"belief in an organic moral order." Their skepticism undermined the moral
basis of their own position: "Political freedom, failing a broad acceptance of the
personal obligation to duty and to charity, is never viable."[2] By contrast
traditionalists, in upholding an inherited social and religious order, neglected
the principle of liberty. Meyer scolded them for being unable to "distinguish

between the *authoritarianism* with which men and institutions suppress the freedom of men, and the *authority* of God and truth."[3]

According to Meyer, "the great tradition of the West has come to us through the nineteenth century, split, bifurcated, so that we must draw not only upon those who called themselves conservatives in that century but also upon those who called themselves liberals." The dialectical tension within the Western tradition produced divisiveness in Europe, but constitutional arrangements were established in America to surmount the Old World dilemma. Those who framed the Constitution overcame "the division, the bifurcation, of European thought between the emphasis on virtue and value and order and the emphasis on freedom and the integrity of the individual person." Whatever their personal and doctrinal differences may have been, the Founding Fathers conducted their own dialectic "within a continuing awareness of their joint heritage." Meyer sums up their achievement thus:

> Out of that dialectic they created a political theory and a political structure based upon the understanding that, while truth and virtue are metaphysical and moral ends, the freedom to seek them is the political condition of those ends—and that a social structure which keeps power divided is the indispensable means to this political end.[4]

Meyer not only expounded a dialectical view of the modern West, but also drew upon the Hegelian tradition for his conception of history. His writings for *National Review* and *Modern Age* indicate that he saw history as the advancing consciousness of freedom.[5] This consciousness allegedly persisted down into our own time, but mostly in the "distorted form of the scientistic and progressivist arrogance of a post-Christian *Weltanschauung*."

Meyer also traced historical consciousness to the "sublime paradox of faith that created the West: the penetration of the transcendent into history, indicating the freedom of men in history" (398). He sought to extricate the true Western sense of history from the distorting influence of modern historical "myths." Coming in the wake of the rationalist assault on traditional religion, modern thinkers, such as Hegel and Marx, Oswald Spengler, and Arnold Toynbee, had created historical systems intended to overcome "the meaninglessness of human life." Their work, by reducing God to a part of the historical process or replacing Him entirely with "laws," had only compounded the spiritual problem.

Meyer did not consider Hegelianism one of the more pernicious examples of historical determinism. The two forms of determinism that most deeply disturbed him were "Marxism and the modern liberal view of progress; both were variants of the intellectually omnipresent modernist dogma of 'scientism.'" Historical systems were progressively vulgarized attempts to restore a transcendent aspect to human existence. Hegel's attempt to rehabilitate God as the immanent principle of history rapidly deteriorated into the pseudoscience of

Marxism and the "progressivist arrogance" of modern liberalism.

In his columns for *National Review,* "Principles and Heresies," Meyer commented on the descent into modern errors. In a debate, for example, with the political philosopher Harry Jaffa on the role of Lincoln as a vindicator of the American ideal of equality, he lamented that egalitarian teachings were upsetting inherited constitutional arrangements. Americans were straying from the idea of ordered freedom, which had originated with the Founding Fathers, into worshipping equality "as an abstract, overarching, unmodified concept" (475). In a tribute to both Karl Wittfogel and Eric Voegelin in *National Review* on 22 June 1957, Meyer contrasted their writings with "the scientism which attempts completely to destroy man's awareness of a divine purpose and meaning to his existence" (401). In a review of Eric Voegelin's *Order and History,* volume II, Meyer further praised Voegelin for seeking "to controvert the two related theories of history which have created the world view that dominates our age, Marxism and the liberal theory of progress" (404).

Although Meyer scorned the liberal, materialist theory of progress, his own scheme of human development emphasized forward movement. His journey from radicalism to what he considered a Christian defense of liberty helps us to understand his approach to this theme. Meyer's journey culminated in the publication of *In Defense of Freedom* (1962), his definitive political-philosophical statement and a critique of "authoritarian" elements on the American Left and the American Right.[6] Two crucial aspects of his conversion were his preference for liberty over collectivist ideals and his turning away from a materialist view of history toward a spiritual one.[7] Meyer always properly viewed himself as being more of a political activist than a historical thinker, but he also looked for evidence to corroborate his moral intuitions. As a defender of the West, he searched for a coherent philosophy of history that would serve as an antidote to liberal and Marxist theories of progress. His enthusiastic endorsement of Wittfogel's *Oriental Despotism* and of Voegelin's *Order and History* resulted from his quest to legitimate his political commitment.

Wittfogel and Voegelin both identified freedom primarily, though not exclusively, with a Western heritage of ideas; both stressed the critical role of spiritual breakthroughs, in contrast to material factors, in analyzing social change. Wittfogel traced the break with the established pattern of hydraulic societies back to the Hebrew, Greek, and Germanic peoples. All of these groups rejected the despotic social organization of older empires for moral and geographic reasons. Voegelin stressed the break with Oriental despotism even more explicitly than Wittfogel, and he focused on the religious dimension of that process. Like Hegel's *Lecture on the Philosophy of History,* Voegelin's *Order and History* opens by depicting the politically monolithic and utterly impersonal condition of ancient Oriental society. China, Egypt, India, and Mesopotamia all exemplified "cosmological empires," in which the cosmic order was seen as coextensive with political authority. No distance was allowed to exist between man's spiritual aspirations and the powers that ruled him. Moreover, a symbolization of religious experience took place in the form of the deification of earthy leaders among the Egyptians and other ancient peoples. This symbolization underscored the unity between political rulers and the very structure of the universe, as imagined in these societies.

The primal, and largely Oriental, political theology received a challenge from the "leaps in being" that occurred around the middle of the first millennium, B.C. The Buddha and other mystics in India and, even more significantly, the Hebrew prophets and Greek philosophers all pointed the way toward a higher level of human consciousness. These figures transcended their societies by showing their openness to the "divine ground of being." Whether through revealed wisdom or speculative truth, Moses, Isaiah, and Plato moved beyond the theophanic symbols of the cosmological empires by reaching for divine truth as individuals. They proved that men were capable of participating in the cosmic order above, even as they remained bound to their earthly condition.[8]

Voegelin did not see any further significant spiritual advances following those leaps in being that he delineated. Neither the pneumatic experience of the Hebrew prophets nor the contemplative vision of the Greek teachers could be perpetuated by their epigones. The generations that succeeded the great teachers felt increasingly alienated from a distant and often inaccessible source of being. Faced by the chasm between the human and divine, the Greeks reverted to the individually undifferentiated life of the polis, and the Hebrews tried to restore meaning to their existence by reaffirming their sense of being a Chosen People.[9] Moreover, once the leaps in being had transpired, the temptation to return to a closed state of consciousness, as well as to a compactly organized society, arose. Voegelin characterized these lapses into closed systems of thought as "derailments [Entgleisungen]." In the modern period such derailments have often taken the form of redemptive myths about the end of history that have come in the guise of a "science of politics."[10] Meyer cited Voegelin as a critic of modern ideology who recognized Marxism for what it was: a fall from philosophy as participation in the divine ground of being into a pseudoreligious adoration of human laws of history.[11]

Meyer was far from being an original thinker, but he interpreted *Order and History* in a way that bore the imprint of his own theorizing. For example, it is possible to find in his writing an emphasis on *continuing* spiritual progress that is generally absent from Voegelin's work. In his review of *Order and History,* Volume II, Meyer attributed to its author his own understanding of the Incarnation of Christ, as being an unqualified advance beyond the leaps into being of the first millennium, B.C. Meyer believed that "only with the ultimate act of grace, the Incarnation, the flash of eternity into time, was it possible for the individual soul truly to recognize itself and its simultaneous existence in two worlds, the world of eternity and the world of time" (407). In contrast to

Meyer, Voegelin views Jesus and St. Paul within a tradition of pneumatic participation in the ground of being that went back to the prophets of Israel. He interprets Christian revelation as a "further differentiation" of the prophetic consciousness of the divine, but a differentiation subject to the derailments characteristic of civilization since the partial but never completed break with the cosmological pattern.

Meyer interpreted Voegelin's theory of history by doing what Voegelin's other Christian disciples—Gerhart Niemeyer, John Hallowell, John East, and others—would also attempt: presenting the Christian moment as a qualitatively separate and higher leap into being than any that had preceded it.[12]

At the same time, Meyer assigned to the Incarnation the historical function that Hegel had bestowed on the same event. Both Meyer and Hegel associated the Incarnation with the principle of subjectivity, which would at last receive full institutional recognition in their own constitutional states.[13] Hegel saw the principle of individual conscience as being in the ascendant throughout the history of Germanic civilization; Meyer thought that "cosmologism" remained politically weak in the West because of the Christian consciousness of individuality. Meyer believed, though, that the full bodying forth of the spirit of freedom awaited the work of America's Founding Fathers: "Western civilization in its European experience did not achieve political institutions fully coherent with its spirit." It was the Americans who reconciled order with liberty, supposedly doing what Hegel had thought the Protestant nations of northern Europe had done. "The establishment of a free constitution," Meyer proclaimed in *Modern Age*, "is the great achievement of America in the drama of Western civilization" (426). It was also an advance in human consciousness for which Christianity, the classical world, and European civilization had all laid the foundations.

The presence of certain recognizable Hegelian elements in Meyer's thinking does not mean that he studied or, even less, approved of Hegel. His earliest and, in some ways, most profound philosophical education occurred while he was still a Marxist revolutionary. One may discern the impact of that learning experience by reading Meyer's implicitly autobiographical *The Moulding of Communists: The Training of the Communist Cadre*. Although obviously critical of the Communist movement, his work puts into relief the compelling power of the Marxist historical view. Those who struggle for moral and existential certainty as Communists can achieve their goal only by developing "faith in History and its avatar, the Party." Communists are taught to believe that "the Party is the Material Force (and for Communists there exists nothing but matter in motion), the chosen vessel of History which embodies the meaning of life.[14] Meyer observes that the will and mind of each Communist novitiate are conditioned through the steady inculcation of the Marxist-Leninist "vision of History." The molding of a Communist mentality requires the implantation of these well-defined beliefs: "freedom is the recognition of necessity; there are no accidents. In human society, in economic development, in political struggle, the dialectical laws of history act with the inexorability of the laws of nature."[15]

These statements, based on Meyer's recollection of his youthful involvement with Communism, indicate how deeply he had believed in an ordered and dialectically controlled history. A dialectical view of history remained operative in his thought even after he had moved to the Right. Indeed this conceptualization persisted in Meyer's thinking despite his affirmation, as a Christian apologist and as an advocate of personal liberty, of the freedom of the individual.

Unlike Herberg and Wittfogel, Meyer as a Communist probably never had more than a nodding acquaintance with Hegel. Yet, in journeying between the two polar positions that shaped his adult life, dialectical materialism and Christian libertarianism, he came to embrace what could pass for a Hegelian theory of history. Meyer spiritualized the dialectical process. He viewed human development as a movement toward freedom that culminated in American regime only after it had passed beyond two confrontations of principle: first, the Voegelinian struggle between the world of compact symbols and the noetic and pneumatic truths of the Greeks and the Hebrews; and second, a new dialectic arising within the Christian age between individuality and the revealed moral-social order. The American Constitution was a response to the second and spiritually higher dialectic that was supposedly inherent in the Christian-Classical heritage. The "Western spirit," as Meyer understood it, achieved its fullest self-realization through the American Constitution as he interpreted that document.

As a contributor to and, later, book editor of *National Review*, Meyer devoted considerable space to philosophers of history. His own analyses of Voegelin Spengler, Marx, Wittfogel, and Toynbee reveal the force of a learned mind accustomed to subtle distinction. Meyer was also, however, a morally passionate thinker who accused others of his generation, and even his political persuasion, of breaking with the "mainstream" of Western tradition.[16] Essential to his political and journalistic activities was his own need for unshakable certainty regarding the rightness of his cause. He tried to anchor those stands he took in the Western consciousness of history, the final point of which had supposedly been reached with the founding of the American government. The militant spirit in which Meyer opposed those who questioned these assumptions became a source of amusement, and sometimes irritation, among the other editors of *National Review*. For more than ten years, Meyer scolded Russell Kirk for failing to appreciate the Founding Fathers as protectors of liberty. He produced large parts of *In Defense of Freedom*, and numerous editorial broadsides, against conservative-authoritarians who, he thought, disparaged the American regime. Nor did his former Marxist soulmate James Burnham, who later helped found *National Review*, escape Meyer's jeremiads. Meyer accused Burnham, often loudly in the editorial offices of *National Review*, of being ungrateful to America's founders, who had reconciled moral order with individual liberty. Burnham, who prided himself on his detached and critical understanding of politics, appeared to Meyer to be a "thoroughgoing cynic." Burnham, as seen by Meyer, treated the American Constitution simply as one instrument of government among others, while refusing to acknowledge the particular genius of that document's framers.[16] From his general historical assumptions and his explicit teachings, it is clear that Meyer considered his age, including many of his colleagues, unworthy recipients of a perfected constitutional system.

Through his censorious view of those who abandoned a perfected government, Meyer expressed another aspect of Hegelian thinking. Hegel and his conservative disciples had believed in the wisdom of supporting regimes that integrated individual and corporate freedoms with social custom and political authority. Hegel had scandalized his radical students by defending both a House of Lords and the practice of aristocratic primogeniture in Prussia.[17] In 1831 he further alienated the political Left when he wrote against the electoral reform of the English Parliament, which was finally passed in 1832.[18] In both cases Hegel argued for what he took as the concrete achievements of Reason in history against unwarranted political tampering. Above all, he feared the specter of "absolute freedom," which he associated with the terror of the French Revolution.

Meyer too expressed misgivings about the French Revolution, though its "massive egalitarian nationalism," not its striving for absolute freedom, was what appalled him most about that event. The French Revolution was the first phase of a growing threat to the work of America's Founding Fathers. The Jacobins and their foreign admirers were the bearers of "cosmologism's twin, utopianism" and combined "mystical statism" with an insatiable passion for social equality (407). The heirs of the French Revolution, Meyer contended, were modern liberals who were seeking to overturn the principle of limited government and subverting traditional social virtues basic to the American dispensation. Liberals taught a materialist, scientist view of history that denied both individual responsibility and human spiritual dignity. They favored bureaucratic and judicial incursions into the body social that Meyer viewed as incompatible with the intent of the Constitution's framers. He opposed most of the civil rights decisions of the fifties and sixties as being a threat to local government from unelected social engineers. He warned against the danger of sacrificing "our constitutional arrangements" to accommodate an aggrieved minority. No matter how genuine some of the grievances of American blacks were, he felt that the civil rights agenda, particularly in the 1960s, could not be squared with the American principle of limited government.[19]

Meyer fought the liberal Left by defending "the true sense of history," which he claimed to find in Eric Voegelin and in what he himself named "Middle America." He ended his career as a popularizer of Voegelin's thought and as the advocate of a by-then inchoate right-wing populism. Meyer's turning toward both roles was apparent from his call in 1964 for a "militant conservatism which becomes necessary when the fibers of society have been torn apart. . . ."[20] In his plea for a "conscious conservatism," he warned against reducing the cause to "a simple piety," yet he also maintained that all true conservatives "must have piety toward the constitution of being." Voegelinian phraseology mixed here with a call for political mobilization on the Right. And though "militant conservatism" would be "more reasoned" and more "consciously principled" than mere traditionalism, Meyer appealed to moral indignation over "that break the revolution has made in the continuity of human wisdom."[21] This use of reason would be intended to achieve, among other ends, a more thoroughly militant response to the loss of historical continuity. Meyer's calls for restoration and preservation should not cause us to disregard the generally progressivist thrust of his historical thinking. What he sought was to preserve that high point of human moral and political consciousness that had been reached in America by the end of the eighteenth century. Rejecting the Marxist view of history as the violent interaction of material forces leading to a classless future, Meyer offered a picture of human development similar in some ways to Hegel's. It was a view of the past as a finished process, a completed work of Spirit that posterity was obliged to uphold in the form in which it was received.

There is no easy way to reconcile Meyer's moral concern with individual responsibility and the dialectical architectonics of his philosophy of history. Although a politically unsympathetic interpreter, John Diggins associates Meyer completely with his defiant aphorism that "freedom depends upon the individual being free to choose freedom." Diggins then observes that "the difference between Meyer on the one hand and Kirk and [Willmoore] Kendall on the other is as great as the difference between [John] Dos Passos and Herberg, between the historian who sides with [Tom] Paine and liberty and the historicist who sides with Burke and order."[22] This statement oversimplifies the tension in both Meyer and Herberg between their faith in history and their belief in the individual. Neither man considered freedom and necessity to be identical, and both expressed support for liberty as a political principle. Yet, their *shared* view of history as a providentially guided series of confrontations remained in tension with their belief that individuals are truly "free to choose freedom." In Meyer's and Herberg's view, human choice was always shaped in varying degrees by one's place in a providential scheme, to which the American people were contributing significantly at the present hour. One of Meyer's most unsparing critics was the atheist libertarian Max Eastman, who, while an editor of *National Review*, attacked the Christian tone of the journal. In January 1964, Eastman denounced Meyer for teaching that "freedom is by itself meaningless without an objective moral order." According to Eastman: "To advocate freedom and then lay down the law as to how men 'should' use it is a contradiction in terms. It is a reversion not to classical liberalism, but to pre-liberal ecclesiastical authoritarianism—or what is left of it."[23]

Eastman may have been unjustly contemptuous of Meyer's attaching an ethical content to the exercise of freedom, but he did recognize properly the persistence of an inherent tension in Meyer's thinking. This thinking often entailed a balancing act intended to keep apparently polarized positions in a state of precarious coexistence on the intellectual Right. Meyer tried to balance traditionalism and libertarianism, individual self-fulfillment and "the belief in an objective moral order." He spoke of the old polarity between traditionalists and libertarians being surmounted by a process of fusion, the beginnings of which he traced back to the founding of America. This fusion, Meyer believed, did not result from the passing exigencies of American politics but was rooted in "the *ethos* of Western civilization from which flow both the traditionalist and libertarian currents. . . ."[24]

In one *National Review* column on 25 September 1962 (to which Eastman responded in his angry blast of 28 January 1964), Meyer appealed to libertarians and traditionalists to recognize their interdependence. Both sides represented parts of a continuing "Western tradition" that would become better clarified through dialogue.[25] Meyer's colleagues objected to his implicit, and often explicit, claim to being the one best suited to grasp the common civilizational "ethos." By what special right did he dictate to others how the Western "spirit" was to be interpreted in twentieth-century America?[26] One might also ask by what special insight Meyer claimed to know that the synthesis of tradition and liberty he described most closely corresponded in the modern West to his own brand of American conservatism. Meyer believed that he viewed history from a privileged position that was not yet fully accessible to Kirk, Eastman, and others on the American Right.

Meyer's choice of Voegelin as a mentor suggests his need for an explicitly anti-Hegelian but also antimaterialist interpretation of evolving human consciousness. Despite the Hegelian aspects of his own thinking, Meyer repeatedly attacked Hegel as a historical determinist and as a worshipper of the State. Voegelin, who levels similar charges against Hegelian determinism, intends his own philosophy of history at least partially as a reaction to Hegel's. In his two essays in *Wissenschaft, Politik, und Gnosis* (1959), the English edition of which appeared in 1968 as *Science, Politics, and Gnosticism*, Voegelin deals at length with the "gnostic speculation" of Hegel. By reviving the immanentism present in gnostic theology and by identifying divinity entirely with human consciousness, Hegel prepared the way for Marx, Nietzsche, and other modern atheists. In the foreword to the English edition of his book, Voegelin notes a fateful linkage that joins Hegel, gnosticism, and "the death of God."[27] The gnostics had replaced a transcendent Deity by the power of the illuminated human mind. Hegel, by reviving this myth under the guise of philosophy, encouraged other moderns to engage in "the murder of God."

In his zeal to unmask Hegel as a corrupter of thought, Voegelin in 1971 published "On Hegel: A Study in Sorcery," a long essay dealing with the "gnostic and magical elements" in his subject's thinking. The study predominantly treats *The Phenomenology of Spirit*, which Voegelin describes as a *grimoire*, or sorcerer's notebook. Hegel, according to Voegelin, set out to affirm the infallibility of his own consciousness as the key to interpreting, and reconstructing, the universe. *The Phenomenology*, he believes, is a "coded" and arcane work, addressed to those moderns who are sympathetic to Hegel's Promethean mission.[28] Although "On Hegel: A Study in Sorcery" reads in some places like a wrathful tirade, unworthy of the brilliant speculative mind that produced it, it leaves little doubt about Voegelin's stated position on Hegel.

From his remarks it is clear that he read *The Phenomenoloy* closely in more than one edition. Voegelin also reveals a keen awareness of the still largely unrecognized influence of Middle- and Neo-Platonists on the construction of that work. Together with the repetitious charges against Hegel as a megalomaniac and falsifier of history, Voegelin makes penetrating comments concerning his conceptual reliance on Plotinus's *Enneads*. Voegelin notes the structural parallel between the journey of the soul in the Platonic mystical tradition and the phases through which the Hegelian Spirit becomes fully reconciled with Itself. He correctly maintains that Hegel had in mind, when he wrote *The Phenomenology*, the movement of the Neo-Platonic soul: from primodial rest (*ēremia* or *hēsuxia*) through alienation (*allotriosis*) and the state of otherness (*heterotēs*), back through the world toward the soul's source in the unity of the divine being (*epistrophē tēs psuxēs*). Voegelin carefully keys these distinctive levels of spiritual ascent to the revelatory moments of Hegel's Spirit, which moves from self-isolation through alienation in otherness, back toward self-identity that is finally regained by Spirit's appropriation of the other to Itself.[29] The parallel between Hegel and the Neo-Platonists rests upon a historically verifiable connection, of which Voegelin was certainly aware by the 1970s.[30] Hegel did study Plotinus and, even more intensively, a later Platonist, Proclus of Athens (A.D. 412–485), before he did most of his speculative work. His construction of the dialectic in *The Jena Logic* and *The Phenomenology* shows the far-reaching influence of two of Proclus's tracts, both of which Hegel read and praised, *Institutio Theologica* and *In Platonis Theologiam*.[31]

Voegelin not only read Hegel with obvious thoroughness, but also drew upon ideas related to his in formulating a philosophy of history. His former colleague at the University of Munich, Helmut Kuhn, has boldly stated an opinion that most of Voegelin's disciples still obdurately resist: "Of all historical thinkers of our age who are known to me, it is Voegelin, the sharpest critic of Hegel and of his philosophy of history, who stands closest to Hegel."[32] Although Voegelin rejected the Hegelian enterprise of plotting the history of Spirit, his own history of human consciousness became an attempt to demonstrate the operation of the divine in human experience. Indeed the progressive series of encounters of great spiritual figures with the divine ground of being was Voegelin's counterpart to Hegel's view of the unfolding of Spirit in history. The theologian Thomas J. J. Altizer, who arrived at the same parallel Kuhn draws after reading *Order and History,* Volume IV, asks the rhetorical question "May we not with far more justice say that Voegelin's hatred of Hegel is an attempted Oedipal murder of his father?"[33] Voegelin denies that he "attacks" Hegel in *Order and History* or in his essay dealing with sorcery in *The Phenomenology.* He claims to have submitted "key passages of his [Hegel's] work to philologically and theoretically the same type of analysis to which I submit the work of other thinkers." Despite his discomfort with Hegel's "process of dialectics," Voegelin, according to his own testimony, had been deeply impressed as a young man by Hegel's "political acumen" and by his "qualities as a German man of letters." Hegel was, in fact, someone "whom I consulted at every step of my own work because of his vast historical knowledge and his powerful intellect. . . ."[34]

Two critical reviews of *Order and History* suggest an awareness of the connection between Voegelin and Hegel. Both reviews were published in 1958, after the appearance of Voegelin's third volume. The shorter and less profound of these critiques, by Moses Hadas in *Journal of the History of Ideas,* covers the first three volumes, all published in 1956 and 1957. Hadas rails against Voegelin for confusing order with authority and for teaching "not a return to religion but emulation of the towering figures of history who used religion as an instrument for manipulating lesser men." Hadas closes his review with a malevolent taunt: "'Sure we'll have fascism in this country, but we'll call it something else.' Leap in being?"[35] Despite the crudity of this invective, Hadas stresses some of the salient characteristics of Voegelin's exposition of "the history of order." Voegelin identifies history with a progressively unfolding vision of order that emanates from the conceptions of a spiritual elite. His historical landscape, like Hegel's, is peopled by world historical figures, who despite the "in-betweenness" of the human condition manage to understand and communicate divine knowledge.

In a probing and detailed review of *Order and History,* Volumes II and III, in *Review of Metaphysics,* Stanley Rosen accuses Voegelin of being insensitive to the Greek world because of his progressivist and teleological outlook. Observes Rosen: "Strictly speaking Voegelin is not interested in the Greeks except insofar as they may be used to assist his Toynbeean march through history toward God. . . . He reads the Classical authors with at least one eye turned elsewhere in, and beyond, history. Nor in all accuracy is it philosophy which he admires, except insofar as it may be transformed into theology."[36] Rosen turns the tables on Voegelin by scolding him for some of the same faults that Voegelin imputes to progressivist ideologues: a lack of openness to Classical thought and a presentist reading of the past. In *Order and History,* Volume II, Voegelin defends the Greek *polis* only insofar as it prefigured later historical developments. So too, in Volume III, in which he evaluates Plato and Aristotle in terms of their "openness" to the Christian experience of faith and, ultimately, to his own philosophy of history. According to Rosen, Voegelin forces Greek philosophy and political thought into the rigid categories of his own Providential historicism. Accordingly, Voegelin reads Augustine and Aquinas back into Plato and Aristotle while approaching Thucydides as an essentially Christian historian. Voegelin is a "quasi-Hegelian" Christian presentist:

> Despite his talk of "a leap into being," he does not allow for the possibility that development in man's understanding of Being is in a fundamental sense independent of empirical history. Nor does he ever consider history itself from any but; the contemporary viewpoint. . . . The empirical continuity of Hellenism and Christianity in our civilization is no proof for the superiority of Christianity; nor for their theoretical compatibility, unless we are Hellenists.[37]

Rosen's review of *Order and History* stands out among studies devoted to this work not only by its size (it fills more than twenty pages in the December 1958 issue of *Review of Metaphysics*) but also by its independent and perceptive judgments. Rosen stood athwart both Voegelin's detractors and most of his admirers. Unlike Hadas's review and an even more vitriolic one on *Order and History*, Volume I, that had appeared in the *New Republic*, Rosen's was not a leftist polemic directed against an avowed defender of inherited social and religious order.[38] Nor did he write, as did Frank Meyer in *Modern Age* and Gerhart Niemeyer in *Review of Politics,* to acclaim a philosophical godsend.[39] Rather, he treated his subject as a versatile scholar who had committed two major conceptual errors: imposing a vulgarly Hegelian historicist framework on the study of Greek thought and institutions, and evaluating the Greek world from the implicit perspective of Christian revelation. The two charges that he made (in 1958) were obviously related for Rosen, who considered the "superiority of Christianity over Hellenism" a view common to Hegel, Voegelin, and the modern Western world. Although the idea of a Christian civilization no longer appeals to our militantly secularist intelligentsia, Rosen attributes to Voegelin what was the dominant, though not exclusive, Western historiographical view at least from Augustine down to Hegel.

Rosen fails to recognize, however, that Voegelin gained adherents, such as Frank Meyer, not for defending widely cherished opinions but for supporting a position under assault. A theological approach to the study of history and a "Christian" understanding of Classical philosophy were hardly the rage among American scholars in 1958. One may also question whether Voegelin applies alien theological concepts to Plato's philosophy. Rosen's own implied assumption of a necessary disjunction between *philosophia* and *philomythia*, or between speculative knowledge and theological truth, may not in fact have reflected Plato's belief. The school of philosophy that Plato founded, produced, after its brief involvement with political reform, many generations of mystics.

These Platonic mystics faithfully studied the cosmogonic myth in *Timaeus* and the Myth of Er, which Socrates recounts in *The Republic*, about the expiatory wanderings of the soul. Although the Middle- and Neo-Platonists usually did not take Platonic mythology literally, they studied Plato for his possible theological lessons. This may not provide definitive proof that Plato and Socrates had also assigned real theological weight to their accounts of God and the soul. But since many of Plato's ancient admirers took these accounts for religious teachings, Rosen's generalizations about the nonreligious character of Greek philosophy may not be entirely accurate. Voegelin may therefore be right when he infers overlaps from the "empirical continuity of Hellenism and Christianity." Hellenistic culture did provide indisputable philosophical and ethical bridges between Classical thought and Christian theology. It is surely possible to recognize these bridges, such as Neo-Platonism and Stoicism, without practicing Christian condescension toward the Classical world.

Despite his overgeneralizations Rosen is right to focus on the historicist and; theological aspects of Voegelin's thinking. He properly notes that Voegelin often collapses any distinction between philosophy and theology and that he evaluates the Classical world, or its greatest minds, from a post-Hellenic perspective. Rosen remarks that Voegelin's historicism combines "quasi-Hegelian," "Christian-existential," and distinctly modernist elements. He uncovers characteristics in Voegelin's historical outlook that more partisan reviewers neglect. Finally, he helps locate, without specifically naming, what is probably a major inspiration for this outlook, the transcendental idealism of Hegel's youthful collaborator and later rival philosopher of history, F. W. J. Schelling.

Although his nineteenth-century contemporaries, such as Ferdinand Christian Baur, and many modern scholars have linked Schelling to gnostic Christianity, Voegelin has kind words for Schelling in obvious contrast to his remarks on Hegel.[40] In an essay, "Toward a Theory of Consciousness," published in 1943, Voegelin comments favorably on "process theology," which he associates with Schelling. Such a theology as the one found in Schelling "deals with the development of a system of symbols which expresses the relationship between consciousness, as transcendent and innerworldly classes of being, and the world-transcending ground of being in the language of an immanently understood process." Voegelin then renders the following judgment: "I am inclined to believe that the theological attempt and, by extension, the metaphysic which interpret worldly transcendence as the immanent process of divine substance is the only significant systematic philosophy." Only this sort of philosophy could render the experience of transcendence comprehensible by interpreting it from within, in humanly understandable language.[41] Voegelin, in the course of elaborating on this view, provides a defense of Schelling's two most famous philosophical questions: "Why is there something? Why is there not nothing?" Voegelin considers both questions unanswerable from the standpoint of the critical epistemology that Kant had developed in the *Critique of Pure Reason*. Kant's method of focusing on the apparatus of perception lost sight of the forest because of the trees. By limiting their study to the structure of consciousness, scholars may ignore those questions about existence itself to which our minds have led us inescapably. Nor can one appreciate questions of being by approaching knowledge from a naturalist perspective, that is, by examining biochemical processes.

Voegelin finally raises doubts about whether another school of thought, phenomenology, can respond to the ontological issue that he and Schelling address. The phenomenologist, who grouped first around Edmund Husserl at the University of Marburg in the interwar years, dreamt of pushing back philosophy from Kant's critical method to a pure analysis of the contents of perception. Husserl and his disciple Alfred Schütz, one of Voegelin's closest friends, attempted to categorize objective phenomena once having stripped them of purely subjective residues. Voegelin was highly skeptical of this attempt to describe the world from without. He warned that the phenomenological search for an appropriate method for examining the objective world might quickly degenerate into a form of scientism. He accused the phenomenologists of being insensitive to the spiritual possibilities of human consciousness.[42]

Voegelin tries to validate ontological values by calling attention to their relationship to human consciousness. By meditating on experience, men are ultimately drawn beyond the world's contents as mere data, or *cogitata*, into recognizing the ground of being as the basis of all knowledge. The search for truth, argues Voegelin, evoking Plato's ascent of the soul, carries its participants beyond sensory experience toward a world-transcending source. Process theology fulfills this function by plotting the ascending order of being "as a series of phases in the unfolding of the identical substance that achieves clarification in human consciousness."[43] Schelling had tried to grasp the ground of being as present and operative in consciousness. Although Schelling could not demonstrate his findings empirically, his "ontological speculation is a legitimate philosophical undertaking that is anchored in precisely describable experiences and supports its interpretation by means of 'understandable' process-categories." Voegelin compares Schelling's conception of being to Kant's analysis of logical or cosmological infinity, which also undertook to express the otherwise Ineffable symbolically. Schelling's "something" is a "symbol that finds its justification in rendering transparent, through finite language, the ground of being which is experienced in meditation as real."[44]

This praise of Schelling, though often couched in convoluted phrases, merits attention for two reasons. First, Voegelin accords to Schelling the respect that he pays to the greatest philosophers of antiquity, crediting him with the attempt to give coherent form to a genuine experience of the ground of being. Second, Voegelin, in honoring Schelling, suspends the withering judgments that he elsewhere makes of Hegel as a gnostic pantheist. The connections between

Schelling and Hegel, however, are obvious, particularly after Hegel's arrival in Jena in 1801. In that Saxon university town he rallied to Schelling's cause, to the point of defending his "philosophy of identity" against the prominent post-Kantian philosophy professor Johann Gottlieb Fichte. Hegel also helped edit Schelling's *Kritisches Journal der Philosophie*. In 1802 in constructing his *System of Ethics*, Hegel abandoned his triadic dialectic for a bipolar one. This too was an accommodation to Schelling, who had developed dialectical polarities to explain the nature of the Absolute and Its relationship to the world.[45] Despite the later disagreements between the two thinkers, Schelling personified to a greater degree than Hegel the gnostic worshipper of the historical process so offensive to Voegelin. Unlike Hegel, Schelling actually delved into gnostic and occult writings in order to understand world history. In the 1820s and 1830s he described history as the progressive unfolding of the divine personality. The by-then celebrated lecturer at the University of Munich hoped to clarify the stages of this process by reference to his own consciousness.

Despite all this, Voegelin's attraction to Schelling may be easily explained, in that Schelling had anticipated some of his own stands. As a philosopher-mystic, Schelling had deplored ever since the late 1790s the divorce between theology and philosophy. By the end of his career as a celebrated professor at Berlin, where the king of Prussia had summoned him in 1841 to "extract the dragon-teeth" of revolutionary Hegelianism, Schelling mocked rationalists who tried to imprison the divine substance within all-encompassing systems.[46] He initiated the practice that Rosen would later criticize in Voegelin, when, in *The Ages of the World* and in *The Gods of Samothrace*, Schelling explored the history of consciousness through religious mythology. Over the years he became increasingly intolerant of discursive approaches to learning, and he affirmed the need to remain open to the power of intuition and the exalted but often hidden truth of myth.

Finally, like Voegelin, Schelling thought himself to be living in an "age of crisis."[47] The Enlightenment and industrialization had changed Europe's cultural-religious landscape, so that philosophers were thereafter obliged to consider religious as well as intellectual problems. In one particularly enthusiastic tribute, Voegelin hails Schelling as the creator of "a new level of consciousness and critique; and by virtue of this achievement, [his work] becomes of increasing importance in a time of crisis as the point of orientation for those who wish to gain a solid foothold in the surrounding environment of decadent traditions, conflicting eschatologies, phenomenal speculations and obsessions, ideologies and creeds, blind hatreds, and orgiastic destructions."[48] The German scholar Jürgen Gebhardt has summed up Voegelin's opinion of Schelling in these words: "In Schelling, Voegelin recognizes a kindred mind whose ideas 'can be a point of orientation for the understanding of the crisis because they are not engulfed in the crisis themselves.'"[49]

In view of Schelling's pantheistic and millenarian writings, the opinion cited shows in Voegelin a spirit of indulgence born of admiration. Gebhardt remarks that Voegelin saw in Schelling's activities a model worthy of imitation in an age of spiritual crisis. In the essay "Last Orientation" in 1945, Voegelin dwells on Schelling's abiding relevance for those seeking to comprehend the present age. Faced by the cult of science, Schelling had made the "grandiose effort . . . to reestablish a philosophy of substance."[50] Although his work "failed to become the starting point for civilizational restoration," it underscored the need to re-construct a science of man that takes account of the soul and of transcendent reality. As he read Schelling, Voegelin turned from his earlier interest in the his-tory of political theory toward the study of the philosophy of history as the his-tory of consciousness. Gebhardt suggests that one must look to Schelling in order to understand by what path Voegelin came in 1952 to make the assertion that introduces *The New Science of Politics:* "The existence of man in political so-ciety is historical existence; and a theory of politics, if it penetrates to princi-ples, must at the same time be a theory of history."[51]

One might note an aspect of Voegelin's education that has still not been suf-ficiently appreciated but one that helps explain his respect for Schelling. As a student and academic in Vienna, where he lived between 1912 and 1938, Voege-lin read Kant on epistemology and ethics. In 1931 he contributed a thirty-seven page essay, "Ought in Kant's System," to a Festschrift in honor of the distin-guished German jurist Hans Kelsen. This study is noteworthy not only for what it reveals about Voegelin's knowledge of Kant, but also for re-erecting the bridge between Kantian philosophy and post-Kantian idealism. In an existen-tial sense, Voegelin rediscovered part of the path by which Schelling and Hegel arrived at their views of "transcendental intuition" and came to identify the Absolute with the world.

Then a young doctor of law, Voegelin stared into the gulf that Kant had uncovered, between the apparatus of consciousness and "the thing in itself." Kant's critical method had reduced empirical knowledge to an interplay between raw sensory data and the organizing instruments that were allegedly present in human understanding. As for lofty metaphysical notions such as God, immortality, and the soul, Kant conceded their reality but denied that one could understand them through sensory experience. Only Reason could penetrate "the thing in itself," that is, achieve knowledge of reality independently of the intervening presence of our cognitive apparatus, which was the source of time, space, causality, and the other "a priori conditions" of perception. Reason produced universal judgments whose validity did not depend upon changing sensory perception. Theoretical Reason, according to Kant, put into our minds "regulative ideas," such as infinity, God, and immortality. Although none of these ideas was empirically demonstrable or logically indisputable, they enabled us to comprehend the universe more fully. Reason performed a second and more "practical" function, of impressing upon our consciousness the content of ethical absolutes. Only through Reason could men arrive at moral imperatives that were unconditional or "categorical," that presented themselves as binding upon everyone regardless of shifting circumstances. Through Practical Reason men became able to do what they ought, notwithstanding the passions and interests that normally affected them.

Voegelin approached the Kantian conception of Reason respectfully but critically. He praised Kant's attempt to draw Reason into the world of human experience. By trying to prove the transcendental aspect of ethical decisions, Kant was in effect answering certain existential questions that Voegelin thought basic to man's understanding of himself: "How do we know about the Logos of being? How do we know that an ethical law obligates? How do we know that there is intelligible Reason?"[52] A proper response to these questions required further knowledge of the "elucidating experience *[Aufschlusser-lebnis]*,"[53] through which one became aware of "the binding nature of commandments in the form of obligation." Kant, without fully recognizing the implications of his own insight, associated this elucidative experience with a "deeply stirring consciousness of the spontaneity of action and moral obligation."[54] He erred, however, by imagining that men could will the good independently of the empirical conditions surrounding human actions. What Voegelin considered the "experiential core of Kantian metaphysics" was for Kant the unintended concomitant of the activity of the moral will; the rational-moral sphere, or the Kantian "thing in itself," operated necessarily within nature and society, despite what Kant considered to be its separate and higher ontological status.

Voegelin agreed with the young Hegel and Schelling that Kant's attempted dissociation of Reason from nature and history was experientially indefensible. All three philosophers viewed Reason, or what Voegelin calls the "Logos of being," as present in the world of human experience. Schelling and Hegel conceptualized this activity of Reason as the self-expression of an absolute subject. The Kantian dualism between Reason, theoretical and practical, and the phenomenal world had given way by 1802, in the metaphysics of Schelling and Hegel, to a dialectic operative within a self-revealing universal subject. Thematic and interpretive differences later arose between the two former friends. Schelling studied the self-revelation of his subject primarily in nature, art, and religious myth, while affirming the ultimate harmony of the divine personality beyond dialectical relationships. He treated "systems" as provisional, fluid attempts to crystallize human perceptions of transcendental consciousness. Hegel, by contrast, stressed the dialectical unfolding more than the essential harmony of his Absolute Subject, and he considered the observation of nature less philosophically useful than the study of logic and political institutions. He presumed to attach a degree of definitiveness to his dialectical system that struck Schelling, as it later did Voegelin, as impious and pretentious.[55]

All three thinkers, however, tried to move beyond the Kantian dualism (1) by identifying subjective consciousness and the objective world and (2) by studying the proposed identity in terms of a dialectically structured history. Although these moments are probably less apparent in Voegelin than in Schelling and Hegel, the same conceptual turning points mark his development as well as theirs. In describing the experiential core of the ethical act in Kant, Voegelin identifies "man as the thing-in-itself" with "the rational personality that is revealed in the experience of spontaneity."[56] But whereas Kant insisted on the ultimate separation of a "corpus mysticum of rational beings" from the sensible world to which they related but by which presumably they were not to be influenced, Voegelin affirms the spiritual value of human interaction with the outer world. Only by beginning with sensory experience does the individual consciousness ascend toward awareness of the ground of being. Voegelin denies that one who performs an ethical act can or should view "the sensory world as a mere object of pure Reason in its practical function."[57] The ethical man advances through his dynamic and active relationship to the world toward the discovery of an "intelligible, noumenal reality."

Voegelin sees man appropriating the Kantian "thing-in-itself," as a percipient and acting entity. Yet what lies outside human consciousness is not a mere adjunct to ourselves that acquires meaning only when our minds experience it. In interacting with the external world, human consciousness moves toward the ground of being that shapes and informs it. It, moreover, advances in this course not by prescinding from sensory experience but rather by opening itself to transcendence in nature and history and, then, finding provisional, symbolic expression for the resulting encounter.[58] From these remarks, it should be clear why Voegelin remained sympathetic to Schelling the process theologian as well as to Schelling the cultural critic. Like Schelling, Voegelin is a "transcendental empiricist," who attempts to approach the Absolute through careful observation and through studying consciousness as an object of history. In exploring the history of consciousness, Voegelin applies a Schellingian, and even Hegelian, criterion of progress. He undertakes to classify the experiences of transcendence in terms of the growing openness to being. The further the historian moves from the compact symbols of the cosmological empires into the age of "the leaps in being," the more comprehensive become the visions of ultimate reality. Thus Voegelin, while interpreting Christian revelation as being one of many "symbolic" expressions of religious encounter, asserts that St. Paul's "experience of the God of the beyond" was a fuller one than that of Isaiah and Plato.[59,60] In his letter to Alfred Schütz of 1 January 1953, Voegelin disagrees with a hypothetical possibility that Schutz earlier raised that a modern may do serious philosophy from a platonic rather than Christian standpoint. Voegelin insists that the movement from platonism to Christianity produced irreversible changes in cultural consciousness. He also doubts the wisdom of retreating from the vantage point of a "more differentiated experience" of being into a less comprehensive and intense one.[61]

It may be useful to observe that a certain dialectical aspect is present in Voegelin's picture of the "leaps in being." Each stage in "the further differentiation of the experience of being" represented an achievement to be preserved against regression. Most importantly, the cumulative spiritual result of these leaps was always in danger of being lost or submerged wherever the attraction for compact symbols became culturally overwhelming.[62] Voegelin believes that this temptation may take different forms in different epochs and suggests that civilizations are sometimes derailed by more than one characteristic fixation. For example, Western intellectuals since the French Revolution have not only refurbished the gnostic transformational myth, but have also replaced theophanic symbols with egophanic ones. Modern intellectuals have come to assign quasi-divine status to their own thinking, while moving from Hegel's alleged sorcery to the more mundane task of planning ideal societies through social engineering.[63]

Voegelin's dialectic is certainly not Hegel's, or the one Frank Meyer read into *Order and History*. In his own understanding of history, Voegelin, unlike Meyer, stands much closer to Schelling than to Hegel. Whereas Hegel believed that almost all conflicts were swallowed up in the march of Absolute Consciousness (in Meyer's case, divine Providence) through men's minds and across history, Schelling (and later Voegelin) held to a dualistic view of the structure of being. Schelling's disquisitions and lectures from about 1809 on keep returning to the story of the Fall as presented in pagan, Christian, and Kabbalistic literature. The ultimate harmony of what Voegelin too calls the "God of the beyond" (the Neo-Platonic *Theos peran tou ontos*) stands in dramatic contrast to the world as it exists. This world was split between mind and force as the result of what ancient civilization correctly imagined to have been a primal cosmic catastrophe.

Schelling examined the recorded accounts of the Fall as symbolic statements of man's continued alienation from the source of being. His preoccupation with this theme came to overshadow his belief in historical progress, as the phased reconciliation of the Absolute with the universe. The human mind fixed in a world that had fallen away from the ground of being could only speculate about the nature of reality. What Hegel viewed as a comprehensive and final system of thought the later Schelling regarded as a blasphemous claim to intimacy with the Absolute. Philosophers struggled for slivers of theological wisdom in a world only barely touched by divine truth. These bits too were often lost and had to be retrieved by later generations. In contrast to Hegel, Schelling saw "the darkness in the world and the evil in humanity," and he warned against desecrating knowledge by turning "personal experience into mere science."[64]

Schelling's quarrel with Hegel anticipated Voegelin's: "The factor Hegel excludes is the mystery of history that wends its way into the future without our knowing its end. History as a whole is essentially not an object of cognition; the meaning of the whole is not discernible. Hegel can construct, then, a meaningfully self-contained process of history only by assuming that the revelation of God in history is fully comprehensible."[65] Such a critical stance does not stem, as most of Voegelin's American interpreters contend, from the doubtful supposition that Voegelin rejected German philosophy starting with Kant. Nor does the preceding view indicate the antimodernist, medieval-Christian outlook that others have ascribed to the author of *The New Science of Politics*.[66] Voegelin's battle against Hegel proceeds from an analysis of consciousness that had definite roots in German idealism. Voegelin castigates Hegel for rashly misrepresenting, and simplifying, the necessarily problematic relationship between consciousness and being.

Yet his investigation of being from the standpoint of the self-discovering subject and the further pursuit of this investigation from a historical, developmental angle suggest that Voegelin shares with Hegel a common terrain; their quarrel occurs within the context of a partly shared philosophical tradition. Although Schelling was the German thinker whom Voegelin most explicitly praises and Hegel the one whom, next to Marx, he mostly roundly condemns, Voegelin as a historian makes striking structural concessions to Hegelianism. The pattern of civilizational development in *Order and History* follows the Hegelian model; it moves from the despotic impersonal Orient (the cradle of an incipient human self-awareness for Voegelin and for Hegel), toward the Hebrew and Classical cultures as the points of entry into higher forms of religious and moral consciousness. Thomas J. J. Altizer emphasizes the degree to which Voegelin replicates Hegel's "negative portrayal of Hinduism and Buddhism as undifferentiated and nonhistorical expressions of consciousness in quest of precosmic totality."[67]

Rosen believes correctly that Voegelin's modernity greatly outweighs his debt to antiquity. Moreover, Voegelin's ties to German philosophy, particularly to Schelling, may explain more about his thinking than his occasional but well-publicized tributes to medieval theology. In the fourth (belated) volume of *Order and History*, the author often departs from his survey of ancient world empires in order to affirm the indispensability of history for clarifying ontological questions. In a speculative essay, "What is Consciousness?" he also observes that

> history is above all not a field of indifferent, objective materials from which we may choose from any standpoint. . . . Rather, history is made up of consciousness, and the logos of consciousness must decide what is or is not historically relevant.
>
> It is especially worthy of note that the time of which history is composed is not that of the outer world in which the corporeal life of man leave its traces, but the dimension of seeking the ground [of being] that is inherent in consciousness.[68]

Voegelin is here discussing the conditions for constructing a universal history based on the universality of man's quest for the ground of being. Undergirding his statements are the assumptions of German idealist philosophy: the view of time and of the contents of perceived reality as the functions of consciousness, and the equation of world history with consciousness as seen on the universal level. According to Thomas Molnar, who often cites Voegelin in analyzing modern culture: "Out of Tübingen [site of a renowned university and Protestant school of theology] were to come Hegel's and Schelling's idealist philosophies, probably outlined at that time in the conversations of the two young students. Through them and others, Tübingen also engendered, indirectly, the vastest intellectual movement of the last two centuries which lifted History to the throne vacated by God."[69] Although one must allow, in reading this assertion, for the antihistoricist fervor characteristic of many of Voegelin's most devoted disciples, Molnar correctly notes the demonstrable link between German idealism and the interest, starting in the late eighteenth century, in history as process. In light of our investigation, it is possible to conclude that Voegelin himself partly exemplifies this link. Like Meyer he too may have been to Tübingen without even knowing it.

# 7

# A CONSERVATIVE FAREWELL
# TO HISTORY

THE PRECEDING CHAPTERS HAVE FOCUSED ON THE RELATIONSHIP between the Hegelian view of history and modernity and the intellectual foundations of postwar American conservatism. I have argued that Hegelian assumptions about the dialectical nature of reality, the unique Western heritage of freedom, and the legitimacy of political power informed the conservative intellectual movement that arose after the Second World War. Whether these assumptions came from exposure to Hegel's writings or to the unwitting absorption of Hegel's thinking by way of Marx or of German universities, Hegelianism became a shaping influence on postwar American conservatism. To a large extent, this occurred despite the ritualistic anti-Hegelianism found among some conservative theorists, and even among those most clearly marked by Hegelian concepts.

This adaptation of Hegelianism resulted from conservatism's theoretical and programmatic needs. The conservatives' Hegelianism provided a historical perspective that united East and West, antiquity and the modern world, and paganism and Judeo-Christianity within an unfolding divine plan accessible to human understanding. It endowed specific struggles and political decisions with world-historic significance. Small wonder that the conservative social thinker Robert Nisbet has recently argued for a renewed sense of historical purpose within Western bourgeois society. Despite his nostalgia for an age of organic social bonds, Nisbet, who has praised Hegel as a teacher of social theory, makes the plausible case that a spiritually confident Western middle class requires a belief in progress based on social evolution. Perhaps it is less significant that Nisbet himself in his other writings has cast doubts on the doctrine of historical progress than that he now defends that doctrine for its alleged therapeutic value.[1]

In explaining why the postwar Right adapted Hegelian thinking, one should stress that a sense of history was long basic to the conservative movement. The Burkeans Russell Kirk, Peter Viereck, Peter Stanlis, and the later Will Herberg; Southern conservatives such as Allen Tate, Andrew Lytle, and Richard Weaver; the historian of order Eric Voegelin; the neo-Machiavellian James Burnham; and even the Christian libertarians Frank Meyer and Karl Wittfogel all appealed to the historical past in order to vindicate their political-cultural values. Anyone who reads conservative publications of the midfifties will be struck by the recurrent invocations of Western history and "the lessons of the Western heritage." By the midseventies these appeals became less frequent, and not only because the founding generation of the conservative renascence were by then either dead (e.g., Weaver, Tate, Herberg, and Meyer) or journalistically less active. Also essential to this thematic change was what Stephen Tonsor has called the "political activism of the conservative second generation."[2] Like Marx in his critical confrontation with Hegel, conservative activists wished to change the world and no longer to philosophize about it.

One may observe that conservatism underwent a cultural narrowing together with the discovery of politics as a vocation. As the gap between liberal social promises and the results of applied liberal policies (e.g., government regulation of the economy, mandatory busing to achieve racial integration, and quotas for minority hiring) aroused public controversy, conservative and neoconservative journals turned their attention increasingly to administrative and economic questions. Although defenses of the free market and complaints about expanding bureaucracy had certainly appeared in conservative publications in the early and midfifties, policy questions were not dominant there.[3] By the late seventies, the setting and criticizing of government agendas became the raison d'être of most conservative enterprises in America. The functioning and growth of thinktanks such as the Heritage Foundation, the Hoover Institution, and the more centrist (neoconservative) American Enterprise Institute, all with multimillion-dollar annual operating budgets, have helped push the conservative movement further in a nontheoretical direction. As a result, conservative intellectuals have been subtly discouraged from addressing philosophical questions and persuaded to focus on those with obvious and immediate political relevance.[4] One sign of the times is that Intercollegiate Studies Institute (ISI), once the best known institution for supporting conservatively oriented scholarship, has now fallen dramatically behind other, in some cases newer, conservative foundations, both in money and in visibility. ISI made the admirable though financially disastrous decision to support primarily moral-philosophical studies.[5]

The preceding explanation suggests some of the reasons that theoretical conservatism flourishes less now than twenty-five years ago. But we should also recognize that even where a theoretical conservatism still survives today, it is less and less concerned with a philosophy of history. The battle against Hegelianism, once waged by some conservatives, has led into the more grandiose struggle against "historicism," and this call to arms has served to weaken the historical-mindedness of much of the American intellectual Right. The word *historicism* by now has become a synonym for social-cultural determinism and has been linked to the teaching of moral relativism. Such an association, which some conservatives have helped to popularize, reflects an exceedingly narrow understanding of the phenomenon in question. Indeed I would have difficulty in trying to relate this biased representation to most of the thinkers in Hans Meyerhoff's anthology of the writings of historical theorists, *The Philosophy of History in Our Time*. According to Meyerhoff and Karl Löwith, historical-mindedness has been a source of intellectual creativity in Western civilization for at least several centuries. Historical consciousness has distinguished Western civilization from other cultures and is, moreover, firmly rooted in the Judeo-Christian vision of time.[6] Although Löwith in particular recognizes the tendencies toward moral determinism and hero worship in Hegel's exposition of the dialectic, both he and Meyerhoff point to more than one type of historicism, that is, conceptual attempt to analyze culture and thought from a developmental standpoint. Thinkers strongly influenced by Hegel, such as Wilhelm Dilthey and Benedetto Croce, nonetheless criticized his mechanistic view of progress and his rigid determinism. The modern opponents of historicism attack the defects of the Hegelian system not only because they seek to discredit a particular thinker and his particular kind of historicism. As I have suggested, the intended target of these repeated attacks is often Western historical consciousness.

Let us note that the three Central European émigrés with perhaps the deepest impact on the conservative intellectual movement, Friedrich Hayek, Eric Voegelin, and Leo Strauss, wrote against Hegel and, in Strauss's case, against historicism.[7] In *The Counter-Revolution of Science* Hayek links historicism in its Hegelian and Comtean forms to the assault on a free society made by social scientists. Voegelin's disciples have presented Hegelian historicism not only as something antithetical to freedom but also as a gnostic distortion of Christianity. Historicists such as Hegel, by treating the course of human events as a self-enclosed and self-propelled process, have allegedly substituted History for God. By claiming a privileged position for themselves as interpreters of a deified History, both Hegel and Marx revived the gnostic pretension of claiming an illuminated historical consciousness for the members of an elect body.[8]

Despite the overzealousness of their epigones, Hayek and Voegelin have usually qualified their own attacks on historicism. Hayek has criticized Hegel, but he has also professed admiration for Edmund Burke and the Historical School of the nineteenth century. Voegelin has affirmed the need for a philosophy of history in order to grasp the nature of reality. Of all the European mentors of postwar conservatism, none castigated historicism so sternly and effectively as Leo Strauss (1899–1973). His grim warnings against taking History too seriously continue to guide the second and third generation of his school. The repugnance for historicism and the waning of historical conservatism on today's intellectual Right indicate in part the apparent cogency of the Straussian critique. By the same token, the continuing appeal of Straussian political philosophy may stem from the concern about "the historicization of truth" that Strauss and his many followers have by now been deploring for over thirty years.

From his six Walgreen Lectures at the University of Chicago in 1949 until his death in November 1973, Strauss decried the value relativism in what he saw as a morally disintegrating American society. He urged a return to the study of the established classics in political thought and violently rejected the assertion that no modern can recapture the true meaning of an ancient text. Of all forces that apparently stood in the way of a return to serious learning, he considered "historicism" to be the most destructive and pervasive. Strauss gained lifelong disciples in the political center, and even occasionally on the Left, as well as on the moderate Right. Both the traditionalist *Modern Age* and the neoconservative *Commentary* have extolled his teaching mission, and his fervent admirers contribute often to both journals.

Strauss's most thoroughgoing attack on historicism appeared in his collection of essays *What is Political Philosophy?* In that work, published in 1959, he repeatedly links the demoralization of political philosophy to its unsuitable marriage to history. Starting in the late eighteenth century, presumably with German idealist philosophy, political thought and ethics began to be seen as mere functions of a changing human condition. Finally, "in our time it [political philosophy] is frequently rejected in favor of historicism, i.e., of the assertion that the fundamental distinction between philosophic and historical questions cannot in the last analysis be maintained. Historicism may therefore be said to question the possibility of political philosophy." Moreover, "historicism is not just one philosophic school among many, but a most powerful agent that affects more or less all presentday thought. As far as we can speak at all of the spirit of a time, we can assert with confidence that the spirit of our time is historicism."[9] This spirit marks a revolutionary change. In the ancient world, he notes, history was esteemed by rhetoricians, not philosophers: "The history of philosophy in particular was not considered a philosophic discipline: it was left to antiquarians rather than to philosophers."[10]

The crystallization of the new outlook, although anticipated by Burke, Kant, and others of the late eighteenth century, came with Hegel's "synthesis of philosophy and history" and later was continued by the Historical School of the nineteenth century. Because of these cumulative influences, it became necessary to substitute "historical jurisprudence, historical political science, historical economic science for a jurisprudence, a political science, an economic science that were evidently 'unhistorical' or at least 'a-historical'." Behind this development lay two root assumptions. One was the belief that history could be made into an "object of study" independently of a normative nature (*nature* here being understood in the philosophical and ethical rather than in the modern naturalist sense). The second historicist assumption was that "the restoration of earlier teachings is impossible or that every intended restoration necessarily leads to an essential modification of the restored teaching . . . [and] that every teaching is essentially related to an unrepeatable 'historical situation'."[11]

Two characteristics of Strauss's broadside merit further attention. First, he identifies the "spirit" of the present age as historicist. Such a reduction or equation is not consistently found in Strauss's other published observations on the contemporary world. Most of those remarks are directed against such various targets as behaviorism, "value-free science," positivism, and moral nihilism. His attribution of other modernist problems to historicism may have been a provisional attempt to get to the ultimate source of the alleged perversion of political thought. His casual analysis may also indicate more about Strauss's reaction to Hegel and to such German social thinkers as Wilhelm Dilthey, Heinrich Rickert, and Max Weber than about contemporary American culture and higher learning. Even if one does assume *arguendo* (since the underlying thesis is open to question)[12] that the American intelligentsia are value relativists, should we blame this problem on the discovery by Heinrich Rickert that historical causation, unlike its experimental scientific counterpart, is unrepeatable? Furthermore, what demonstrable relationship is there between the attempt of Karl von Savigny, a progenitor of the Historical School, to study the evolutionary dynamics of ancient Roman law and the modern disparagement of Classical political theory? Perhaps we should not assume a causal relationship where Strauss intends to stress long-range influences. Yet, his incrimitory tone implies that he somehow blames nineteenth-century German academics for modern disasters. Another characteristic of Strauss's attack is that he directs it against those often perceived as traditionalists. Most of the major figures of the Historical School, which studied the "spirit" of evolving social and legal institutions, were men of the nineteenth-century Right. Yet, according to Strauss and his disciples, it was they, and not "the radicals of the eighteenth century," who practiced the "more extensive form of modern this-worldliness." By historicizing thought and ethical values, putative traditionalists, far more than the Jacobins or Marx, prepared the way for the modern assault on transcendent values.[13]

Strauss suggests a similar argument in the closing section of *Natural Right and History* (which came out of his Walgreen Lectures), in his comments on Edmund Burke. In all fairness, it must be said that Strauss spreads the blame for the alleged disappearance from Western thought of a normative view of nature widely. He regards, for example, the natural right teachings of John Locke (and implicitly of Thomas Jefferson) as a surrender to "political hedonism," and he laments the replacement of an older view of nature, which implied moral duty, by the state of nature as Locke defined it, to wit, a situation characterized by the absence of external constraint.[14] He identifies Macchiavelli, Hobbes, and Locke with a modernization of political theory that removed ethical values from consideration of the good life. Strauss also finds already present in J. J. Rousseau, particularly in his *Second Discourse,* an intimation of later progressive historicism. While disputing the possibility that man could achieve sovereignty over his own actions, Rousseau had proposed replacing "freedom" by "perfectability" as an attainable social goal.[15]

Despite his criticisms of earlier thinkers, Strauss assigns a special blame to Burke for modern value relativism. He applies this censure not to the whole Burke but to whatever part of him was drawn to history. In short: "Whereas Burke's 'conservatism' is in full agreement with classical thought, his interpretation of his 'conservatism' prepared an approach to human affairs which is even more foreign to classical thought than was the very 'radicalism' of the theorists of the French Revolution." Strauss reproaches Burke for taking his moral bearings from the course of history rather than from nature. Burke justified the English constitution too often as being prescriptive without taking into account a higher standard of measurement. He thereby implied that "transcendent standards can be dispensed with if the standard is inherent in the process; 'the actual and the present is the rational.'" What could appear as a return to the primeval equation of the good with the ancestral is, in fact, a preparation for Hegel."[16] Burke allegedly possessed a secularized understanding of Providence that was incompatible with resisting victorious evil. Denying "the nobility of last-ditch resistance," he came close to suggesting that "to oppose a thoroughly evil current in human affairs is perverse if that current is sufficiently powerful." Indeed, in the midst of the French Revolution, which Burke fought relentlessly, he argued that if "the system of Europe" did go down, "they, who persist in opposing this mighty current in human affairs . . . will not be resolute and firm, but perverse and obstinate."[17]

Strauss's assault on historical conservatives of the past as radicals in disguise coincided with a growing interest in Burke on the postwar Right, starting in 1949 with the scholarship of Ross J. S. Hoffmann and continuing through the writings of Peter Stanlis and Francis Canavan. Russell Kirk's *The Conservative Mind* (1953) was the most widely read book to come out of this revival. It extols Burke as a defender of ancestral virtue and as a paradigmatic opponent of revolution. Meanwhile, conservative Burke scholarship of the period, from Hoffmann down to Stanlis and Canavan, stressed Burke's awareness of a "continuity between nature and law" as an alternative to Lockean natural right.[18] Strauss criticized Burke at the beginning of this revival, for even then he may have regarded historical conservatism as detrimental to his educational mission. He believed that Burke and his disciples were engaged in a depreciation of reason, even though they ascribed a kind of corporate reason to institutions. Unlike Plato they rejected the belief that the individual human mind might by its own means apprehend the Good and the Just. Even worse, Strauss claimed that historical conservatives such as Burke ignored the infinite distance between the conventional and customary and what the best philosophical minds had judged to be good.[19]

Notwithstanding his profound learning and critical acumen, Strauss generally attacks a straw man in his polemics against Burke and historicism. His treatment of Burke is particularly suspect, since he makes his most damning charge by quoting his subject out of context. Burke never taught that one must surrender to a "mighty [but evil] current in human affairs," if that current is "sufficiently powerful." Strauss was obviously referring here to the last paragraph of "Thoughts on French Affairs," a long letter on the inroads of the Revolution outside France that Burke had sent to an aristocratic friend in December 1791. The merit of this letter, according to the great English literary critic Matthew Arnold, lies in Burke's attempts to survey the international scene from the perspective of his hated enemy.[20] Once having noted the opportunism of Europe's rulers, the decrepitude of many European states and the widespread appeal of the revolution's majoritarian doctrines, Burke concludes "that the remedy must be where power, wisdom, and information, I hope, are more united with good intention than they can be with me." The tone is one of resignation and in no way suggests an ecstatic affirmation of fate. Burke goes on to observe that "if a great change is to be made in human affairs, the minds of men will be fitted to it, the general opinions and feelings will draw that way. Every fear, every hope will foward it, and then they who persist in opposing this mighty current in human affairs will appear rather to resist the decrees of Providence itself than the mere designs of men."[21] Burke is here commenting on the way in which cataclysmic changes occur whether for good or for ill. He is not urging anyone to change course with the winds of history. He is simply reminding his reader how opponents of the Revolution (such as he) "will appear" (a phrase inappropriately deleted from Strauss's quotation), if the other side triumphs. Given this situation the antirevolutionaries would *seem* "perverse and obstinate."

We may also challenge Strauss's strictures about the historicist tendencies that Burke supposedly foreshadowed. Did the practice of justifying constitutions as works of history represent a break with Classical political thought? We can answer in the affirmative if we disregard that part of the Classical heritage that exalted evolutionary regimes and that interpreted filial piety as a proper source of public virtue. Strauss suggests that Classical philosophers treated history merely as a branch of rhetoric, yet Aristotle thought it was more than that when he prepared the histories of two hundred political regimes. Aristotle included the topic of *historia* in *The Rhetoric* to tell us that a statesman should study "the information of those who write about the activities of political councils." Such a pursuit, he concluded, "is political rather than rhetorical."²²

Strauss states correctly that Aristotle, and presumably Plato, who viewed the writing of history as a mere "skill [*technē*]," considered philosophical "knowledge [*epistēmē*]," a superior form of truth. It is also indisputable that among ancient Greek historians were certainly teachers of rhetoric. In fact, as Paul Pédech has demonstrated, it was by studying the techniques of courtroom advocacy as developed by rhetoricians such as Isocrates of Athens that Polybius and other Hellenistic historians arrived at a complex understanding of historical causation.²³ What is equally significant is that Greek historians came to distinguish their activity from mere art by virtue of their quest for "precision [*akribeia*]" and "demonstrable knowledge."²⁴ Polybius, for example, despised his fellow historian Phularxos for imitating tragedians and for appealing to his readers' pity rather than to their passion for truth. Instead of "terrifying and arousing his listeners through the most evocative words [διὰ τῶν πιθανωτάτων λόγων ἐκπλῆξαι καὶ ψυχαγωγῆσαι]," the historian must "teach and persuade the lover of learning at all times by means of real deeds and actual words [διὰ τῶν ἀληθινῶν ἔργων καὶ λόγων εἰς πάντα τὸν χρόνον διδάξαι καὶ πεῖσαι τοὺς φιλομαθοῦντας]."²⁵ The comments in Polybius and Plutarch about the defects of rhetoric resemble Plato's animadversions on sophistry and artistic imitation. Hellenistic historians, like earlier Greek philosophers, understandably felt compelled to distinguish their *ergon*, or activity, from the act of entertaining, impressing, or informing. Hellenistic historians attempted to raise their form of inquiry to the *apodictic*, or demonstrable, a term that Aristotle had applied to philosophical knowledge.

One obvious result of this undertaking was that Hellenistic scholars of the second century B.C. had a deeper and more informed historical sense than had most of the Greek world of two centuries earlier. Strauss remarks that Cicero compared Rome's organic constitution quite favorably with the Spartan regime of Lycurgus.²⁶ Cicero, who studied a by-then already extensive Greek and Roman historiography, had a sense of the continuity of generations and customs. And though generally an unoriginal Platonist in his philosophical speculation, he may have seen the past more fully than his master in philosophy. Although Plato approached the past as an ambiguous and therefore adaptable backdrop for his own invented regime in the *Critias*, Cicero dealt with expanding and adapting political forms.

Strauss does indicate that Cicero praised the old Roman republic, which he considered to be declining in his day. In so doing, according to Strauss, Cicero modeled himself on Plato, who had also relegated "the best polity" to an ideal past. For Cicero as for Plato this past need never have existed and was invoked only to demonstrate that the best regime "could have become actual at some place and at some time."²⁷ But such an assertion ignores an obvious difference between Plato and Cicero as political theorists. Whereas Plato consciously invented an ideal regime, Cicero identified the best government with the political practices of his own ancestors. The favorable comparison of Rome's evolutionary republic to the Spartan model originated in Book Six of Polybius's *Histories*. Describing the Roman regime "while still at its zenith," Polybius enumerated the political advantages that had enabled the Romans to recover from the initial defeat at the hands of Hannibal and eventually to win the Second Punic War. The Roman state drew its strength not only from its embodying aristocratic, monarchial, and democratic features, but also by preserving its character even while changing.[28] Although no single lawgiver had created the Roman regime, Polybius considered it to be remarkably well suited to the social and military needs of its people. Cicero and later Roman historians identified their country's republican past with a society that was politically adaptable while remaining loyal to ancestral customs.

Strauss ultimately concedes that "Cicero preferred the Roman polity which was the work of many men and many generations to the Spartan polity which was the work of one man." He then, however, assumes a fallback position: Cicero (and Polybius, whom he cites in the footnotes) did not despise the Spartan constitution. Furthermore, unlike Burke, these ancient writers never understood political developments "to be processes unguided by reflection." Yet, there is no reason to assume that Burke admired unreflective governments. His parliamentary speeches appeal repeatedly to prudence. He distrusted majoritorian doctrines because he doubted that the majority of people in his or any other society could be sufficiently sober and disciplined to rule themselves.

Polybius, who anticipated Burke's praise of prejudice as inbred moral sentiment, presented Roman "superstition [δεισιδαιμονία]" as essential for public virtue. Contrary to "wisemen" who mocked the Roman fear of gods and adoration of ancestors, Polybius defended these attitudes "for holding Roman institutions together [συνέχειν τὰ ῥωμαίων πράγματα]."[29] In his view: "the ancients or so it would seem to me, were not rash to introduce among the masses notions about gods and ideas about Hades; indeed it would be far more reckless for someone now to dislodge them."[30] Polybius says that Roman officials were more honest than Greek administrators because the former feared divine retribution. He traced the greater martial valor of the Romans to the manner in which they buried their war heroes. At these funerals Romans, with customary pomp, eulogized the deeds of fallen soldiers and invoked the spirits of courageous ancestors.[31] Although Polybius sometimes treated "superstition" as an intellectually questionable restraint on the "lawless passions" of the masses, he, like his Roman admirers, deeply respected filial piety. He commended this quality in others, such as the Syracusan prince Gelo "who had set for himself the most beautiful goal in life by obeying his own progenitor."[32] Polybius did not make these judgments condescendingly, from the alleged high ground of an ideal polity. In considering the best constitutions, for example, he sardonically dismissed Plato's republic: "Just as we do not admit into an athletic competition those artists or athletes who are neither prized nor trained, so too is it not proper to introduce this [constitution] into a contest of champions unless it has first truly shown something of its operation."[33]

Was Polybius any less of a "Classical" political thinker than Plato? Did his historical consciousness or his assessment of piety disqualify him from teaching true political philosophy? Strauss probably would have responded that thinkers remained in agreement with Classical standards only if they judged existing societies by the ideal standards of human reason. Yet, like Kant's mystical body of moral absolutes removed from any empirical context, Strauss's ideal state relates to the world of flesh and blood like a disembodied wraith. His remedy seems worse than the disease, relativism, that he sets out to cure. Since individuals have used history to relativize values, he would have us do away with historical consciousness or, at least, treat it as a modern blemish on the body of Western thought. Although such a plan has been called reactionary, its implications are radically antitraditional. Strauss and his disciples have no more respect for ancestral custom and the virtue of *pietas* than do the "value-free social scientists" whom they often berate. In place of "the primeval equation of the ancestral with the good," they wish to substitute one possible lesson of Plato's *Euthyphro:* individuals should do what their minds demonstrate to be Just rather than what divine law prescribes for us.[34] Such a teaching may be intellectually opportune but hardly a recipe for restoring "the permanent things."

Strauss may also have protested too much against those cultural limits that prevent us from reading Plato and Aristotle as they understood their own statements. Nineteenth-century Hegelians and, more recently, the modern historicist Han-Georg Gadamer argue that a richer meaning may be infused into an ancient text by the mind of a later interpreter.[35] The conservative historicist Claes G. Ryn, in a debate with the Straussian Eugene F. Miller, eloquently describes these benefits: "Our own experience and knowledge stream into our efforts to understand a certain thinker, and they are expanded in turn by the activity of interpretation. Nothing can ever be read in the same way twice, not even a theorem and proof in Euclid. Our consciousness is changed, however imperceptibly, by each new moment."[36] Ryn goes on to expound a dialectical hermeneutics strongly influenced by Hegel and Croce. He speaks of concepts fraught with undiscovered possibilities and of how every single moment of thought "both replaces and develops the past." Just as the notion of the triangle has yielded to our consciousness meanings that were not apparent to Euclid, so too has there been an increasing enrichment, without abandonment, of Classical political philosophy. In reading Plato, according to Ryn, a modern can grasp more fully the character of political regimes than was possible in ancient Greece. The educated modern, unlike even the wisest of ancient Athenians, has an extensive historical frame of reference and is aware of governmental distinctions (for example, "between plebiscitary majoritarian democracy and constitutional representative democracy") that had no place in most ancient societies.[37]

I believe that Ryn's polemic may go too far in the direction of what Miller calls "a sanguine progressivism that nonetheless denies the possibility of a culminating 'absolute moment' in history because of man's finiteness."[38] Ryn in his response to Miller may also be confounding complexity with philosophical and spiritual progress. The experience of modern democracy, as Ryn himself admits, does not disprove Plato's warnings, made with reference to ancient democracy, about the dangers of majoritarian oppression or of a morally irresponsible citizenry. Representative government (which the ancients also had) does not render Plato's observations about "democratic man" obsolete.

According to Eugene Miller, a Straussian, historicism fell into sin less through a doctrine of progress than an insistence that all "knowledge is inescapably historical."[39] I disagree. Historicism became intellectually serious only when it abandoned a facile teleological optimism (however important that optimism may remain as a spur to social action). The achievement of German historicists such as Leopold von Ranke and Wilhelm Dilthey was to divorce the recognition of the historicity of knowledge from the mechanical progressivism of Comte, Marx, and unfortunately even Hegel. Ranke and Dilthey recognized that all consciousness was marked, if not totally determined, by the age out of which it came. By a leap of understanding *(Verstehen)* the scholars and political leaders of one generation or society may gain insight into those of an earlier one. Yet, according to Dilthey, "time-boundedness *[Zeitbedingtheit]*" is the inherently limiting framework in which all applications of historical understanding and historical imagination occur.[40] The sense (and even reality) of a living past in some societies, and so vivid in the rhetoric of Burke, may help to bridge the distance described. And yet, for scholars the recovery of the values and attitudes of a temporally remote thinker and age must always remain problematic: and all the more so for those who reject their time-boundedness.

In fact, a scholar who rejects, or is unaware of, his time-boundedness is likely to succumb to an unreflective presentism that precludes the very possibility of a true understanding of the past. Like the Renaissance painters who depicted the Holy Family like their own contemporary Italians, the antihistoricist may try to overcome temporal distance by projecting his own views and concerns onto those whose meaning he claims to retrieve. I for one believe that the Straussians' attempted recovery of the lost meanings of "great political thinkers" has often allowed them to blur distinctions between their own *modern* values and the values of earlier generations. The interpreters studiously ignore the historical distance between themselves and what they study. Moreover, because Strauss and his students claim that thinkers of the past, out of moral prudence or fear of political reprisal, often concealed their true meaning, they undertake to reveal the esoteric core of those texts they interpret.[41] The subjects of Straussian studies, whether medieval Talmudists or eighteenth-century French aristocrats, were allegedly religious skeptics and philosophical antitraditionalists who supported the established powers of their time *faute de mieux.*[42]

The radical antihistoricism of some Straussians, though not of Strauss himself, has taken other far more questionable expressions. One disciple of Strauss has written extensively on the "Aristotelianism" of FDR, a form of praise that would no doubt have perplexed the former president.[43] Another admirer of Strauss's has tried to explain the student radicalism of the 1970s by minutely examining Locke's understanding of liberty. Because Straussians consider the "American regime" almost entirely derivative from Locke's conception of the social contract, it apparently follows that all American political and social crises have their origin there too.[44] A Straussian picture of history often consists of a succession of regimes and their "founding principles." By avoiding questions about specific religious, cultural, and social contexts, we are supposedly brought closer to grasping the philosophical foundations of functioning governments.

These critical remarks, it should be emphasized, are not directed at a group that is either dullwitted or insignificant. Among the Straussians are some of the most intellectually prolific and academically respected critics of the political-cultural Left. Such Straussians as Walter Berns; Joseph Cropsey; Harry Jaffa; Martin Diamond; Harvey Mansfield, Jr.; and Alan Bloom have contributed decisively to the current identification of theoretical conservatism with political philosophy. Whether or not their views are in fact conservative is arguable, yet there can be no doubt that Strauss's students and admirers, by being on the cutting edge of political debate with the New Left and academic Marxists, have gained the deep respect of the postwar conservative intellectual movement. The close ties to their camp of neoconservative journalists such as George Will, Irving Kristol, and Norman Podhoretz have also served to popularize the Straussians' ideas.[45] However wrong-headed and dogmatically presentist may be the Straussian attacks on historicism, it would be foolish to underestimate their pervasiveness and impact.

The discussion of Strauss and of his school may contain part of the answer to a question recently posed by Thomas Molnar: "Why is it that Marxists, unlike conservatives, can inspire students with their vision of history?"[46] Part of the answer is that the American intellectual Right has largely lost the sense of a living past. Too many conservatives prefer to capitalize on transitory policy issues or to declaim against the historicization of values and knowledge. Thirty years of attack on historical approaches and methods by Straussians, neo-Thomists, libertarians, and others on the intellectual Right have driven a wedge between conservatism and the study of history. The very term *historical conservative* has now fallen on hard times. Whether that term is applied to the author of *The Philosophy of Right*, the eloquent defender of the "historical liberties" of Englishmen, or the Historical School in early nineteenth-century Germany, the critics of "historicism" can be expected to pronounce the same warnings. The study of historical continuities and contexts diverts us from the examination of eternal truths; by stressing the historicity of knowledge, we stumble inescapably into relativism. In 1952 Russell Kirk, at the end of a defense of Burke's evolutionary, organic conception of the state, noted "the gulf that separates Burke from Hegel."[47] Kirk made a similar distinction at the beginning of *The Conservative Mind*, published in 1953, between German historicists and the Anglo-American traditionalists treated in his book.[48] His apparent attempt to guard Burkean historical conservatism from the critics of Hegel proved fruitless. By 1952, Frank Meyer, despite his own unacknowledged historicism, was castigating Burkeans as crypto-Hegelians. Even three years earlier in his Walgreen Lectures, Strauss had already proposed the provocative thesis that Burke and the Historical School in early nineteenth-century Germany were the most extreme radicals of their age. By producing historicism they had helped demoralize the Western world.

Self-declared historical conservatives nonetheless remain, for example, Kirk and survivors of the Southern Agrarian movement like the aged but still contentious Andrew Nelson Lytle. There are even self-avowed conservative Hegelians, such as Henry Paolucci (of St. John's University in New York) who has tried to relate *The Philosophy of Right* to the American political experience.[49] The neo-Crocean philosopher Claes G. Ryn, together with his colleagues and graduate students at Catholic University of America, has tried to reconcile nature and history, by constructing a "value-centered historicism."[50] In an ongoing synthesizing task, Ryn and his group have tried to clarify how "the transcendent moral order becomes historically immanent and is experienced by man in particular good actions." Drawing upon Burke's (and Russell Kirk's) concept of moral imagination, Croce's intuitionism, and Irving Babbitt's attempt to link will and imagination epistemologically, Ryn calls for recognition of "the continuing manifestation of the universal in forever changing circumstances." In conscious reaction to others on the intellectual Right, he (like Strauss's former student Stanley Rosen) has defended the value of Hegel's logic; Ryn has also praised Edmund Burke as "a conservative 'modern' in that he [Burke] sees history at its noblest as manifesting the transcendent, if only imperfectly, and thus as an invaluable guide in the realization of man's moral destiny."[51]

One may also point to two conservative Catholic historians, Stephen Tonsor of the University of Michigan and John Lukacs, a Hungarian émigré at Chestnut Hill College, as remaining links to nineteenth-century historical theory. Tonsor, through his articles and the numerous dissertations that he has directed, has tried to call attention to the indispensability of historical consciousness to the Western understanding of man. Although Tonsor has criticized the slide into moral relativism among the disciples of Hegel and Ranke, he has also praised the attempts of these and of other theorists to view historical time providentially.[52]

Despite his reputation primarily as a diplomatic and social historian, Lukacs has manifested most of the same interests as those of Tonsor, like him a former president of the American Catholic Historical Association. Perhaps Lukacs's most reflective work is *Historical Consciousness,* which affirms the evolutionary and time-bounded aspect of all memories of the past. Although his book may best be remembered for its stress on national character as the key to causation, it also dwells on the autobiographical aspect of our thinking about the past. Rejecting the notion of a finished historical past, Lukacs observes, "And the past is still working. We keep working and reworking it in our minds. We are, all, prophets about the past. Historically and existentially speaking we do not solve our problems: we, rather, overcome them."[53] Lukacs, who holds no brief for either Marxists or Straussians, considers the spiritual and ethical dimensions of life to be the productive agents of material and political situations. He believes spiritual developments occur within the framework of national character. Moreover, the study of these developments is further filtered by the personal, ethnic, and generational associations and loyalties of the historian himself. Lukacs goes far indeed in contesting the idea of historical objectivity and the methodological value of universal, as opposed to civilizational or national, norms, but his statements are obviously a defiant response to both Marxist materialism and the attempt to deny man's historicity.[54] Lukacs makes a critical distinction between historical thinkers who, like Leopold von Ranke, aspired to "objectivity" in their research and those who, like Dilthey, recognized the necessarily experiential core of their investigations. In a letter to the author on 15 January 1984, he objected to my treatment of Ranke, Dilthey, and him as inventors of a common historicist tradition. *History and Consciousness,* according to Lukacs, was written partly as an argument against Ranke. I would nonetheless argue that those here grouped as adherents of the historicist tradition do share a common perspective, which the Straussians and many others reject. All of these historicist believe—or believed—that human knowledge is, whatever else it may be, necessarily historical and, within the same civilization, cumulative. It is less important for our purposes whether they also accept, as did Polybius and Ranke, the feasibility of "objective" or "demonstrable" historiography.

It might here be in order to note the significance of conservative academic historians in the American South. The Southern Historical Association has proportionately more members who define themselves as conservatives than any other regional professional historical society.[55] The Center for the Study of Southern History and Culture at the University of Alabama, under the leadership of Grady McWhiney and Forrest McDonald, has focused on ethnic and regional culture in interpreting the American past. McWhiney and McDonald have doggedly challenged materialist interpretations of southern history.[56] In the University of South Carolina history department, the John C. Calhoun scholar Clyde Wilson has helped initiate two explicitly traditionalist and regionalist publications, *The Southern Partisan* and *The Southerner.* Wilson, a disciple of Melvin E. Bradford and an admirer of Andrew Lytle, has defended the agrarian and chivalric values of the antebellum South. Wilson has ridiculed the tendentious efforts of writers to "refound" America historiographically after each alleged national crisis. Such refoundings, he argues, are attempts to alter historical memory that historians undertake to justify their pet notions of progress.[57]

Despite the pride of southern historians in their regional agrarian past, it would be erroneous to generalize from their example about a resurgence of historical interest on the Right. The predilection for southern antiquities of Wilson, McWhiney, and Melvin E. Bradford of the University of Dallas is related to an older southern tradition, one that goes back to the Southern Agrarians of the 1930s and ultimately to such early twentieth-century southern historians as Ulrich B. Phillips. Although provocative antimodernist historians, most notably the Agrarian F. L. Owsley, have defended the South against its critics, the southern defense has been primarily literary and ethical and only derivatively historiographical. Of the original twelve Agrarians, only one, Owsley, became a full-time historian. The South's conservative intellectual tradition has favored literary creativity and the interpretation of literary texts more than the study of history. That same tradition has looked to the southern past as Livy did to the Roman republic, for models of social and public virtue. Southern filial piety has been more instinctive than philosophical, more of an inspiration for poems, novels, and eloquent manifestoes than for sustained and systematic reflection on the meaning of history.[58] Southern historians have ever looked to Rome in order to celebrate their region. Melvin Bradford has cited Livy and Polybius in describing American southern character. He has repeatedly compared antebellum southern society to the picture of the early Roman republic, with its cult of ancestor worship, found in the works of the French historian Numa Denis Fustel de Coulanges.[59]

Outside the South, it must be stressed, there are proportionately fewer conservatives in the history departments. Most American historians are politically and philosophically far to the left of the general population and share this tendency, as indicated in surveys by the Carnegie Institute, with other teachers in the humanities and social sciences.[60] This state of affairs may partly result from the fact that most conservatives prefer commerce and politics to academic life. Yet, another hypothetical explanation deserves to be considered. A tension exists between postwar conservatism and history as a sense of the communal past, the origin of which may be sought in the *American* conservative outlook. History, seen as the examination of human actions within particular epochs and in relation to evolving societies, tells more about man's cultural dependence than his autonomy. History deals with the continuing power of past events and provides little support for two values that have long been associated with a specifically American conservatism, individual initiative and personal responsibility.[61] As the record of our bonds with communities past and present, history fits together uneasily with the American conservative emphasis on the individual's freely shaping his future.

American conservatism, save for its southern and Burkean manifestations, seeks to defend old modernity against postmodern culture. The modernity American conservatives still uphold is the one created by eighteenth-century revolutions, which challenged without totally eradicating the institutions of an older Europe. Some American conservative principles have more in common with the French Revolution's Declaration of the Rights of Men and of Citizens than with Burke's pointed attack on that document. American conservative political heroes, from Hoover and Taft to Goldwater and Reagan, have often unknowingly embraced the values and slogans heard in the French National Assembly of 1789. American conservatives have claimed personal and property rights as inalienable human possessions. Like the French revolutionaries of 1789, they have championed the liberty and rights of the individual stripped of corporate and historical identity.

Despite their affinity with eighteenth-century radicalism, American conservatives are not merely followers of the ideas of the French Revolution. Locke's teachings on natural right influenced revolutionaries in both America and France, but other principles—Judeo-Christian, Classical, and even medieval—also contributed to the American government's founding and growth. Classical modernity, as Hegel brilliantly perceived, came out of the Christian sense of the individual's spiritual worth, which gained increasing theological and cultural importance through the Protestant Reformation. The first cataclysm of modernity, unleashed by Luther, Calvin, and their followers, far more than the second produced what became the established virtues of traditional American society: devotion to one's calling, a pursuit of worldly success as a form of service to God, the careful nurture of children, and the view of marriage as a means of perfecting virtue all formed the shaping ideals of middle-class civilization. They were also ideals, as Ernst Troeltsch and Max Weber have argued, that lay germinating in the Reformation's teachings of "justification by faith" and the spiritual equality of all honorable vocations as opportunities for religious service.

The rejection of capitalism and property rights, particularly in America, has usually proceeded in lockstep with assaults on both "Puritanism" and "Victorian morality." The format of these combined denunciations was already present in Friedrich Engels's *Outline of a Critique of Political Economy*, which joined observations on the structural defects of industrial capitalism to remarks on the "self-righteous" Protestantism of early capitalists.[62] Although Engels included Protestant moral values (such as individual spiritual freedom) in the mere "superstructure" of capitalist society, the necessary link between capitalism and Protestant morality was as obvious to him as it was to Max Weber and to the American New Left. In his multivolume biography of Herbert Hoover, George Nash dwells on the modernist aspect of his subject's conservatism.[63] According to Nash, Hoover believed that America was unique among the nations of the world and indeed of all ages by virtue of its dedication to "equality of opportunity." Yet, he thought the pursuit of upward mobility could be morally justified only as it contributed to character formation.[64] Nash observes that Hoover's strict upbringing as a Quaker in Iowa, and later in Oregon, left an indelible imprint on his personality and outlook.[65]

A comprehensive picture of conservative modernism must take into account a critical change that has occurred during the last thirty years: the total secularization of the conservative modernist outlook. A secularizing process was already operative in middle-class Protestant culture in early modern times. This process involved a gradual shift of religious emphasis from the quest for individual salvation to the means by which salvation was sought or existentially verified, hard work, self-improvement, and service to the community. Yet, this secularization of Protestant moral theology was until recently never total. The Western middle class and its religious and political leaders paid honor to biblical morality and spoke of serving God through civic, educational, and professional activities. Despite the agenda of the Moral Majority (which has generally received condescending if not hostile treatment from intellectual conservatives), the direction of today's theoretical conservatism is increasingly toward a secularist and utilitarian interpretation of freedom. It is libertarians such as Milton Friedman and Thomas Sowell, and the defenders of democratic capitalism grouped around *Commentary, Policy Review,* and *The Wall Street Journal,* who now receive the broadest hearing among domestic and foreign critics of the Left. It may be that only those on the Right who share the materialist and secularist assumptions of the contemporary world can communicate with other intellectuals.[66]

Irving Kristol, a leading light of American neoconservatism and a frequent contributor to *Commentary* and *The Wall Street Journal,* has outlined his movement's "distinctive characteristics" in the Spanish traditionalist journal *Razón Española.* Kristol declares democratic capitalism to be the guiding principle of American neoconservatives, whose "modest enthusiasm" for market economics and popular government distinguishes them from both the Old and New Right. Unlike the ancients, neoconservatives believe in the possibility and desirability of continuous material growth, but unlike libertarians, they do not support an unregulated market economy. They advocate a "conservative welfare state," which helps shape private economic choices while guaranteeing minimal material security for all citizens. The neoconservatives are seen as temperamentally different from Southern Agrarians by virtue of their "antiromantic" attitude. Unlike the utopian Left and romantic Right, his movement, Kristol claims, thinks in a way that is "more rabbinic than prophetic." Moreover, its roots are in classical political thought: neoconservatives have embraced "the teachings and writings of Leo Strauss whom many consider contemptuous of the modern world." Accordingly, they "admire Aristotle, respect Locke, and distrust Rousseau."[67]

This invocation of Strauss by Kristol and other neoconservatives as an author of choice may not be entirely defensible. If neoconservatives consciously dissociate themselves from older conservative movements and from ancient social teachings that are politically reactionary or economically anachronistic, in what way is their movement anchored in the premodern world? The neoconservatives' claim to ancient roots may have come through the "teachings and writings of Strauss," but a qualification must be made before we can establish such a link. Unlike the neoconservatives, Strauss disliked Locke, respected Rousseau, and preferred Plato to Aristotle. In rating Locke as a political teacher, Strauss was clear in stating his judgment: "Locke's teaching on property, and therewith his whole political philosophy, are revolutionary not only with regard to the biblical tradition but with regard to the philosophic tradition as well. Through the shift of emphasis from natural duties and obligations to natural rights, the individual, the ego, had become the center and origin of the moral world since man—as distinguished from man's end—had become that center of origin."[68]

The largely hand-to-mouth political philosophy devised by the neoconservatives is largely the work of certain Straussians—for example, Walter Berns; Harvey Mansfield, Jr.; and Ralph Lerner—who have conspicuously identified the American regime and the American cause with Lockean "natural rights." Contrary to the sentiments of their own teacher, Straussians extol Locke's essential decency," while applying his criterion of individual self-interest to social ethics and family morality.[69]

One need not disagree with Kristol's specific economic prescriptions in order to recognize the provisional, contrived nature of his appeal to past authorities. He makes light of speculative thinking and archaic visions but appeals to rabbinic Judaism and the "classical wisdom" of Leo Strauss. But outside of certain counsels to pursue a worldly vocation (together with study of the sacred law), it is hard to see exactly what Kristol has extracted from the Talmud. Beyond a few phrases he has drawn from Strauss's students about the value of John Locke, it is also problematic whether he has taken anything from Strauss save a marked distaste for historical conservatism. The point of these observations, let me repeat, is not to disparage either Kristol's journalistic talent or his persuasiveness as a political advocate. Rather, we are trying to understand the difference between his personal ability as a political journalist and the theoretical thinness of the movement he has helped launch. Despite his own celebrity, Kristol's movement still gropes awkwardly for historical and philosophic roots as it seeks to justify American society as it is presently constituted. The task, we might note, is not entirely dissimilar to the one that engaged Hegel, Vera, the St. Louis Hegelians, and, finally, Will Herberg. They too undertook their own defenses of the *juste milieu* and argued the need for social and political stability. What distinguishes them from the neoconservatives are the sense of historical perspective and the philosophical breadth that they brought to bear on their labors.

The postwar disintegration of the classical European Right of monarchists and clericalists has aided the change in outlook described. The neoconservative exaltation of Lockean natural rights (as opposed to traditional moral duty) and of democratic capitalism (of Locke plus parliamentary democracy) has by now found an echo among the ideologically drifting European opponents of the Left. Anticommunist newspapers such as *Le Figaro, The Daily Telegraph,* and *Il Giornale di Sera* have rallied rhetorically to the neoconservative defense of a secularist, pluralistic, and democratic-capitalist West. The French academic and journalist Guy Sorman recently published a commercially successful book, *La révolution conservatrice américaine,* which celebrates the surging power of the New American Right. The conservatism that, according to Sorman, is making inroads among even European intellectuals and bureaucrats is mostly economic, utilitarian, and individualistic.[70] A conservatism based on cultural revival or on the sense of spiritual continuity no longer has much appeal in today's Western society.

One of the most bitter critics of this situation has been the French author Alain de Benoist, who has mocked the dehistoricized "American anti-model."[71] Benoist believes that liberal America, with its atomistic and entirely presentist conception of the individual, poses a greater threat to European civilization than does Soviet Communism. Both Marxism and Western liberalism (i.e., democratic capitalism) rest upon "antihistorical myths": one, upon the hope of a future classless society with a transformed humanity, and the other, upon the ideal of self-actualizing individuals freed of communal ties except those that are freely accepted. There is, however, a critical difference between those who hold to these two antihistorical myths. All "communist societies are constantly required to project into the more and more distant future the arrival of the 'classless society,' whereas liberal societies affirm the imminent realization of their myth."[72] This is because the need for cohesion in collectivist societies compels their leaders to resurrect communitarian values and to refurbish symbols from the national past (note the official honor paid to Frederick the Great in Communist East Germany but not in liberal Western Germany). By contrast, liberal societies recognize only the sovereignty of individual hedonism and the transitory material desires that emanate from the electorate and the marketplace.

Although there may be considerable merit in these observations, Benoist himself typifies the problem of one who looks for historical continuity in a time of cultural dislocation. His hatred for the American "anti-model" is so intense that he urges Europeans, if faced by the choice, to support the Soviets rather than the Americans. Soviet militarism reminds Benoist of Rome, and America's self-indulgent materialism recalls the decadent Carthaginians, who were dependent upon mercenary armies during the First and Second Punic Wars. He leaves no doubt that men of character will always "declare for Rome and against Carthage."[73]

When Benoist presents his alternatives to the modern Western "retreat from history," he reveals a cranky mind more than a penetrating one. He advocates a politics of spite against the Americans in the form of closer European ties to the Soviet Union and to anti-American Asian and African states. He exhorts European countries to reaffirm their ancestral traditions, but when he defines these traditions, he excludes from the outset *"Judéo-Christianisme,"* which, like Nietzsche, he associates with vulgar and effeminate egalitarianism. The living and spontaneous tradition of the European soul, before it had been forced into Christian ritualism, was the Indo-European culture found "at the dawn of the neolithic revolution."[74] Benoist believes that the survival of European tradition and order hinges upon the reappropriation of pre-Christian Indo-European religious symbols and attitudes, although he assumes incorrectly that a basic harmony existed between the Roman civil cult, Celtic animism, and various non-Christian mystery religions. The absence of *Judéo-Christianisme* from all pre-Christian religions once practiced in Europe supposedly indicates that their ways of life were the same or at least similar. If this idea is difficult to swallow, it may be less so than Benoist's entire understanding of Western tradition, as "something that lives within us" but must be rediscovered by archeological investigation and retrieved from its place in time "at the dawn of the neolithic revolution."

Despite his whimsical cures for a disintegrating civilization, Benoist puts into relief what may be today the chief obstacle to historical conservatism: the disappearance or continuing radicalization of those cultural and social institutions whose growth and survival conservatives in the past contemplated with pride. The secularization and liberalization of institutional Christianity have obviously removed one keystone of a hierarchical and organic society. Moreover, in America historical conservatives, particularly outside the South, have always faced the difficulty of looking for continuity in a regime founded upon a rupture with the European, premodern past.[75] Historical conservatives have argued that although the American regime incorporates modern elements, it also carries forward an older heritage. But there is a difficulty integrating the past into a regime whose founders declare it to be a *"novus ordo seclorum* [new order for the ages]."

As the American social order becomes increasingly identified with post-modern tendencies—for example, feminism, secularism, and governmentally mandated social equality—it may grow ever harder for historical conservatives to sustain the argument that Russell Kirk offers in *The Roots of American Order.*[76] In that work intended originally as a history textbook, Kirk maintains that the present government and society have their legal and spiritual origins in Jerusalem, Athens, and Rome. That "living past" to which Kirk appeals may have already died at some time when modern was giving way to post-modern cultures. Some conservatives have argued, however, that a welfare state committed to egalitarian and materialist propositions is an effort to return us to precapitalist norms. George Will and Peter Viereck have created a veritable cottage industry denouncing heartless capitalism in the name of Tory democracy.[77] Will and Viereck are right in emphasizing the modernist element in the American conservative cause, yet they have deluded themselves by believing in nonexistent historical alternatives. Democratic capitalism in the second half of the twentieth century is not likely to be replaced by an updated version of eighteenth-century England. The only likely successor to capitalism is the postmodern welfare state, to which Viereck, and by now Will, have gradually given their allegiance.

Indeed one danger for all historical conservatives is the belief that we can revivify what has ceased to be the "living past." Benoist, and the French New Right for which he speaks, and Viereck and Will all commit this error, however much they may differ in their day-to-day politics. A far greater thinker than any of these, Charles Maurras, a frustrated French monarchist, supported the Vichy government after the German occupation of France. Maurras was convinced that the highly centralized Pétain administration (operating with the sufferance of Hitler) would restore, as Marshall Pétain had promised, the prerevolutionary autonomy of the old French provinces. Maurras's misjudgment was pathetic and excusable only in view of his advanced age and physical infirmity, yet it exemplified a pitfall of historical conservatism, believing that modern society will eventually yield to what has been irretrievably lost to the past. Unlike Will and Maurras, who wait confidently for the impossible, Benoist at least prepares for an improbable future by excavating and inventing "historical myths."

The present American culture holds out little promise for a historicism of the Right: for a philosophy of order based on historically validated traditions that are made to endure amid change. One should at the outset distinguish such a view from proceduralism, because the mere survival of forms from an earlier period need not guarantee the transfer of a substantive heritage. For example, the present English constitution, in view of the virtual powerlessness of the monarch and House of Lords, bears little substantive resemblance to the English regime as it existed in 1800. Some may wish to dote on old forms and vestigial rituals, but we should recognize antiquarianism for what it is. Antiquarian proceduralists mistake forms for their long-vanished contents. Such minds do not represent the conservative historicism attributable to Burke and found even in parts of *The Philosophy of Right*. In what is probably the most arresting statement of historical conservatism, and conservative historicism, that has ever been written, Burke characterized the English regime as

a mode of existence decreed to a permanent body composed of transitory parts, wherein, by the disposition of a stupendous wisdom moulding together the great mysterious corporation of the human race, the whole, at one time, is never old or middle-aged or young, but in a condition of unchangeable constancy moves on through the varied tenor of perpetual decay—fall, renovation, and progression.[78]

Such a view of political society as the one given previously did not reflect either presentism or a belief in human perfectibility. Burke believed in the English constitution as the embodiment of a living past, that vital structure in which his own society perdured in the form of a unity of generations. His observation fully anticipated Hegel's comment in *The Philosophy of Right* that a true constitution was "not merely a contrivance *[ein bloss Gemachtes]*, but the work of centuries." Yet Burke presented this idea without paying tribute to the Left-historicist principle of progress that is present in Hegel. The historicism that Burke expressed emphasized not the self-enclosed discreteness but the organic interrelatedness of generations. Only within that continuum could men behave honorably and decently, for good behavior was the result not of individual reason but of the exercise of moral imagination. Burke saw European civilization as a spiritual-political legacy. At its best, it engaged man's corporate nature, by disciplining emotions and appealing to sensibilities as well as by shaping intellects. He loathed the French Revolution for stripping human relations of the "superadded" mystique of place and degree that he believed necessary for instilling social duties. He attributed whatever bonds had held society together to the ongoing "spirit of religion" and "the spirit of a gentleman."[79]

The historicism of the Right that Burke expounded has never enjoyed more than marginal support in America's highly mobile and success-oriented culture. Although Russell Kirk and, more recently, Melvin E. Bradford have tried to identify a Burkean outlook, replete with filial piety and admiration for Cicero and Polybius, with America's Founding Fathers, their interpretations have made little headway outside a few traditionalist journals.[80] Despite the merits of their scholarship, Bradford, Kirk, and southern conservative historians have little chance of sounding credible in a society that values progress and mobility above all else.

Another type of historicism has fared perhaps better, that of Voegelin, Herberg, and others. It reflects the influence of the Hegelian-idealist tradition of thought, which developed especially among Italian and German Hegelians and which by now has been partially revived in the value-oriented historicism of Ryn. This second form of historicism has shifted the focus away from social continuity toward the nature of consciousness. Instead of seeking social permanence within a changing world, it associates "the stupendous wisdom moulding together the great mysterious corporation of the human race" with leaps of consciousness or with spiritual evolution. This school of thought considers human consciousness a self-renewing or, in Ryn's neo-Crocean phrase, a self-enriching continuum that preserves an internalized living past. The exponents of this historicism stress the role of spiritual heroes who enhance civilization by further illuminating the ground of being or by boldly applying inherited truths.

These historicists see knowledge as the product of intuition, or of human minds operating in concrete situations as the creative bearers of traditional values. Almost all of them, once having wrestled with the Kantian dualism between sensory experience and moral-rational principles, have affirmed the unity of these two sources of knowledge. Voegelin has insisted on the "reality" of the perceived world as a precondition for the "attunement of human consciousness to the divine ground of being." Ryn has tried to show the unity between universality and changing historical circumstances by depicting ethical acts as transactions involving will, reason, and imagination. Although not himself concerned with Kantian dualism, Herberg also taught that ethical maxims acquired their ultimate validity in practice. He cited approvingly the Jewish theologian Franz Rosenzweig, who distinguished mere law (*Gesetz* or, in Hebrew, *din*) from a commandment (*Gebot* or *mitzvah*). Only by internalizing a law and acting upon it does a person bestow upon it a personally binding character as a divine commandment.[81] In his remarks on history, Herberg spelled out the implications of his religiously grounded ethical activism. The past, he asserted, was made to live through the ethical deeds of those who acted as the guardians of the "funded wisdom" of civilization. No individual could actualize himself as a moral being without seeking to appropriate the past.

A third form of historicism continues to appeal to at least some conservatives: a methodological historicism that prescribes that events, movements, and personalities be interpreted within the framework of an unrepeatable configuration of circumstances. Some Straussians and disciples of Voegelin associate this historicist method with moral relativism, and even with a certain receptivity to totalitarian dictatorship. For example, the Straussian political writer Harry V. Jaffa has stated that Americans must either be "committed" to equality or remain "open to the relativism and historicism that is the theoretical ground of modern totalitarian regimes."[82] Yet, the object of this attack is a Teutonic fossil, the by-now largely abandoned nineteenth-century attempt to overcome presentist bias by studying the past in its own terms. The polemics against methodological historicism are usually aimed at the predominantly German creators of historical science and social scientific methods, who are saddled with yet another unproven (and unprovable) burden of guilt. Rickert, Dilthey, and their disciples paved the way for Hitler (according to some German émigrés) by refusing to be socially engagés. They also led Western

academics, we now learn, into abandoning their democratic faith. Unfortunately for this proposition, the Marxist historicism now fashionable in our universities has little to do with the methodological historicism of nineteenth-century German universities.

Marxism, which is often presented in a popular, only vaguely economic
form, is by now the only kind of historicism with wide appeal among the
Western intelligentsia. The Marxian promise of a totally transformed society
with a reconstructed human nature is the intellectual's alternative to what
John Lukacs has properly called the "passing modern age." The Rumanian
anthropologist and traditionalist Mircea Eliade has paid tribute to "one of the
great eschatological myths of the Asiatic-Mediterranean world," the
redemptive role of the Just (the elected, the anointed, the innocent, the
messenger, in our day the proletariat) whose sufferings are invoked to change
the ontological status of the world."[83] Eliade recognizes the power of Marxism
both as a secularized adaptation of the Christian myth of the end of days and as
a "social scientific" restatement of the cosmic hope for a victory of the
"suffering Just." He insists that Marxism is not just one of a number of
historical hypotheses, but the overshadowing transformational myth of a post-
Christian culture, such as ours, that is still affected by Christian eschatology.[84]
Today's social-science faculties in Germany, Italy, and elsewhere in Western
Europe are filled not with just any historicists, but almost exclusively self-
labeled Marxists. American conservative intellectuals, however they may rail
against historicism in general, seem to be insensitive to this condition. They
trivialize Marxism by reducing it to a subform of Hegelianism or, far more
indefensibly, to an outgrowth of classical German historiography. Such
genealogical explorations have no more value than those attempts (still
unfortunately made by some commentators on German culture) to hunt for
proto-Nazi tendencies in Martin Luther's table talks or in Frederick the Great's
statecraft.

It is curious to what extent the European mentors of postwar American
conservatism neglect the distinction between leftist and rightist historicism. In
fact, it might be more accurate to state that European thinkers—particularly
Voegelin, Molnar, and Strauss—seem much more concerned about the
influence of Nietzsche and Heidegger than about the impact of Marx and the
revolutionary Left. When Strauss, for example, speaks of "radical historicism,"
he refers specifically to the Nietzschean-Heideggerian "commitment to the
creation and transformation of values." It was not the Marxian (left-Hegelian)
hope of a socially homogenized humanity created by revolutionary practice
but the Heideggerian quest for commitment, or for "being based on belief,"
that Strauss considered the most catastrophic and extreme form of modern
historicism. A similar concern can be found in Thomas Molnar, who still calls
Nietzsche "the most dangerous" thinker for our time. Voegelin does have harsh
words for Marx, particularly in *Science, Politics and Gnosticism,* and in *The New*

*Science of Politics,* but he nonetheless wedges him in between Hegel and Nietzsche in a discussion of modern gnosticism that ends in an utterly abrasive judgment of Heidegger.

Perhaps Voegelin, Strauss, and other European thinkers of their background had less regard for Marx than Hegel, Nietzsche, and Heidegger. They considered Marx derivative, a crude epigone of the great Hegel, who had extracted historical conceptions from an existing body of ideas. By contrast, Nietzsche and Heidegger (and to some degree Heidegger's teacher Edmund Husserl) were seen as towering minds whom Voegelin and Strauss felt it necessary to refute.[86]

Another explanation for the relative neglect of Marx and of leftwing historicism generally in the critical observations about revolutionary ideologies made by Strauss (until the end of his life) and by Voegelin (at least into the 1970s) might be related to their encounters with tyranny. Both men suffered personally from the Nazi ascent to power, but neither was forced to endure Communist tyranny. Their most vivid encounter with totalitarianism came through the Nazis, who undertook a return to the "old gods" by means of war and merciless extinction. Paul Norton, in "Leo Strauss: His Critique of Historicism," notes the persistence of Strauss's concern with "the meaning of 1933." Strauss remained up to the end of his life deeply, and even obsessively, disturbed by the temporary defection of Martin Heidegger to the Nazi cause while chancellor at the University of Freiburg in 1933. A cursory glance at a bibliography of Voegelin's publications should suffice to indicate how many of his writings of the thirties and forties deal with the German catastrophe. But unlike other European émigrés of his generation, he did develop ultimately a genuine interest in the historical mythology of the intellectual Left. His book *From Enlightenment to Revolution* deals with the utopian vision that originated in the Age of Reason and helped shape Comtean positivism and Marxian socialism.[87] In this book too, though, Voegelin dwells on the common etiology of Nazism and Communism and purports to be studying a gnostic explosion that produced Nietzsche and the Nazi movement as well as revolutionary socialism. Such an attempt to associate Communism with Nazism, which one also encounters in Erik von Kuehnelt-Leddihn, John Lukacs, and other Central Europeans, is not the deliberate counterrevolutionary tactic that some intellectuals often consider it. If Central European conservatives, especially those who grew up in the thirties, "tar" Communism with a Nazi or Fascist brush, the reason may have more to do with the trauma of Nazism than their hatred of Communism. They interpret Marxist revolutions and Communist dictatorships by analogy to the Nazi experience that so grievously affected their youths.

To the degree that leading theorists of the American Right have bewailed the radicalizing effect of the genus historicism, while having relatively little to say about Marxism or about historicism of the Left, they have helped obscure the pedigree of European conservatism and of the postwar American Right. Historicism played a critical role in both of these developments.[88] Historically grounded defenses of inherited authority undergirded most arguments against revolution and "abstract" human rights that were raised in Europe from the French Revolution down to the twentieth century. By opposing this line of reasoning, modern conservatives have rejected the heart of traditional European conservatism from the eighteenth century almost to the present day.

Historical conservatism has at least temporarily resurfaced in the more recent utterances of the classical liberal and Nobel Laureate, Friedrich von Hayek. Addressing the assembled guests of the policy-oriented Heritage Foundation on 29 November 1982, Hayek ridiculed a "misleading belief," which it may be inferred from the subsequent questioning, was widely shared by his audience: that man "by his supreme intelligence" invented and adapted moral rules and social codes. According to Hayek, who here paraphrases the view of historical conservatism, "We do not owe our morals to our intelligence; we owe them to the fact that some groups uncomprehendingly accepted certain rules of conduct—the rules of private property, of honesty and of the family—that enabled the groups practicing them to progress, multiply and gradually to displace the others."[89] Hayek does not attribute this evolutionary process to Burke's "stupendous wisdom" or to Hegel's "World Spirit," but he has obviously reappropriated the European conservative sense of reverence for the natural cohesion and spontaneous order of a traditional, deferential society. In an essay in *New York Tribune,* (7 January 1984), Thomas Molnar criticizes Hayek's remarks for reducing society to "economic facts and organization." According to Molnar, "Conservatism, adopting Hayek's creed, would be unable to generate either values or the understanding of these values; it would encourage bright young robotized individuals, good at their jobs but onesided cogs in the mechanism." My own reading of Hayek's speech differs from Molnar's, which seems to reflect his revulsion for Hayek's "puritanical" and classical liberal values. Hayek's picture of "man, society, morality, and God" is far from being "devastating," as Molnar states. Like Burke's, and to some extent Hegel's, historicism, it attempts to reconcile moral and social tradition with individual property rights. Though the resulting synthesis may not mesh well with Molnar's Thomistic perspective, I see no evidence that what Hayek is teaching is either morally dubious or inconsistent with historical conservatism.

Although it was not historical conservatism, but the historicism of consciousness and the Hegelian theory of civilizations that had the more crucial impact on the postwar conservative movement, what remained essential for both American and European conservatives was the motif of cultural continuity. The postwar American Right no less than classical European conservatism sought some notion of a living past. By presenting their own society in the broad context of an evolving, cumulative Western civilization or consciousness, conservative intellectuals attempted to instill in their countrymen a sense of historical destiny and responsibility. This exposition of a historicism, often Hegelian in content, took place as conservatives looked about anxiously at those they might offend. Hardly ever did postwar American conservatives identify themselves as Hegelians and only rarely as historicists. But the evidence of their debt to Hegelian and other forms of historicism is both abundant and clear.

Perhaps a few final remarks are in order to clarify exactly the relationship assumed to exist between our subjects and Hegelian ideas. Hegelianism, it has been argued, affected postwar conservative thinking by serving as a conceptual paradigm, as a way of understanding historical reality. Postwar conservative thinking was not historicist in a purely generic sense. Its conception of history was Burkean, Hegelian, or sometimes a combination of both. The present study has treated the Burkean historicist model only in passing. By choosing to focus on the conservatives' *Hegelian* heritage, we have been forced to limit the discussion of other contributing factors in our analysis of historical conservatism.

One may, however, note that contrary to an established misconception, postwar conservatives were no more unified in their praise of Burke than in their condemnation of Hegel. Richard Weaver wrote scathing attacks on Burke's "rhetoric of expedience." A reading of Frank Meyer's *In Defense of Freedom,* moreover, reveals that Burke's exaltation of the state offended its author far more than Hegel's thinking. Burke was a controversial hero even for postwar conservatives.

It may further be argued that postwar conservatives generally did not study Burke deeply at a formative stage in their political thinking. Reinhold Niebuhr, who recommended him to Herberg, began to read Burke in midlife and was in any case not strictly speaking a conservative. There is praise of Burke, especially of his appeal to moral imagination, in the essays of Irving Babbitt. This favorable opinion of Burke may have affected some readers of Babbit, but their impact on postwar conservatism was probably minimal, except for that of Russell Kirk and possibly Peter Viereck, who did in fact come to Burke largely through Babbitt. But even Kirk, the most illustrious Burkean conservative in America, developed his present understanding of Burke only after he had established himself as a political thinker. In *The Conservative Mind,* Kirk praised Burke, in the tradition of Babbitt, for his conception of the moral imagination, but only after he had read Stanlis in the late fifties did Kirk present Burke as a Christian Aristotelian teacher of natural law. This interpretive shift suggests how fluid was even Kirk's conception of the thinker to whom he tried to give a central role in the postwar conservative movement.[90]

The Burke revival that did attract the most attention in postwar America was primarily the work of a small band of Catholic traditionalists. Centered around Ross J. S. Hoffmann, Thomas Mahoney, Peter Stanlis, Francis

Canavan, and Carl Cone, the "natural law" Burkeans publicized their views through numerous books and, from 1959 through 1967, through *The Burke Newsletter,* which was later renamed *Studies in Burke and His Times.* This group managed to associate Burke in America with a coherent body of ideas. He was no longer linked to mere denunciations of eighteenth-century rationalism or to a particular rhetorical reaction to the French Revolution. One commentator, noting the changing "reputation of Edmund Burke" in America, observed in 1962 that his stock had risen remarkably in about ten years' time. Before the fifties American thinkers had rarely read Burke, except a few selected passages from *Reflections.* By the early sixties Burke was shown "to have a relevance for us now that we ourselves would not have expected half a century ago."[91] The author notes the journalistic and scholarly vigor of Burke's natural law interpreters who had won acceptance for their views among American conservatives. Nonetheless, this mission to the unconverted and half-converted took place only after the worldviews of most postwar conservatives had already been formed.

By contrast, our subjects came into contact with Hegelian ideas as part of the nurturing environment in which their thinking developed. Discussing Cambridge University before the First World War, Bertrand Russell observes that Hegelianism was so prevalent there that only those who doggedly resisted could escape its sway. Russell and one of his classmates at Cambridge, the later neonominalist G. E. Moore, worked on their own consciousness to overcome the effects of the Hegelian idealism of their teachers, F. H. Bradley and J. E. MacTaggert: "[W]e reverted to the opposite extreme, and thought that every-thing is real that common sense, uninfluenced by theology and philosophy, supposes real."[92]

Hegelianism flourished as much in Central European and American universities as in the Cambridge that Russell describes. The bitter complaints of Merle Curti, Leo Strauss, Irving Babbitt, and Sidney Hook may be exaggerated, but they point to the fact that Hegelians did influence higher learning in twentieth-century America.

The spread of Hegelian ideas in nineteenth-century America was massive enough to extend into the early decades of this century. Whereas Hegelian epistemology by the late nineteenth century gained footholds at Michigan, Harvard, Yale, Johns Hopkins, and University of California, Hegelian theology and social theory had gained distinguished American adherents even before the Civil War. Concord, Massachusetts; Milwaukee; Cincinnati; and St. Louis all had groups composed of prominent citizens devoted to Hegelian studies. The most successful Hegelian educator, William Harris, had studied Hegel as a theology student at Yale. He thereafter began a career that brought him to the positions of superintendent of schools in St. Louis, lifetime director of the National Education Association, and U.S. Commissioner of Education from 1889 to 1906. From his writings it is clear that Harris, like Denton J.

Snider and other American Hegelians, sought administrative power in order to create public policy. The St. Louis Hegelians pressed for a national program of public education that would stress individual discipline and the transmission of inherited cultural values. Harris himself was explicit in advocating the study of Hegel's social philosophy in public schools.

Nor is there any mistaking the emphatically anti-Marxist, antisocialist tone of the publications and speeches that the St. Louis Hegelians produced on social questions. Snider scolded the socialists for their "negative anti-Hegelian dialectic" and accused Marx of being a primitive who wished to shove the Western world back into Oriental despotism. Harris took a similarly critical position on Marxists in educational speeches and in his numerous articles for *Philosophical Review, Forum, Journal of Social Science,* and *Educational Review.*[93] He defended private property, the bourgeois family, and the teaching of individual self-reliance in his roles as an administrator and leader of the National Educational Association. He also took these stands as a Hegelian, indeed as America's best-known Hegelian until his death in 1909.

Such historical data show that Hegelian thinking was not a piece of exotica in American higher education by the time that our subjects went to school. American educators and philosophers once viewed Hegelianism as a possible civil religion and as a highly attractive system of ideas. That young radicals who later became conservatives had imbibed Hegelian thinking together with Marx seems to be a highly probable assumption. The presence of recognizably Hegelian views in the thinking and statements of postwar conservatives lends even further weight to the premise.

The passing of the historicist tradition of thinking from the postwar conservative movement has left a theoretical void that may eventually embarrass American conservatives. The intellectual Right has generally grown cold to the study of history, except as a means of assailing the far Left's revisionism.[94] Having by now largely lost a shared vision of the past, conservatives may soon find themselves without any vision except that of dehistoricized persons who seek to enrich themselves and the gross national product through the tireless pursuit of self-interest. Nor has the attempt to recover ancient truths by ignoring historical consciousness provided the intellectual Right with greater depth. John Lukacs notes the futility of trying to exclude historical memory from a historical civilization such as ours. In a comment that may be aimed at antihistorical conservatives and neoconservatives, he states, "My point is that there may be, after all, no such thing as 'pre-historic' and 'post-historic' man, but only historic man. . . ."[95] Leo Strauss's enterprise, raising spiritual horizons through an unmediated return to the ancients, was the most publicized attempt on the intellectual Right (or at least non-Left) to defuse social and cultural radicalism while dispensing with historical consciousness. It has produced results that Strauss himself might well have deplored. Observing the distance between abstract, ideal justice and human political practice, Strauss's students have easily reconciled themselves with the modern world. Their thinking has led not to a platonic contemplation of the Good, but into celebrating Lockean materialism, without even the older American leaven of Protestant moral theology.

Perhaps the solution to that problem and other problems addressed in this chapter may come from taking seriously Molnar's question about why the Left, unlike the Right, can inspire with its view of history. However much the Left may manipulate data to shape its version of a "meaningful past," it properly recognizes that men are influenced by knowledge of their antecedents. From the sixties on, the New Left has tried to revise American history; its supporters are certainly aware that what passes for "history" can affect human behavior and self-esteem. Both pride of identity and self-rejection often result from the way that we view our own group's past. Such radical historians as Howard Zinn, who depict white, middle-class male America as forever oppressing virtuous minorities, rely also on the sense of historical continuity.[96] By retelling our past differently from the way traditionalists, patriots, or even moderate reformers have done, radical historians seek to alter the perception, and therefore nature, of the national heritage. They understand that although historical interpretations do change, people continue to identify with their collective past. In the late nineteenth century, the educated and politically active elements in Western societies were predominantly in favor of overseas expansion into Asia and Africa. Today the same social groups lament, and even exaggerate, the uniquely Western evils inflicted on their countries' former colonial empires. But even Westerners who bitterly deplore Western imperialism deplore what they consider *their own* nation's or civilization's past. They, no less than the admirers of the West, recognize their inherited ties to a set of events and traditions that they have done little to bring about.

The major subjects of this study thought that they and their countrymen belonged to an evolving civilization that provided a moral legacy rather than a burden of guilt. None of them was a self-defined Hegelian, yet most of them, particularly Herberg and Voegelin, held to historically based theories of consciousness. They all accepted a belief that Sidney Hook ascribed to Hegelians, "No individual can make history de novo," although none of these thinkers embraced the social determinism that Hook also associates with Hegelianism.[97] Their history-mindedness stemmed not only from their understanding of reality as process, but also from their view of what moved others in Western society. As Herberg never tired of pointing out, the historical past mattered; what men thought about it would determine the regard in which they held themselves, their families, and their communities. According to Karl Löwith, Hegel viewed his schematization of history as a defense of "Christian bourgeois society."[98] Hegel's schematization was intended as a theoretical support for that integration of moral virtue, political authority, and individual freedom that he believed had developed out of his own civilization. The subjects of this investigation rallied also to a "Christian, bourgeois society" and through all their intellectual wandering and inconsistencies remained loyal to that cause.

# NOTES

## INTRODUCTION

1. See David Levy, "On Being Right: Reality, Utopia, and Tradition," *Continuity* 4/5 (Spring/Fall, 1982), 200.

2. Ibid., 201.

3. Burnham's references to the divine Logos, the Gospel of John, and the platonic-Christian heritage of the West were in a speech that I heard him deliver at the Ingersoll Prize Dinner in Chicago on 8 December 1983. His remarks were reprinted in *Chronicles of Culture VIII*, April 1984, 4–5.

4. See, for example, Karl A. Wittfogel, "Karl A. Wittfogel, "A Stronger Oriental Despotism," *China Quarterly* 1 (1960), 32; and "How Happy Are the Peasants?" *National Review*, 3 March 1972, 214–16.

5. James Burnham, "Why Does a Country Go Communist? (Bombay, 1951), 2.

6. Herberg's speech was subsequently published as "The Biblical Basis of American Democracy," *Thought* 30 (Spring 1955), 37.

7. "Why Does a Country Go Communist?," 3.

8. Quoted in William F. Buckley, Jr., ed., *Did You Ever See a Dream Walking? American Conservative Thought in the Twentieth Century* (New York, 1970), 216.

9. James Burnham, "Selective, Yes. Humanism, Maybe," *National Review*, 12 May 1972, 514.

10. Samuel T. Francis in a letter to the author, 6 May 1984.

11. Samuel T. Francis, *Power and History: The Political Thought of James Burnham* (Washington, D.C., 1984), 118. I rely here on Francis's recently published study because it broadly coincides with my own interpretation of the relationship of historicism to postwar conservatism.

12. See, for example, Peter Berger, "Democracy for Everyone?" *Commentary* 76 (September 1983), 31–36.

CHAPTER 1

1. Edmund Wilson, *To the Finland Station*, 2d. ed. (New York, 1956), particularly 188–98. This quotation can be found in Karl Marx's *Capital: A Critique of Political Economy*, trans. Ernest Untermann (New York, 1906), 25.

2. For statements of this view, cf. Herbert Marcuse, *Reason and Revolution: Hegel and the Rise of Social Theory* (Boston, 1960), 323–74; and Georg Lukács, *Die Zerstörung der Vernunft, György Lukacs Werke* (Neuwied am Rhein, 1962), vol. 11.

3. Isaiah Berlin, *Karl Marx*, 3d ed. (Oxford, 1963), 57.

4. Henning Ottmann, *Individuum und Gemeinschaft bei Hegel* (Berlin, 1977), particularly the introduction.

5. Ibid., 222–40.

6. Ibid., 300–37. For a centrist interpretation of Hegel in English, see my "On the Social Implications of the Hegelian Dialectic," *Journal of the History of Ideas* (July 1980), 421–32.

7. G. W. F. Hegel, *Werke in zwanzig Bänden*, vol. 7 (Frankfurt, 1970), 407–8.

8. Ibid., 501–6.

9. Ibid., 17:526.

10. Ibid., 535.

11. Ibid., 531.

12. For a representative statement of the mature Hegel's views on ecclesiastical polity, see *Werke*, 7:415–20.

13. This point is made most emphatically in the concluding section of Hegel's *Phenomenology of the Spirit*, in *Werke*, 3:589–91.

14. Hegel, *Werke*, 1:206.

15. G. W. F. Hegel, *Frühe politische Systeme*, ed. Gerhard Gohler (Frankfurt, 1974), 67–68.

16. Ibid., 74–77.

17. Ibid., 94.

18. Cf. Georg Lukács: *The Young Hegel*, trans. Rodney Livingston (London, 1975), 168–76.

19. Hegel, *Werke*, 7:388–98.

20. See Joachim Ritter's penetrating but unfortunately still untranslated essay "Subjektivität und industrielle Gesellschaft," *Subjektivität* (Frankfurt, 1974), 11–35.

21. Hegel, *Werke*, 12:529.

22. Ibid., 533.

23. Ibid., 531.

24. Karl Rosenkranz, *Hegel als deutscher Nationalphilosoph* (Leipzig, 1870), introduction and 300–47.

25. Ibid., 162.

26. Augusto Vera's plea for middle-class hegemony is found in his essay "La Souveraineté du Peuple," *Mélanges philosophiques* (Paris, 1862), 242–69.

27. Guido Oldrini, *Primo hegelismo italiano* (Florence, 1969), 82; and Guido Oldrini, *Augusto Vera e la corrente orthodossa* (Milan, 1964), passim.

28. See John Diggins, *Up From Communism* (New York, 1975), 290–91. Diggins correctly discerns the basic components of the Herbergian Weltanschaaung: biblical messianism and the Hegelian dialectic.

29. Augusto Vera, *Essais philosophiques* (Paris, 1864), 224.

30. See Will Herberg, "Historicism as Touchstone," in *Christian Century*, 16 March 1969, 311.

31. Augusto Vera, *Essais philosophiques*, 223–24, 226–44.

32. For a trenchant study of Gentilian epistemology, see Fazio Allmayer, *Ricerche hegeliane* (Florence, 1959), especially 30–42. The most comprehensive and intelligently sympathetic study on Gentile in English is H. S. Harris, *Social Philosophy of Giovanni Gentile* (Urbana, Ill., 1960).

33. Cited in *Ricerche hegeliane*, 32.

34. This attempted reduction of objective reality to the "constructive [actually self-constructing] process" of the subject takes place at the beginning of chapter 3 of *Theoria generale dello spirito come atto puro*, 4th ed. (Bari, 1924). An English translation, *The Theory of Mind as Pure Act* (London, 1922), was made by Wilden Carr soon after the appearance of the third edition.

35. See *Social Philosophy of Giovanni Gentile*, 22–65.

36. Giovanni Gentile, *Genesis and Structure of Society*, trans. H. S. Harris (Urbana, Ill., 1966), 121–34, 174–94.

37. In stated opposition to European conservatives, Gentile defined the state as "an eternal process of self-criticism" (*Genesis and Structure*, 168). See also *Social Philosophy of Giovanni Gentile*, 131–59.

38. Two essays that focus on Lukács's vitalism are Lee Congdon, "The Unexpected Revolutionary: Lukács' Road to Marx," *Survey* 20 (1974), 176–205, and my own "Lukács' *Young Hegel* Revisited," *Marxist Perspectives*, Winter 1979–1980, 144–56.

39. Two examples of this critical perspective can be found in Thomas Molnar, *Theists and Atheists: A Typology of Non-Belief* (The Hague, 1980), and in Molnar, "Au Coeur du Marxisme: La Dialectique," *La pensée catholique*, November 1978, 33–53.

40. For examples of conservatives who assume a priori the validity of a Marxist-Hegelian reading of Hegel, see Barry Cooper, "Ideology, Technology, and Truth," in *The Ethical Dimension of Political Life: Essays in Honor of John H. Hallowell* (Durham, N.C., 1983), 138–56; and , in the same volume, Gerhart Niemeyer, "Communism and the Notion of the Good," 156–66.

41. Denton J. Snider, *Social Institutions* (St. Louis, 1901), 279–80.

42. See Konrad H. Jarausch, *Students, Society, and Politics in Imperial Germany: The Rise of Academic Illiberalism* (Princeton, 1981), 161, 209; and Charles McClelland, *State Society and University in Germany, 1700–1914* (Cambridge, 1980).

43. See William H. Goetzmann's introductory essay to *The American Hegelians*, ed. Goetzmann (New York, 1973), 3–19; and Frances Harmon, *The Social Philosophy of St. Louis Hegelians* (New York, 1943), 4–7.

44. Denton J. Snider, *Social Institutions*, 277.

45. W. T. Harris, "The Definition of Social Science and the Classification of the Topics Belonging to Its Several Provinces," *Journal of Social Science* 22 (June 1887), 1–2.

46. *Social Institutions*, 277.

47. N. K. Krupskaya, *Reminiscences of Lenin*, trans. Bernard Isaacs (New York, 1970), 180.

48. I have consulted the Italian edition of this wartime work, which seems more comprehensive than the English one. See V. I. Lenin, *Quaderni filosofici* (Milan,

1958), 92.

49. Lucio Colletti, *Il Marxismo e Hegel* (Rome), 2:167–69.

50. Two attempts to correct the abuse of Hegel's picture of the master-slave relationship in the *Phenomenology* (a relationship that Hegel saw as a timeless problem of consciousness, not as a function of economic conflict) are "Lukács' *Young Hegel* Revisited," *Marxist Perspectives* 2 (Winter 1979–1980), 148–49; and Quentin Lauer, *A Reading of Hegel's Phenomenology of the Spirit* (New York, 1976), 109.

## CHAPTER 2

1. Robert A. Nisbet, *Tradition and Revolt: Historical and Sociological Essays* (New York, 1970), 4–5.

2. Ibid., particularly 76–84.

3. Thomas Molnar, *Le dieu immanent: La grande tentation de la pensée allemande* (Paris, 1982), 49; see also ibid., 31, 46–48.

4. Max Eastman, *Reflections on the Failure of Socialism* (New York, 1955), 73.

5. André Glucksmann, *Les maîtres-penseurs* (Paris, 1977), replicates Eastman's argument that Marx was "the son of Hegel," yet there is no evidence that Glucksmann plagiarized Eastman, whom he may never have read.

6. On Morris's thinking and activities, see M. E. Jones, *George Sylvester Morris: His Philosophical Career and Theistic Idealism* (New York, 1948).

7. John Dewey, *Experience and Nature* (Chicago, 1925), 402.

8. John Dewey, *Psychology* (Chicago, 1887).

9. See Richard Bernstein, *John Dewey* (New York, 1966), 11–16.

10. Sidney Hook, John Dewey: An Intellectual Portrait, 2d ed. (Westport, Conn., 1971), 13.

11. Ibid., 14–15.

12. Sidney Hook, "Dialectic in Social and Historical Inquiry," *Journal of Philosophy* 36 (6 July 1939), 371.

13. Ibid., 378.

14. John Dewey, "From Absolutism to Experimentalism," in *Contemporary American Philosophy,* ed. G. P. Adams and W. P. Montague (New York, 1930), 2:18.

15. See William H. Goetzmann's introductory essay in *The American Hegelians,* 8–9.

16. G. W. F. Hegel, *Werke in zwanzig Bänden* (Frankfurt, 1970), 12:114.

17. *The American Hegelians,* 14. The earliest detailed account of the Movement is Denton J. Snider, *The St. Louis Movement in Philosophy, Literature, Education, Psychology, with Chapters of Autobiography* (St. Louis, 1920).

18. Denton J. Snider, *The State,* 529–30.

19. See, for example, ibid., 485–96.

20. Denton J. Snider, *Abraham Lincoln* (St. Louis, 1908); and *The American Ten Years War* (St. Louis, 1906), 50–53.

21. See David Herreshoff, *American Disciples of Marx: From the Age of Jackson to the Progressive Era* (Detroit, 1967), especially 30, 54, and 57, for a sketch of Marx's relationship to early American socialists, including Willich.

22. Quoted from Lloyd D. Easton, *Hegel's First American Followers* (Athens, Ohio,

1966), 320.

23. For the most widely studied product of late-nineteenth-century English Hegelianism, see T. H. Green, *Lectures in the Principles of Political Obligation* (London, 1985).

24. See Irving Babbitt, *The New Laokoon: An Essay on the Confusion of the Arts* (Boston, 1910), 217–52. An attempt to reconcile Babbitt and Croce through a historically tested doctrine of moral will can be found in Claes G. Ryn's *Will, Imagination, and Reason* (Chicago, 1985).

25. Merle Curti, *Social Ideas of American Education* (New York, 1935), 312–13.

26. Ibid., 329.

27. A product of the World War I Teutonophobia that prefigured and influenced the later American wave of anti-Hegel polemics was L. T. Hobhouse's *The Metaphysical Theory of the State* (London, 1918).

28. Herbert Marcuse, *Reason and Revolution: Hegel and the Rise of Social Theory* (New York, 1941), vii.

29. See the review of Sidney Hook's *Philosophy and Public Policy* by Werner J. Dannhauser, *Commentary* 70 (October 1980), 74–77; and the one by Constantine Fitzgibbon, *Encounter* 55 (November, 1980), 71–74.

30. Sidney Hook, *From Hegel to Marx: Studies in the Intellectual Development of Karl Marx*, 2d ed. (New York, 1950), 36.

31. Ibid., 35.

32. Ibid., 42–43.

33. Ibid., 52.

34. Ibid., 57.

35. This theme of the non-Marxist materialist, Engels, who corrupted Lenin can be found in the work of Max Horkheimer, George Lichtheim, and other thinkers once associated with the Frankfurt School for Social Research. Recently the same idea has been revived by a historian who obviously admires the Frankfurt School but who has had the temerity to try to prove an untenable proposition. See David McLellan, *Friedrich Engels* (New York, 1977).

36. See Licio Colletti, *From Rousseau to Lenin: Studies in Ideology and Society*, trans. John Merrington and Judith White (London, 1972).

37. See Sidney Hook, *Marxism and Beyond* (Totowa, N.J., 1983), 96.

38. Ibid., 9.

39. G. W. F. Hegel, *Werke in zwanzig Bänden* (Frankfurt, 1970), 8:177.

40. See Carl J. Friedrich, *The Philosophy of Law in Historical Perspective* (Chicago, 1958), 131–36.

41. Hegel, *Werke*, 7:83.

42. See Louis Dumont, *La civilisation indienne et nous* (Paris, 1964), 36–42.

43. See, for example, Hook, *Marxism and Beyond*, vii–ix. The same tendency to cover up Marx's belief in violence by depicting him as a humanitarian democrat who lived in unjust times is unmistakably present in Hook's *Toward the Understanding of Karl Marx* (New York, 1933).

44. Hook, *Marxism and Beyond*, ix.

45. Will Herberg, "Parties under Workers' Rule," *Workers Age* IV (4 May 1935), 5. See also Sidney Hook, "On Workers' Democracy," *Modern Monthly* 8 (October 1934), 529–44.

46. Will Herberg, "Workers' Democracy or Dictatorship," *Workers Age* 3 (15 December 1934), 3.

47. *Workers Age* 4 (4 May 1935), 5.

48. Sidney Hook, *The Hero in History: A Study in Limitation and Possibility* (New York, 1943).

49. Quoted in Leon Trotsky, *In Defense of Marxism* (New York, 1973), 207.

50. For a probing study of Hook's political and intellectual evolution, see Lewis S. Feuer, "The Pragmatic Wisdom of Sidney Hook," *Encounter* 44 (October 1975), 37–45. Although my analysis of Hook largely coincides with Feuer's, I have emphasized more than he has the palimpsest quality of Hook's thinking. Whereas Feuer sees distinctive stages in Hook's philosophical development as he went from Marxism to pragmatism, I have been struck by Hook's retention of early beliefs. Feuer too is aware of these doctrinal overlaps but stresses them less than I do.

## CHAPTER 3

1. W. H. in conversation with the author, 12 October 1971.

2. Will Herberg, "Theory of Relativity and Dialectical Materialism," *Revolutionary Age* 2 (27 December 1930), 3, 4.

3. For an account of the birth of American Trotskyism, see Theodore Draper's *American Communism and Soviet Russia* (New York, 1960), particularly 375–76.

4. W. H. in conversation with the author, 20 March 1972.

5. Although a prominent spokesman for the Young Communist League in the twenties, Herberg was reduced to a nonperson in post-1929 American Communist annals. William Z. Foster's official *History of the Communist Party of the United States* ignores him entirely and refers only in passing to Herbert Zam and Benjamin Gitlow, both leading Lovestoneites. Foster was the American Communist whom Stalin chose to replace Charles E. Ruthenberg, the first party chairman, who had died in 1927. Moscow's choice was ultimately imposed after American Communists had opted for a Lithuanian Jewish intellectual and friend of Herberg's, Jay Lovestone.

Theodore Draper's *American Communism and Soviet Russia* (New York, 1960) provides useful information on Herberg's career, first in the Young Communist League and later among the Lovestoneites. So, too, does John Diggins's *Up from Communism* (New York, 1975), which perceptively notes—see especially page 156—the hollow quality of Herberg's Lovestoneite defense of intellectual dissent in light of his (and Lovestone's) intolerance of the Trotskyists. According to Lewis Coser and Irving Howe, *The American Communist Party: A Critical History* (Boston, 1957), 144–75, the Stalinist campaign against Herberg and other Lovestoneites was part of an attempt to "bolshevize" the American organization. The Soviet choice of Foster and the subsequent hounding of the Lovestoneites from the Communist Party took place after Stalin had triumphed over Trotsky and while he was still fighting Bukharin. These actions were taken at a critical juncture: while Stalin was still solidifying his support against an opponent who had attacked his first Five Year Plan and his centralization of the Russian party structure.

6. As John Diggins correctly observes: "Herberg and the Lovestoneites wanted Stalinism without Stalin." Cf. *Up from Communism*, 157. See also Herberg's "The

Case of Leon Trotsky," *Workers Age* 6 (18 December 1937), 3–6.

7. This fact should be stressed since the biographical note on him in *Contemporary Authors* (Detroit, 1978), 115, states that "after leaving the Communist Party in 1929, he became an outspoken conservative." Perhaps the author of this entry may consider "conservative" Herberg's outspoken opposition to Moscow. Nonetheless, from 1929 down to the late thirties, Herberg remained a Marxist, albeit one critical of the Soviet regime.

8. See James O. Morris, *Conflict within the A.F.L.: A Study of Craft vs. Industrialism, 1901–1938* (New York, 1958).

9. *The C.I.O. and Labor's New Challenge* (New York, Communist Party, U.S.A., 1937), 19, 20.

10. Ibid., 13. For information on the Knights of Labor, see Chapter 3 of Gerald N. Grob, *Workers and Utopia: A Study of Ideological Conflicts in the American Labor Movement, 1865–1900* (New York, 1961).

11. W. H. in conversation with the author, 20 March 1972.

12. *The N.R.A. and American Labor* (New York, Communist Party, U.S.A., 1933), 11.

13. Ibid., 18.

14. *The C.I.O. and Labor's New Challenge*, 12. One the relationship of the Communist Party to the American union movement, see Bert Cochran, *Labor and Communism* (Princeton, 1977).

15. *The C.I.O. and Labor's New Challenge*, 20.

16. Ibid., 23.

17. Interview with the author, 20 March 1972.

18. *Antioch Review* 3 (Spring 1943), 132.

19. Ibid., 131.

20. Ibid., 127. The distinction I have made between Hegel's and Marx's dialectic follows primarily from my reading of Marx's *1844 Manuscripts (Die Pariser Manuskripte)* and the *Grundrisse* to the first edition of *Capital*. On the divergent meanings that Marx and Hegel assigned to the term *Aufhebung* ("rescinding" or "sublation"), see my essay "On the Social Implications and Context of the Hegelian Dialectic," *Journal of the History of Ideas* 61, no. 3 (Fall 1980), 421–32, and Karl Löwith, *Von Hegel zu Nietzsche* (Stuttgart, 1950), 151–53, 301–4. A countertendency can be found among some Marxist intellectuals who associate communist society, once the state has truly withered away, with a return at a higher level to primitive communitarianism. Such a view may possibly be inferred from Engels's *The Origin of the Family, Private Property, and the State,* which takes from the American anthropologist Lewis H. Morgan an idyllic picture of communal life among the Iroquois. Yet, such musings on social life before even the earliest, or patriarchal, mode of production played no discernible role in Marx's thought. His *Grundrisse* deals with the five modes of production and contains no idealization at all of primitive communitarian life. Indeed, Marx spent many years fighting such an idealization, which prevailed among the anarchists, and affirming the unique, modern character of his own "scientifically" predicted communism.

Two more points may be relevant for any consideration of Marx's possible belief in a future return at a higher level to prepolitical communitarianism. In the first place, Engels wrote most of *Origin of the Family* after Marx's death, publishing it in 1884. It is also doubtful whether even this work attempts to depict a primeval foreshadowing of life under communism. The main themes for Engels here are the institution of monogamy and the rise of the state. The latter is tied to the former, since, according to Engels by way of Morgan, the struggle for property between the patrilinear and matrilinear descendants of the same families ends in the victory of the strong, the privatization of property, and the establishment of the state to enforce these arrangements. Engels saw primitive communism as an intermediate phase between nomadic tribal life and the emergence of the state and monogamy. Whether Engels viewed this gentile society (in which property was vested collectively in the matrilinear *gens*) as a blueprint for the socialist future is entirely open to question.

21. Aileen S. Kraditor recalls (in converstation with the author 27 July 1983) that when she was a Party member in the late forties and fifties, it was the belief propagated by the Party that once the proletariat had achieved its revolution and dictatorship, society would return to a *nonpolitical* form of communism, but at a higher level than in Engel's primitive matriarchy. In Herberg's case this teaching may have been grafted onto an essentially Hegelian vision of the dialectic, although, according to Adam Ulam, communist parties have usually emphasized antimodern themes to capture the working class, particularly in France, from the anarchists. Marx's appeal to scientific progress and to a rationally organized industrial world has always been less attractive to European workers than the anarchist myth (which the communists have occasionally appropriated) of a return to some preindustrial, prepolitical community. See Adam Ulam, *The Unfinished Revolution* rev. ed. (Boulder, Colo., 1979), 318.

22. *Antioch Review* 3 (Fall 1943), 406.

23. *National Review* 29, no. 30 (5 August 1977) 880–86.

24. Herberg, "From Marxism to Judaism," *Commentary* 3 (January 1947), 25.

25. These sermons have been published in Will Herberg, *Faith Enacted as History: Essays in Biblical Theology*, ed. Bernhard W. Anderson (Philadelphia, 1976).

26. Will Herberg, "Historicism as Touchstone," *Christian Century* 77 (16 March 1960), 313.

27. John Diggins, *Up from Communism*, 290.

28. Will Herberg, *Judaism and Modern Man* (New York, 1973), 193–95.

29. Ibid., 155.

30. Ibid., 157.

31. Ibid., 161

32. Ibid., VII.

33. Ibid., 137.

34. Ibid., 243–52.

35. Ibid., 225.

36. On Hegel's understanding of the Trinity in the *Phenomenology,* see Quentin Lauer's *A Reading of Hegel's Phenomenology of the Spirit* (New York, 1976), 246–55. Although Lauer downplays the total identification made between the divine personality and the historical process, this connection seems to be basic to Hegel's theologizing.

37. See "The Biblical Basis of American Democracy," *Thought* 30 (Spring 1955), 37.

38. Will Herberg, *Protestant, Catholic, Jew* (Garden City, N.Y., 1959), 270.

39. Ibid., 269.

40. Ibid., 1–5, 245–49.

41. For a summing up of the critical objections raised to Herberg's thesis about America as a national community with "three religious subdivisions," see J. A. Winter, *Continuities in the Sociology of Religion* (New York, 1977), 197–229; also Gerhard Lenski, *The Religious Factor: A Sociological Study of Religion's Impact on Politics, Economics, and Family Life* (Garden City, N.Y., 1963).

42. Andrew Greeley and Peter Rossi, *The Education of Catholic Americans* (Chicago, 1966), contains both empirical evidence and historical observations on this topic.

43. On contemporary American Jewish society, see Jacob Neusner, *Stranger at Home: The Holocaust, Zionism, and American Judaism* (Chicago, 1981). An indication of the growing dissatisfaction of Jewish intellectuals with the hyphenated identity "American-Jewish" is the spate of historical literature, mostly by American Jews, that either stresses the pervasive anti-Semitism of American society since the nineteenth century or implicates the American people and government in the Nazi Holocaust. Lucy S. Davidowicz, in *Commentary* 75, no. 6 (June 1983), 36–45, discusses how the American Jewish Commission on the Holocaust, organized under Arthur Goldberg in 1981, unfairly indicted American Jews and American Christians for responsibility in allowing the Holocaust to occur. She astutely observes that cooperation took place between anti-American radicals and certain right-wing Zionists in producing the commission's widely publicized findings. On the growing tendency of American-Jewish historiography to focus on the Jewish experience of persecution in America, see the comments of Jonathan D. Sarna in *Commentary* 71, no. 3 (March 1981), 42–47. Regarding recent trends in the interpretation of American Jewish history (mostly by Jews), Sarna notes: "As these books demonstrate, we have moved in just half a century from the myth that America is different to the myth that America is not different at all. By itself this transformation speaks volumes about loss of faith in American institutions and dreams" (46).

44. See, for example, "Civil Rights and Violence," *National Review* 17, no. 36 (7 September 1965), 769–76; "The Case for Heterosexuality," *National Review* 21, no. 39 (7 October 1969) 1007–9; and "Limits of Pluralism," *National Review* 23, no. 7 (23 February 1971), 198–9. Nathan Glazer, in a published eulogy, noted accurately, "Herberg saw the virtues of the American way of life (even when capitalized) as he also saw its distance from religious faith." *National Review*, 29, 30 (5 August 1977), 882.

45. G. W. F. Hegel, *Werke in zwanzig Bänden* (Frankfurt, 1970), 7:424–6.

46. Peter J. Stanlis, *Edmund Burke and the Natural Law* (Ann Arbor, 1965), 3–14.

47. Will Herberg, "Natural Law and History in Burke's Thought," *Modern Age* 3, no. 3 (Summer 1959), 325.

48. See Frank S. Meyer's worried libertarian response to this revival of Burke within what he styles the New Conservatism in *In Defense of Freedom* (Chicago, 1962), 40–53, 132–34. Meyer scolds the New Conservatives for, among other things, being Hegelians entrenched behind Burkean slogans.

49. See *Edmund Burke and the Natural Law*, especially 195–230.

50. Will Herberg, "Natural Law and History in Burke's Thought," 328.

51. Ibid., 327. Stanlis, in point of fact, makes exactly the same argument as Herberg about Burke as a historical conservative. Although Stanlis overlooks certain interpre-

tive distinctions between, on the one side, Aquinas and, on the other, Burke and Rudolf Stammler, his own reading of Burke is entirely consistent with Herberg's. For example, according to Stanlis, "Burke conceived of Natural Law with a changing content and dynamic method, guided by the principles of prudence, subject to growth by the recognition of new values, emerging from the historical development of civilization." See *Edmund Burke and the Natural Law*, 112.

52. It is of course true that Stammler, according to the French jurist, François Geny, rebelled against Hegelian thinkers of the late nineteenth century and admired Immanuel Kant for his universalist legal and moral teachings. All the same, Stammler's doctrine of "natural law with a changing content" and his attempted mediation between the Enlightenment's rationalism and romantic historicism have caused him to be sometimes identified with the historicist interpretations of law. See John C. H. Wu's appendix "Stammler and His Critics" in Rudolf Stammler's *The Theory of Justice*, trans. Isaac Husik (New York, 1925), 553–87.

53. Herberg, who had read Husik's translation of *Lehrbuch der Rechtsphilosophie*, respected Stammler's attempt to define universal ethical norms within changing cultural circumstances.

54. Will Herberg, "Reinhold Niebuhr: Burkean Conservative," *National Review*, 11, no. 22 (2, December 1961), 379.

55. See, for example, the comment about progress that Herberg cites from Jacques Maritain and then applies to Aquinas and Burke, in "Natural Law and History in Burke's Thought," 327. In 1973 both Peter Stanlis and I held discussions with Herberg (at different times) about Ruth A. Bevan's *Marx and Burke: A Revisionist View* (LaSalle, Ill., 1973). Although we deplored what seemed Bevan's forced attempt to find a parallel between Burke's view of historical continuity and Marx's dialectical materialism, Herberg, by contrast, found her discussion "extremely fruitful."

56. The outline, which I received from Herberg, was for a graduate tutorial scheduled at Drew for the first semester, 1973–1974.

57. Herberg's graduate student Donald G. Jones states in a eulogy for *National Review* (5 August 1977), 886: "Many of us learned in a dialogue with Will Herberg not just the structure of Hegel's system or the thought of Augustine, but equally important the historical, philosophical and theological bearing of our own thought." This comment is noteworthy since Herberg considered both Augustine and Hegel to be major influences on the Western historicist tradition.

In all fairness, it should be mentioned that Herberg delivered a paper critical of Hegel at the Princeton Theological Seminary in fall 1969. This address, "Hegel and His Influence on Biblican Theology," is included in the anthology *Faith Enacted as History*, whose distinguished editor, Bernhard W. Anderson, discusses it in the introduction. In the address Herberg held Hegel accountable, in varying degrees, for distorted explanations of Scripture. Implicit in the Hegelian view of history were supposedly nationalist understandings of the Old Testament, dialectical theories of the primitive church, and modernist and selective readings of Scripture or its identification with "the endless process of development itself" (128). Among those descendants of Hegel whom Herberg criticizes is Gerhard von Rad, a German exponent of process theology. Despite von Rad's earlier influence on Herberg's view of redemptive history, Herberg now faults him for understanding Scripture as "development without a historical religious center." In this failing von Rad resembled Buber, who "saw the Old Testament as a religious movement without a center."

Anderson is justified in calling to our attention Herberg's explicit reservations about Hegel during his later religious phase. He also properly observes, in his introductory essay (22), that Herberg, unlike von Rad and even Buber, was concerned with the "concrete historical reality" of biblical narrative. Yet, must one assume that Herberg's concern with the facticity of Scripture in 1969 held the same overriding importance for him when he composed *Judaism and Modern Man* in 1951? What evidence, if any, is there that he distrusted Hegel throughout his religious period for corrupting biblical commentators, including Martin Buber? Significantly, Herberg's brief against Hegel even in 1969 ends with the scales tilted in the philosopher's favor. Although "his influence on biblical studies has not been an unequivocally happy one," the author notes, "the incredible extent of his knowledge, the breadth, penetration, and depth of his thinking, his unparalleled capacity for system-building—these constitute one of the chief glories of the Western mind" (129–30).

58. This essay is reprinted in *Faith Enacted as History*, 132–37.

59. Ibid., 135.

60. See especially Benedetto Croce, *My Philosophy and Other Essays on the Moral and Political Problems of Our Time*, trans. E. F. Carritt (London, 1949).

61. Giovanni Gentile, *Teoria generale dello spirito come atto puro* (Bari, 1924), 172, 173.

62. Ibid., 179.

63. *National Review* 29, no. 14 (15 April 1977), 429.

64. The socialist scholar Lucio Colletti has criticized the romantic naturalist strain in the thinking of Hegel, Engels, and Lenin. See Colletti's two-volume work *Marxism and Hegel*, trans. Lawrence Garner (New York, 1973).

65. *Revolutionary Age* 2 (27 December 1930), 3.

66. Sidney Hook, *Marxism and Beyond* (Totowa, N.J., 1983), 217.

## CHAPTER 4

1. The initials of *Kommunistische Partei Deutschlands* (German Communist Party).

2. Although Hegel did see Judaism, Christianity, and Hellenism as all contributing to the Germanic world, he associated their origins with earlier civilizations. By contrast, Wittfogel has usually presented the Jews and Greeks as prototypically Western.

3. *Unter dem Banner des Marxismus* 5, no. 3 (1931), 347; this journal is henceforth cited as *U.B.M.*

4. Ibid., 348.

5. Ibid., 349.

6. Ibid., 351–54.

7. Wittfogel had developed his germinal views on the Asian mode of production as early as 1924. See his comments on the Chinese and Indian bureaucratic states, both of which are called *"Wasserbau-bürokratische Regierungen* (hydraulic-bureaucratic regimes)," in *Geschichte der bürgerlichen Gesellschaft* (Vienna, 1924), 116–19.

8. *U.B.M.* 5, no. 3, 361; see also Wittfogel's study "Karl Marx über China und Indien," *U.B.M.* 1, no. 2 (1927), 274–389.

9. Wittfogel's longest work on China, *Wirschaft und Gesellschaft Chinas* (Leipzig, 1931),

contains sparse but complimentary references to Hegel; see especially 19–20.

10. *U.B.M.* 3, no. 1 (1929), 485–92.

11. Ibid., 494.

12. Ibid., 495.

13. See *U.B.M.* 2, no. 3, 361. Wittfogel enumerates all the references to Chinese civilization found in Hegel's published writing and also makes learned allusions to *The Science of Logic*. He recommends Hegel's voluminous comments on China and notes that their quantity is sufficiently distinctive and specific to reach that point at which, in Hegelian logic, mere bulk acquires a qualitative aspect. Such erudition obviously resulted from a serious study of Hegel's thought, and certainly not from memorizing those stock phrases from his work that Communist partisans may trot out *dans les grandes occasions*.

14. See G. L. Ulmen's short biographical sketch in the preface to his *Society and History: Essays in Honor of Karl August Wittfogel* (The Hague, 1978).

15. Although the Hegelian simile is my own, Wittfogel approved of it. On the existential background of his *chef d'oeuvre*, see the 1962 preface of *Oriental Despotism: A Comparative Study of Total Power* (New Haven, 1963).

16. Although *Oriental Despotism* treats the Hebrews and Western European Christians as peoples who avoided the "massive theocratic structures" characteristic of hydraulic societies, Wittfogel linked this good fortune to the geographical environment in which they settled. For a more "idealistic" and sympathetic view of the Western religious heritage, see Karl Wittfogel's remarks in *Relations between East and West in the Middle Ages*, ed. Derek Baker (Edinburgh, 1973).

17. *Oriental Despotism*, 197, 209–10.

18. Ibid., 91–92, 150–51.

19. Ibid., 139–45, 149, 448–49.

20. Ibid., 77, 91–92, 194. Wittfogel offers a provocative contrast between the differing fates of China and Europe. Although those nomadic tribes that periodically overran north China were eventually absorbed into the "agro-despotic power structure," "the marginal hydraulic society of Western Rome collapsed under tribal attacks, and non-Oriental forms of government and society emerged" (194).

21. Wittfogel makes these points explicit in *Oriental Despotism* (369–401). He contends that Marx and Lenin abandoned their theories of an Asian form of production for tactical, revolutionary reasons. Both came to believe that the possibility for revolutionary activity outside the West required them to swallow theoretical-scientific scruples and to draw exaggerated comparisons between Western and non-Western social development.

22. Wittfogel, "Marxism, Anarchism, and the New Left," *Modern Age* 14, no. 2 (Spring 1970), 122.

23. Karl Popper, *The Open Society and Its Enemies*, 2 (New York: Harper Torchbook Edition, 1962), 27–80.

24. See, for example, David Levy "Karl Popper: His Philosophy of Politics," *Modern Age* 22, no. 2 (Spring 1978), 151–60.

25. F. A. Hayek, *The Counter-Revolution of Science: Studies on the Abuse of Reason* (London: Free Press Paperback, 1964), 191–206.

26. *Oriental Despotism*, 370.

27. Ibid., 372.

28. Ibid., 416.

29. Two German classics that treat the continuity of Hegel's impact on Marx's social theory are Johann Plenge, *Marx and Hegel* (Tübingen, 1911), and Paul Vogel, *Hegels Gesellschaftsbegriff und seine geschichtliche Fortbildung durch Lorenz Stein, Marx, Engels, und Lassalle* (Berlin, 1925).

30. The Wittfogels made these remarks about Godwin during a conversation with me on 8 February 1974. The only printed discussion of Godwin published by Wittfogel that I can find is in "Marxism, Anarchism, and the New Left," *Modern Age* 14, no. 2 (Spring 1970), 116–17.

31. Hayek, *The Counter-Revolution of Science*, 192–94.

32. Ibid., 199. Although Hayek does express an intellectual debt to Popper on the page cited, the study of Popper's to which he alludes is not the stridently anti-Hegelian *Open Society and Its Enemies*, but the more subdued *Poverty of Historicism* (London, 1961). The latter work, which sets out to refute historical determinism, began as a seminar paper delivered before Hayek at the London School of Economics in the late thirties. Although Popper was then a democratic socialist and Hayek a classical liberal, the two men thereafter became lifelong friends.

33. Cf. F. A. Hayek's introductory essays to J. S. Mill's *Spirit of the Age* (Chicago, 1942). Admiration for Adam Smith abounds in most of Hayek's work on social theory; see, for instance, his best-selling *Road to Serfdom* (Chicago, 1944), 13, 34, 39.

34. Other scholars have stressed Adam Smith's and J. S. Mill's significance for Marx's theory of an Asian mode of production, while totally ignoring Hegel's *Philosophy of History*. See, for example, Boris I. Nicolaevsky, "Marx and Lenin on Oriental Despotism," in Ulmen, *Society and History*, 85–91. Nicolaevsky, a social democratic émigré who wrote this essay originally in Russian in 1958, may himself have been affected by the discrediting of Hegel that started during the Second World War. Although Popper's polemics against Hegel were among the most widely read, other anti-Hegelian tracts were published between 1941 and 1945. Herbert Marcuse's *Reason and Revolution*, which was written during the war, sought to reclaim Hegel for the Left, but not necessarily for the democratic Left.

Another essay in the aforementioned festschrift, which mentions but fails to analyze Hegel's contribution to Wittfogel's thought, is Angel Palerm, "Sobre el mondo asiatico de produccion y la teoria de la sociedad oriental: Marx y Wittfogel," in Ulmen, *Society and History*, 15–85. Nicolaevsky and Palerm may both have been following Wittfogel's lead. Wittfogel's essay, "The Ruling Bureaucracy of Oriental Despotism: A Phenomenon That Paralyzed Marx" in *Review of Politics* 15, no. 3 (July 1953), 350–59, goes beyond his later volume on this subject in totally ignoring Hegel's putative role in the formation of Marx's theory of oriental despotism. Nor does he refer, as he later will, to his earlier views on Hegel, even for the purpose of admitting a "mistake."

35. George Nash, *The Conservative Intellectual Movement in America since 1945*, 112–14, 273, 295–98, 375–76, 432–33.

36. John Diggins, *Up from Communism*, 430, 504.

37. See the appeal to American destiny in the opening editorial note of the *Journal of Speculative Philosophy* 1, no. 1 (1867), 1.

38. Lee Benson, *Turner and Beard* (Glencoe, Ill., 1980), 50–72.

39. See Jeffrey Hart, *The American Dissent* (New York, 1966), 189.

40. David Collier in conversation with the author, 30 June 1983.

## CHAPTER 5

1. Jeffrey Hart, *When the Going Was Good! American Life in the Fifties* (New York, 1982), 3–16, 270–92.

2. See especially David Riesman, *The Lonely Crowd*, 8th ed. (New York, 1958), 36–52; and Helmut Schelsky's fine introduction to the German edition, *Die einsame Masse. Eine Untersuchung der Wandlungen des amerikanischen Charakters* (Rembek, 1962).

3. A work that investigates the background of "liberal" anti-Communism, mostly in the 1930s, is Frank Warren, *Liberals and Communism* (Bloomington, Ind., 1966). Sidney Hook, in *Political Power and Personal Freedom* (New York, 1959.), tries to make the case that democratic socialists are the most principled and reliable anti-communists. The Congress for Cultural Freedom (CCF) in the 1950s provided a *point de ralliement* for anti-Communist, Left-democratic intellectuals such as Arthur M. Schlesinger, Jr., Sidney Hook, Irving Kristol, and (for a short time) even J. K. Galbraith, as well as for more conservative writers like John Chamberlain and James Burnham. For a critique from the Left of the CCF, see Christopher Lasch, *The Agony of the Left* (New York, 1969).

4. On the question of conservative cosmology, see my "On the European Roots of Modern American Conservatism," *Thought* 55, no. 217 (June 1980), 196–206.

5. This statement on Niebuhr's influence can be found in, among other places, John Diggins's *Up from Communism*, in the captions below the photographs of Niebuhr and Schlesinger opposite page 300.

6. Reinhold Niebuhr, *The Irony of American History* (New York, 1952), 128.

7. Reinhold Niebuhr, *Man's Nature and His Communities* (New York, 1959), 157.

8. Reinhold Niebuhr, *The Structure of Nations and Empires* (New York, 1959), 157.

9. Ibid., 156.

10. G. W. F. Hegel, *Werke in zwanzig Bänden* (Frankfurt, 1970), 1:577–81.

11. Ibid., 7:500.

12. Niebuhr, *The Structure of Nations and Empires*, 152–153.

13. Ibid., 168.

14. Ibid., 158, 166.

15. Hegel, *Werke*, 3:348.

16. Quentin Lauer, *A Reading of Hegel's Phenomenology of the Spirit* (New York, 1976), 186.

17. Niebuhr, *The Structure of Nations and Empires*, 242.

18. Hegel, *Werke*, 12:52–56.

19. Reinhold Niebuhr, *The Nature and Destiny of Man*, one-volume ed. (New York, 1974), part 2: 167, 301.

20. Joachim Radkau, *Die deutsche Emigration in den U.S.A.: Ihr Einfluss auf die amerikanische Europapolitik 1933–1945* (Dusseldorf, 1971), 214–23, 268–81.

21. See Hans Morgenthau, "The Evil of Politics and the Ethics of Evil, *Ethics* 56, (October 1945), 4.

22. See Hans Morgenthau, *Science: Servant or Master?* (New York, 1972), 70; and John Coffey, *Political Realism in American Thought* (Lewisburg, 1977), 133.

23. For Rosenstock-Huessy's demand for a "harsh peace" against Germany, see *Christianity and Crisis*, 24 July 1944, 8.

24. Stephan Possony, "Defeatism," *Review of Politics* 4 (January 1942), 52.

25. See George Nash, *The Conservative Intellectual Movement in America since 1945*, 268–73,

370–71. Nash adds Gehart Niemeyer, the Christian philosopher and interpreter of Eric Voegelin, to the list of Central European émigrés who called for bolder policies to stop Soviet imperialism. Because of the philosophical emphasis of most of Niemeyer's work, I have not listed him among the conservative realists who devoted themselves largely to international relations.

26. James Burnham, *The Machiavellians: Defenders of Freedom* (Chicago, 1963), especially 251–305.

27. See Stefan Possony , *A Century of Conflict: Communist Techniques of World Revolution, 1848–1950* (Chicago, 1953), especially the concluding admonitions (419–22).

28. See Strauz-Hupé's contribution to *Protracted Conflict* (New York: Harper Colophon Edition, 1963), 4. That volume is the fruit of a seminar sponsored by the Foreign Policy Research Institute.

29. Ibid., 5.

30. As illustrations of the "hardline" anti-Soviet policies advocated by conservative realists, see the epilogue to *Protracted Conflict*, 152–78, which calls for turning the NATO defense into an "enduring partnership" and for resisting "psychological manipulation" by the Soviets. These positions also represent the boldest points in Possony's plan for a war of attrition against the Soviets in *A Century of Conflict*. Another anti-Communist émigré, Stephen Kertesz, in *East Central Europe and the World* (Notre Dame, 1962), 1–21, likewise stresses the need for a propaganda initiative against the Soviets. Moreover, in the wake of the brutally suppressed Hungarian uprising of 1956, Burnham proposed a deal with Soviet Russia to achieve the neutralization of Central Europe. See Burnham's comment "Sighting the Target," *National Reivew* 2 (29 December 1956), 12.

31. James Burnham, *The Machiavellians*, 3–26.

32. Thomas Molnar, "Une Théorie des rapports internationaux: Est-elle formulable?" in *Revue européenne des sciences sociales et Cahiers Vilfredo Pareto* 19 (1981), 225–26.

33. Thomas Molnar, *Tiers monde, idéologie, et réalite* (Paris, 1982), 120.

34. James Burnham, *Suicide of the West: An Essay on the Meaning and Destiny of Liberalism* (New York, 1964), especially 163–87.

35. Stephen Kertesz, *The Fate of East Central Europe* (Notre Dame, 1956), 2–6.

36. See Thomas Molnar, *Le socialisme sans visage* (Paris, 1976); and the exchange of opinions concerning Molnar's work in *Continuity* 3 (Fall 1981), 77–90.

37. Friedrich Meinecke, *Das Weltbürgertum und der Nationalstaat*, ed. Hans Herzfeld (Munich, 1962), 240; and Hegel, *Werke*, 7:503.

38. See my comment on this subject, "History or Hysteria," *The Alternative: An American Spectator* 8 (January 1975), 16–18.

39. Stefan Possony, *Lenin: The Compulsive Revolutionary* (Chicago 1964), 162.

40. Thomas Molnar, *Le modèle défiguré* (Paris, 1978), 78. See David Levy's "Tribute to Thomas Molnar" in *Modern Age* 26, no. 3/4 (Summer/Fall 1982), 290.

41. Among the critical responses to the elitist spirit and scorn for democratic idealism present in *The Machiavellians* were Reinhold Niebuhr, "Study in Cynicism," *Nation* 156 (1 May 1943), 636–38; and Malcolm Cowley, "The Newest Machiavellian," *New Republic* 108 (17 May 1943), 673. Burnham avowed his "deep admiration" for Gentile in a conversation with me on 5 August 1981. Because of his frail health at that time, I made no attempt to pursue the topic.

42. John P. Diggins, *Up from Communism*, 335–37.

43. Paul Gottfried, "The Scholarship That Failed," *The Alternative: An American Spectator* 9 (April 1976), 34–36.

44. James Burnham, *Containment or Liberation? An Inquiry into the Aims of United States Foreign Policy* (New York, 1953), 211–18. See also Raymond Aron's "Postface" to James Burnham, *Contenir ou libérer?*, trans. Helene Claireau (Paris, 1953), 275–323.

45. James Burnham, *The Struggle for the World* (New York, 1947), 215–48.

46. Ibid., 53.

47. Ibid., 132.

48. See Nash, *The Conservative Intellectual Movement in America since 1945, 78–81.*

49. Frank Meyer, *In Defense of Freedom: A Conservative Credo* (Chicago, 1962), 40–63, 127–37.

50. Ibid., 8.

51. See Stefan Possony's contribution to the volume cited previously, 188–210, which emphasizes martial virtue and the importance of the American nation in arms. Although Possony attacks socialist planning for its inefficiency, he views the free market only as an "*instrumental good*" for increasing the material base of the American people.

52. Jeffrey Hart, *When the Going Was Good!*, 292–94. Hart describes Rosenstock-Huessy as "the most influential professor at Dartmouth College during the fifties." In typical Hegelian fashion, this refugee professor told his class: "Lincoln did not know the result of freeing the slaves. But he changed history. When men do what is demanded of them, the results surround us."

53. See Eugen Rosenstock-Huessy, *Out of Revolution: Autobiography of Western Man* (New York, 1938), 560.

54. Cited in Radkau, *Die deutsche Emigration in den U.S.A.*, 263.

## CHAPTER 6

1. Quoted in *National Review*, 17 April 1981, 402.

2. See Frank S. Meyer, "Freedom, Tradition, Conservatism" in *What is Conservatism?* ed. Frank S. Meyer (New York, 1964), 15.

3. Ibid., 15–16.

4. Ibid., 17–19.

5. Most of the citations from Meyer's work in this chapter can be easily located in the anthology of his writings, *The Conservative Mainstream* (New Rochelle, 1969). Parenthetical references in the text are to that book.

6. See George Nash, *The Conservative Intellectual Movement in America since 1945* (New York, 1976), 175–76.

7. Elsie Meyer (Mrs. Frank Meyer) in a letter to the author, 14 February 1974.

8. See Eric Voegelin, *Order and History*, vol. I. *Israel and Revelation* (Baton Rouge, 1956), 1–13, 388–515; and vol. 2, *The World of the Polis* (Baton Rouge, 1957), 1–25.

9. Voegelin, *Order and History*, 1:134–45; 2: 263–77.

10. See Eric Voegelin, *Science, Politics and Gnosticism*, trans. W. J. Fitzpatrick (Chicago, 1968), 3–51.

11. Voegelin uses the Platonic term μέθεξις to describe human participation in the ground of being. Like Plato and the Neo-Platonists, he stresses the "in-between" situation (μεταξύ) of the philosopher mystic who tried to mediate between the human and the divine.

12. Voegelin's view of Christian "soteriological truth" in relation to earlier Hebrew prophecy and Greek philosophy may be pieced together from a number of his writings. His most comprehensive statement on the subject is his letter to the German phenomenologist Alfred Schütz (dated 1 January 1953) in which he presents Christian truth as a precondition for philosophizing in the modern era. Voegelin alludes in this letter to his assertion in *The New Science of Politics: An Introduction* (Chicago, 1952), 76–79, that Christian "soteriological.truth" provides a fuller understanding of the ground of being than did the compact myths of the cosmological empires or even the differentiated "anthropological type of truth" in Greek philosophy. Christianity, by grasping both the "in-betweenness" of the human condition and the transcendence of God, represents a higher level of consciousness than earlier attempts to understand the ground of being.

In *The New Science of Politics*, 164, Voegelin also observes that "in the Mediterranean civilizational area this evolution [of pneumatic experience] culminated in the maximum of differentiation through the revelation of the logos in history." All the preceding levels of consciousness in ancient Mediterranean civilizations were only stages leading to the Christian experience of transcendence. By contrast, a modern, gnostic civilization belongs to the downward part of the spiral of consciousness that has moved back from a more advanced to a less differentiated level of truth.

In his letter to Schütz, Voegelin, referring to his assertions in *The New Science of Politics* about "degrees in the differentiation of experience," presents Christianity as a richer type of truth than Classical philosophy. Although it may still be "possible to philosophize without Christianity," the modern philosopher, he thinks, would be foolish "to base his interpretation on the more compact [pre-Christian] types of experience while ignoring differentiation. . . ." See the copy of the letter to Schütz cited previously in *The Philosophy of Order*, ed. Peter J. Opitz and Gregor Sebba (Stuttgart, 1981), 450.

Despite the apologetic elements of this letter, Harold Weatherby, Bruce Douglass, and other Christian critics of Voegelin have properly noted his highly ambiguous attitude toward the New Testament. Since the publication of *Die politischen Religionen* (Vienna, 1938), Voegelin has explored the connection between Christian revelation and the eschatological nature of modern political religions. In *The New Science of Politics* he plots the development of gnostic myths into revolutionary ideologies. He traces gnostic influences back to the New Testament even while locating them also in post-Christian political religions. In his letter to Schütz, *The Philosophy of Order*, 453, Voegelin makes a key distinction between "essential Christianity and the gnostic and eschatological components." The essential Christianity that he recommends is predominantly a combination of Thomistic theology and Aristotelian ethics.

Voegelin defends Christian doctrines not as historically true but as symbolically appropriate. He upholds the divinity of Jesus for "clearing up" the pagan practice of acknowledging multiple epiphanies: the Christian mediator was "not the incarnation of a god but was God. . . ." Moreover, "just as Christ marks the end of the gods, Mary marks the end of the superhuman vessels of the divine. In both instances the symbolism restores the balance between man's splendor and possibilities and his limitations."

Although Voegelin does defend the symbolism, if not facticity, of Christian dogma, it is also clear that he sees the early church, in opposition to the high medieval one, as a hotbed of gnostic speculation. In reviewing *Order and History*, volume 4, Gerhart Niemeyer complains that Voegelin's treatment of Christianity is "deeply disappointing." See "Eric Voegelin's Philosophy and the Drama of Mankind," *Modern Age* 20 (1976), 34–45. One might add that Voegelin's defense of Christianity, in contrast to his remarks on Platonism, has grown steadily more perfunctory over the last twenty years. See Harold Weatherby, "Myth, Fact, and History: Voegelin on Christianity," *Modern Age* 22 (1978), 144–51; and Bruce Douglass, "A Diminished Gospel: A Critique of Voegelin's Interpretation of Christianity," in *Eric Voegelin's Search for Order and History*, ed. Stephen A. McKnight (Baton Rouge, 1978), 139–54.

13. Hegel asserted that although Christianity developed the principle of individuality, partly out of "the Jewish yearning for inwardness," the ancient world was incapable of overcoming "the cleavage between the inwardness of the heart and existence." Indeed "the completion of this task was left to other peoples, the Germanic ones." See G. W. F. Hegel, *Werke in zwanzig Bänden* (Frankfurt, 1970), 12:387–404 pasim.

14. Frank S. Meyer, *The Moulding of Communists: The Training of the Communist Cadre* (New York, 1961), 25.

15. Ibid., 58.

16. James Burnham in conversation with the author, 5 August 1981.

17. Attacks on *The Philosophy of Right* for defending "reactionary" institutions came not only from Marx and the radical *Junghegelianer*, but even from Rudolf Haym, a politically centrist scholar. See, for example, Haym's work *Hegel und seine Zeit* (Berlin, 1857), 371–78.

18. Haym, who refused to believe that Hegel opposed the Reform Bill of 1831 out of conviction, attributed Hegel's stance to "fear and anxiety"; *Hegel und seine Zeit*, 456. This also seems to be more or less what Franz Rosenzweig suggests in his magisterial *Hegel und der Staat,* 2 (Munich, 1920), 220–21. Although Hegel by 1831 was admittedly concerned with political instability, it is hard to see why this concern should lessen his sincerity or the force of his argument against reforming the English parliament. Eric Voegelin states that he had read Hegel on the Reform Act, while still a young man; he had been intellectually impressed despite his reservations about Hegelian philosophy. See *Eric Voegelin's Thought: A Critical Appraisal*, ed. Ellis Sandoz (Durham, N.C., 1982), 192.

19. See Frank S. Meyer, "The Negro Revolution," *National Review*, 18 June 1963, 496; and "Showdown with Insurrection," *National Review*, 16 January 1968, 36.

20. *What Is Conservatism?*, 10.

21. Ibid., 12.

22. John P. Diggins, *Up from Communism* (New York, 1975), 448.

23. Max Eastman, "Am I a Conservative?" *National Review* 28 January 1964, 57.

24. Frank S. Meyer, "The Twisted Tree of Liberty," *National Review*, 16 January 1962, 26.

25. Frank S. Meyer, "Why Freedom?" *National Review*, 25 September 1962, 225.

26. Russell Kirk raised these questions in conversation with the author, 21 August 1970.

27. Eric Voegelin, *Science, Politics and Gnosticism*, vi–vii and 53–73.

28. Eric Voegelin, "On Hegel: A Study in Sorcery," *Studium Generale* 24 (1971), 335–45.

29. Ibid., 350–60.

30. See Eric Voegelin's comments on his discovery of the Neo-Platonic roots of the Hegelian dialectic in Sandoz, ed., *Eric Voegelin's Thought*, 192–94.

31. See Walther Beierwaltes, *Proklos. Grundzüge seiner Metaphysik* (Frankfurt, 1965), 92–98; Franco Chiereghin, *Hegel e la metafisica classica* (Padua, 1966); and my "Hegel and Proclus: Remarks on a Problematic Relationship," *Thought* 56 (September 1981), 263–71.

32. Helmut Kuhn, "Periodizität und Teleologie in der Geschichte," in *The Philosophy of Order: Essays in History, Consciousness, and Politics*, ed. Peter J. Opitz and Gregor Sebba (Stutgart, 1981), 300.

33. Thomas Altizer's provocative comment, made in the context of a review essay of *Order and History*, vol. *4, The Ecumenic Age*, appears in Sandoz, ed. *Eric Voegelin's Thought*, 186.

34. Ibid., 192.

35. Moses Hadas, review of *Order and History*, vols. 1, 2, and 3, in *Journal of the History of Ideas* 19 (June 1958), 442.

36. Stanley Rosen, review of *Order and History*, vols. 2 and 3, in *Review of Metaphysics* 12 (December 1958), 258.

37. Ibid., 276. A less comprehensive overview of *Order and History*, vols. 2 and 3, and one whose critical thrust coincides with Rosen's, is A. H. Chroust, "Review: The World of the Polis," *Thomist* 21 (1958), 381–91.

38. See H. J. Muller's review of *Order and History*, vol. 1, in *New Republic*, 29 October 1956, 19.

39. See Gerhart Niemeyer, "The Order of History and the History of Order," *Review of Politics* 19 (1957), 403–7; and Niemeyer, "The Depth and Height of Political Order," *Review of Politics* 21 (1958), 588–96.

40. In his response to Altizer (see note 25), Voegelin relates how he came to understand the "experiential premises" of Hegel's philosophy by reading Ferdinand Christian Baur's *Die christliche Gnosis* (Tübingen, 1835). Although the concluding chapter of that work acclaims Schelling as well as Hegel as a latter-day Christian gnostic, Baur's views on Schelling obviously impressed the young Voegelin far less than did his judgment of Hegel.

41. See Eric Voegelin, *Anamnesis. Zur Theorie der Geschichte und Politik* (Munich, 1966), 50–51.

42. Voegelin's most detailed critique of phenomenology in general, but more particularly of Edmund Husserl, is in his letter to Alfred Schütz of 17 September 1943. Voegelin here criticizes Husserl not only for the scientific claims that he makes for his investigative method, but also for imagining that a reconstruction of civilization would take place under a "phenomenological dispensation." Voegelin, who had read Husserl's essay-speech "On the Crisis of the European Sciences," thought that he found in this pep-talk, produced in the shadow of Nazi tyranny, the political aims of Husserl's movement. See Voegelin, *Anamnesis*, 21–37.

43. Ibid., 53.

44. Ibid., 54.

45. See Heinrich Knittenmayr, *Schelling und die romantische Schule* (Munich, 1929), especially 357–441.

46. See Erich Kaufmann, *Studien zur Staatslehre des monarchischen Prinzips* (Leipzig, 1906), 54; and my *Conservative Millenarians*, 114–16, 149–50.

47. Schelling's last published work, *The Philosophy of Revelation*, combines mystical intuitionism with a premonition of the approaching end of secular history. For a meticulous study of this phase of Schelling's work, see Horst Fuhrman, *Schellings Spätphilosophie* (Düsseldorf, 1940).

48. Quoted in Sandoz, ed., *Eric Voegelin's Thought*, 68. Gebhardt here cites an unpublished manuscript of Voegelin's.

49. Ibid. See also Gebhardt's remarks on Schelling in the essay "Erfahrung und Wirklichkeit. Anmerkungen zur politischen Wissenschaft der spirituellen Realisten," in Opitz and Sebba, eds., *The Philosophy of Order*, 341.

50. Quoted in Sandoz, ed., *Eric Voegelin's Thought*, 68.

51. Eric Voegelin, *The New Science of Politics* (Chicago, 1952), 1.

52. Eric Voegelin, "Das Sollen im System Kants," in *Untersuchungen zur reinen Rechtslehre. Festschrift für Hans Kelsen zum 50 sten Geburtstag*, ed. Alfred Verdress (Vienna, 1931), 152.

53. The German words *Aufschluss* and *aufschliessen*, like the Greek *anoiksia* and *anoignunai*, mean both "opening up" and "disclosing." Because of their dual meaning, these terms have been useful to analysts of the structure of being.

54. Ibid., 165.

55. Despite the obtrusive Marxist bias of his treatment of post-Hegelian German philosophy, Herbert Marcuse accurately depicts the magnitude of Schelling's falling out with Hegel in *Reason and Revolution*, 323–27. Marcuse describes the way in which Schelling, starting with his *Munich Lectures* in 1826, backed into a defense of English empiricism as a reaction against "systematic-rationalist" thinking such as Hegel's. Exactly the same tendency can be found in Voegelin, who has reactively defended both English empiricism and American pragmatism. See, for example, Voegelin's autobiographical remarks in *Modern Age* 26 (Summer/Fall 1982), 332.

56. Verdress, ed. *Untersuchungen zur reinen Rechtslehre*, 159.

57. Voegelin challenges the statement cited previously from Kant's *Critique of Practical Reason*. See Jürgen Gebhardt's remarks, in Opit and Sebba, eds., *The Philosophy of Order*, 342–44, on Voegelin's critical reaction to Kant's treatment of ethical imperatives in isolation from the phenomenal world.

58. See Eric Voegelin, "Immortality: Experience and Symbol," *Harvard Theological Review* 60 (July 1967), 235–79.

59. The Pauline experience of repentance *(metagnoia)* involved a correspondingly more dramatic conversion than the Platonic "turning about *[periagoge]*" or the Hebrew prophetic appeal for a national return to piety *(tshuvah)*.

60. Voegelin, *Order and History*, vol. 4, *The Ecumenic Age*, 267.

61. For the translated text of this letter, see Opitz and Sebba, eds., *The Philosophy of Order*, 449–57.

62. In the sense that Voegelin conceives of the possibility, and even probability, of backsliding from a higher to a lower level of religious consciousness within the same civilization, his view of cumulative spiritual advance is less mechanistic than Hegel's.

63. *Order and History*, vol. 4, *The Ecumenic Age*, 267.

64. Quoted from the description of the elder Schelling during his teaching years in Berlin, in Friedrich Heer, *Europa: Mutter der Revolutionen* (Stuttgart, 1967), 179.

65. Voegelin, *Science, Politics, and Gnosticism*, 105.

66. The portrayal of Voegelin as neomedieval and philosophically Teutonophobic can be found in the writings of Thomas Molnar and of other Catholic (and Anglo-Catholic) interpreters. David Levy, in *Realism* (Atlantic Highlands, N.J. 1981), claims Voegelin for his cause in a critical confrontation with German thought from Luther to

Kant and Hegel. See also my review of Levy's book in *Modern Age* 26 (Summer/Fall 1982), 415–418.

67. By selecting this model, which Meyer discovered in Voegelin and Wittfogel, the author of *Order and History* was opting against Schelling's view of history. Unlike Hegel and Voegelin, Schelling profoundly admired the ancient Egyptians, Indians, and Babylonians as the creators of religious mythologies. Schelling followed other European romantics, such as Friedrich Schlegel and Joseph de Maistre, in associating the oldest civilizations with the deepest and most immediate awareness of God. Despite his usual predilection for Schelling over Hegel, Voegelin adapted an explicitly Hegelian scheme of progress in the way that he plotted the cultural background of the emergence of consciousness.

68. *Anamnesis*, 299.

69. Thomas Molnar, *Christian Humanism* (Chicago, 1978), 34.

## CHAPTER 7

1. See Robert Nisbet, *History of the Idea of Progress* (New York, 1980).

2. Stephen Tonsor in conversation with the author on 15 April 1977.

3. In reading Jeffrey Hart's *American Dissent*, I am struck by its emphasis on the nonutilitarian, antimaterialist outlook of most of the founding generation of the postwar conservative intellectual movement.

4. When Adam Meyerson assumed the editorship of *Policy Review*, the Heritage Foundation's quarterly, on 9 August 1983, he wrote to me of his resolve to remove "theoretical questions" entirely from his journal. In view of the thematic preferences of his predecessor, John O'Sullivan, and the policy interests of Heritage Foundation, Meyerson's decision is unlikely to shock either his readers or his employers.

5. In speaking to a Washington gathering of the supporters of the Intercollegiate Studies Institute on 30 September 1983, E. Victor Milione, its president, reaffirmed the commitment of his group to expounding the "moral philosophical" principles of the West.

6. See my "European Roots of American Conservatism" *Modern Age* 26 (Summer/Fall 1982), 303.

7. See Hans Meyerhoff, *The Philosophy of History in Our Time* (Garden City, N.Y., 1959); and Karl Löwith, *Meaning in History: The Theological Implications of the Philosophy of History* (Chicago, 1957), particularly 182–207.

8. See the exposition of Voegelin's thought in Ellis Sandoz's *The Voegelinian Revolution: A Biographical Introduction* (Baton Rouge, 1981). Although Sandoz recognizes the changing and eclectic character of Voegelin's historical speculation, he nonetheless accepts his invectives against Hegel perhaps too much at face value. A more original study of the German background of Voegelin's conceptions about order and history is Eugene Webb, *Eric Voegelin: Philosopher of History* (Seattle, 1981).

9. Leo Strauss, *What Is Political Philosophy?* (Glencoe, Ill., 1957), 57.

10. Ibid., 58.

11. Ibid., 60.

12. Most modern intellectuals are egalitarian, secular materialists (as Strauss also observed); yet if one grants the accuracy of these predicates, one can hardly call intel-

lectuals value relativists. For a discussion of this topic and of other related ones, see Alisdair C. MacIntyre, *After Virtue* (Notre Dame, 1981).

13. See *Six Essays by Leo Strauss,* ed. Hilail Gildin (Indianapolis, 1975), 138.

14. Leo Strauss, *Natural Right and History* (Chicago: Phoenix Edition, 1965), 219–29, 248–51.

15. Ibid., 264–94.

16. Ibid., 318–19.

17. Ibid., 318.

18. See Francis Canavan's essay on Edmund Burke in *History of Political Philosophy,* ed. Leo Strauss and Joseph Cropsey (Chicago, 1963), 619.

19. Strauss, *Natural Right and History,* 313–14.

20. This assessment of Burke's "Thoughts on French Affairs" comes from Matthew Arnold's "The Function of Criticism at the Present Time," which is available in *Criticism: The Major Texts,* ed. W. J. Bate (New York, 1952), 456–57.

21. See *Works of Edmund Burke,* 4 (Boston, 1904): 377.

22. Aristotle, *Ars Rhetorica,* Oxford Classical Text (Oxford, 1959), 1360a. 35–36.

23. Paul Pédech, *La méthode historique de Polybe* (Paris, 1964), 33–52, 54–98.

24. Plutarch's phrase was τὸ ἱστορικὸν ἀποδεικτικὸν ἔχοντα, which he contrasted with words that delighted without instructing the listener.

25. Polybius, *Historiae,* Teubner Edition (Stuttgart, 1962), 2.56.11.

26. Strauss, *Natural Right and History,* 322.

27. Ibid., 321. One link between Polybius and Cicero was Polybius's disciple Panaetius, whom the great Roman orator studied with obvious admiration. The ideal of a Stoicized republican virtue that Polybius identified with Publius Scipio, hero of the Second Punic War (see *Historiae,* 23.14.1–12), was given a more systematic treatment in Panaetius's ethical tract, περὶ τοῦ καθήκοντος. Panaetius, who praised the manner in which Polybius taught the adopted grandson of Publius Scipio (Africanus), Scipio Aemilianus, to be "an active and judicious man [ ἀνήρ πραγματικὸς καὶ νουνεχὴς]" helped to establish a Roman ethical typology operative in both Cicero's *De Officiis* and Titus Livy's *Exemplarēs Virtutis.* In this connection, see M. Pohlenz, "Antikes Führertum, Cicero's *de officiis* und das Lebensideal des Panaitios," *Neue Wege zur Antike* 2, no. 3 (Leipzig, 1934), 110.

28. Polybius, *Historiae,* 6.49.50.

29. Ibid., 6.56.7.

30. Ibid., 6.56.17

31. Ibid., 6.53.55.

32. Ibid., 7.8.9.

33. "ὥσπερ γὰρ οὐδὲ τῶν τεχνιτῶν ἤ τῶν ἀθλητῶν τοὺς γε μὴ νενημένους ἤ σεσωμασκηκότας παρίεμεν εἰς τοὺς ἀθλητικοὺς ἀγῶνας οὕτως οὐδὲ ταύτην χρὴ παραγάγειν εἰς τὴν τῶν πρωτείων ἅμιλλαν ἐὰν μὴ πρότερον ἐπιδείξηται τι τῶν ἑαυτῆς ἔργων ἀληθινῶς."

34. Ibid., 6. 47. 8. The parallel drawn between Socrates' views as expressed in *Euthyphro* and the teachings of *Natural Right and History* should not be carried too far. Although Socrates, like Strauss, disparages "conventional" notions of piety, he also tries to salvage "holiness [ὁσιότης]" as part of an extended concept of justice. Strauss, by contrast,

belabors the distinction between the customary and the ancestral, on the one side, and the rational and the philosophical, on the other. See *Natural Right and History*, 82–108. Strauss's collaborator in organizing *History of Political Philosophy*, Joseph Cropsey, makes, at least for a putative conservative, an utterly shocking statement in *Political Philosophy and the Issue of Politics* (Chicago, 1977), 117–18. According to Cropsey, "If conservatism is respectful of the conventional, the artificial, and the traditional, it may be said to that extent to abjure nature and reason."

35. Gadamer, who is deeply influenced by Hegel's *Phenomenology*, views textual hermeneutics as an ongoing and self-transcending process. See H. G. Gadamer, *Wahrheit und Methode. Grundzüge emer philosophischen Hermeneutik* (Tübingen, 1960), and David E. Linge's introductory essay to an English edition of some of Gadamer's essays, *Philosophical Hermeneutics* (Berkeley, 1976), xi–lvi.

36. See Claes G. Ryn, "Knowledge and History," *Journal of Politics* 44 (1982), 400.

37. Ibid., 403–4. Claes G. Ryn treats the same theme, inter alia, in elaborating his neo-Aristotelian understanding of the state in *Democracy and the Ethical Life* (Baton Rouge, La., 1978).

38. See Eugene F. Miller, "On Rules of Philosophic Interpretation: A Critique of Ryn's 'Knowledge and History,'" *Journal of Politics* 44 (1982), 416.

39. Ibid., 414.

40. An excellent defense of the methodological historicism that developed among eighteenth- and nineteenth-century historians is Hans Meyerhoff's introductory essay to *The Philosophy of History in Our Time*, 1–25.

41. The quest for the esoteric core of political philosophical texts is an essential element of the Straussian method and is followed by Strauss himself in, among other works, *Persecution and the Art of Writing* (Glencoe, Ill., 1952).

42. It should be stressed that I am not denying that political authors, faced by the possibility of persecution or swayed by their own sense of tact, have not tried to address themselves simultaneously to more than one group of readers. The difficulty of Straussian hermeneutics, however, is that it creates what I think is the irresistible temptation to allow the interpreter, in the name of rediscovering hidden truths, to father his own views upon earlier thinkers. For a telling discussion of Straussian methodology, which unfortunately does not raise the preceding point, see Claes G. Ryn, "Strauss and Knowledge: A Rejoinder," *Journal of Politics* 44 (1982), 420–25.

43. I am referring to a work in progress by Morton J. Fisch of Northern Illinois University.

44. See, for example, Harvey Mansfield, Jr., *The Spirit of Liberalism* (Cambridge, Mass., 1979); and Martin Diamond, "The Federalist," in *American Political Thought: The Philosophic Dimension of American Statesmanship*, ed. M. J. Frisch and R. G. Stevens (New York, 1973), 51–70.

45. George F. Will's latest book, *Statecraft as Soulcraft: What Government Does* (New York, 1983), 23–29 and 94–95, retraces the same stages that Strauss included in his picture of the "crisis of modernity." Will also laments the lowering of the West's moral horizons that accompanied the movement from Aristotelian political theory to the "political science" of Machiavelli and Hobbes. Like Strauss but unlike most Straussians, Will takes a dim view of Lockean materialism. He departs from the whole Straussian school, however, in recommending Burke as a better guide for the present age than

Locke. James Nuechterlein, "George Will and American Conservatism," *Commentary* 76 (October 1983), 35–43, attempts to defend both American acquisitiveness and American pluralism in a perceptive neoconservative critique of Will's "Toryism."

46. This question, which is partly rhetorical, is taken from Thomas Molnar's note in *Continuity* 7 (Fall 1983).

47. Russell Kirk, "Burke and the Principle of Order," *Sewanee Review* (April 1952), 14.

48. Russell Kirk, *The Conservative Mind* (Chicago, 1953), 6–7.

49. See Henry Paolucci, *A Separate and Equal Station: Hegel, America, and the Nation State System* (New York, 1978). Although Paolucci is the most explicitly Hegelian post-war conservative, I can find no evidence of his influence on others whom I treat in this work.

50. For an implicit defense of Ryn's historicism done by one of his disciples, see W. Wesley McDonald, "Reason, Natural Law and Moral Imagination in the Thought of Russell Kirk," *Modern Age* 27 (Winter 1983), 15–24.

51. Claes G. Ryn, "American Intellectual Conservatism: Needs, Opportunities, Prospects," *Modern Age* 26 (Summer/Fall 1982), 311.

52. See, for example, Stephen J. Tonsor, "Myth, History and Desacralized Time," *Continuity* 45 (Summer/Fall 1982), 11–19. Although Tonsor in this essay is sharply critical of Ranke for compartmentalizing, and inadvertently secularizing, *die Weltgeschichte*, his own position is almost Hegelian in terms of its insistence on seeing History as the march of Providence.

53. See John Lukacs, *Historical Consciousness* (New York, 1968), 268; and Lee Congdon, "History as Personal Knowledge: John Lukacs and His Work," *Continuity* 3 (Fall 1981), 63–75.

54. Lee Congdon has called my attention to the intriguing comparison made between Lukacs and the existential historicist (and Straussian bête noire) Martin Heidegger in George J. Stack, "The Phenomenon of Historical Consciousness," *Man and World* 2 (November 1969), 626–36.

55. The author in conversation with Grady McWhiney, a former officer of the Southern Historical Association, on 18 November 1980.

56. See *Newsweek*, 10 August 1981.

57. See Clyde Wilson, "American Historians and Their History," *Continuity* 6 (Spring 1983), 1–16.

58. See *I'll Take My Stand* (New York: Harper Torchbook Edition, 1960), particularly Stark Young's "Not in Memoriam but in Defense," 328–60, and Virginia Rock's concluding notes, "The Twelve Southerners: Biographical Essays," 361–85. See also Andrew Lytle, "They Took Their Stand: The Agrarian View after Fifty Years," *Modern Age* 24 (Spring 1980), 114–20.

59. See M. E. Bradford, *A Better Guide Than Reason: Studies on the American Revolution* (LaSalle, Ill., 1972), 3–29.

60. For research data on the politics of American liberal arts faculty, see Everett Carll Ladd and Seymour Martin Lipset, *The Divided Academy: Professor and Politics* (New York, 1975).

61. The connection between the sense of American exceptionalism and the American individualist ethic on the one side, and the rejection of historicism on the other, is treated in John Lukacs, *Passing of the Modern Age* (New York, 1970).

62. Engels, in his *Outline of a Critique of National Economy* in 1844, forcefully identified Protestant ethics with financial manipulation and moral hypocrisy. He interpreted the transition from a Catholic mercantile to a Protestant liberal economy as being a victory for "Protestant duplicity *[Gleisnerei]*" over "Catholic integrity *[Geradheit]*." Engels praised the mercantilists (whom he associated with an older Catholic society) for openly acknowledging the inevitability of commercial competition by excluding foreign imports and traders. By contrast, the Protestant defenders of free trade, such as the "economic Luther," Adam Smith, ascribed fictitious moral value to commerce while denying the necessary savagery of a capitalist economy. See *Marx-Engels Studienausgabe*, vol. 2, ed. Irving Fetscher (Frankfurt, 1975), 16–17; and Marx's contemptuous references in *Economic-Philosophical Manuscripts* to the "ascetic but usurious skinflint," whom he presents as the archetypal industrial capitalist *(Marx-Engels Studiensausgabe*, 2:112).

63. Nash has performed the further scholarly service of reminding a gathering of predominantly southern and Burkean conservatives (in February 1983) of the modernist element in American conservatism. By emphasizing the historical commitment of this movement to mobility, material progress, and the Protestant work ethic, Nash underscored its distance from two other forces, the corporatist, clericalist, and feudal European Right of the nineteenth century and the anti-industrial, redistributionist contemporary Left.

64. See George H. Nash, *The Life of Herbert Hoover: The Engineer, 1874–1914* (New York, 1983), 568–76. In an address in Iowa City, Iowa, on 1 November 1983 sponsored by the Herbert Hoover Presidential Library Association, Nash stressed Hoover's view of America as being unique because of its commitment to social mobility.

65. *The Life of Herbert Hoover*, 1–51.

66. Among a group of prominent young conservative and neoconservative publicists interviewed by *American Spectator* 12 (November 1979), 10–20, the majority expressed no particular interest in religion, while defining themselves politically, mostly in terms of budgetary or administrative issues. The fact that the questions did not aim at eliciting statements of moral or religious commitment told something about the journal's lack of spiritual perspective. But the questions asked were obviously congenial to the interviewees, at least one of whom expressed enthusiastic support for the feminist movement.

67. Irving Kristol, "Neoconservatismo," *Razón Española* 7 (October–November 1984), 325.

68. Strauss, *Natural Right and History*, 245.

69. See, for example, Clifford Orwin and Thomas L. Pangle, "Restoring the Human Rights Tradition," *This World* 1 (Fall 1982), 21–41; and William A. Stanmeyer's critical perception of Bern's secularist, utilitarian understanding of religion in "Walter Berns: Philosopher of the First Amendment," *Modern Age* 21 (Fall 1977), 367–75. In a discussion with me on 10 November 1982, Alan Bloom emphasized the "essential decency" of Locke's political thought. He made this defense in responding to a critical remark that Locke's contractual theory of government rested upon the unprovable assumption of Locke's conception of "the state of nature." One of the most bizarre examples of appealing to Locke as a moral court of last resort is Jan H.

Blits, "What's Wrong With Children's Rights?" *This World* 1 (Winter 1984), 5–19. Blits proposes to clarify the question of children's rights by invoking the judgment of John Locke, "one of the principal founders of the modern natural rights tradition." Blits turns for a defense of the family to Locke's "modified form of self-love," identifying those further left than himself as believers in a Hobbesian rather than Lockean world, that is, in a world characterized by strife between parents and children rather than in one marked by the peaceful pursuit of self-interest. Both the affiliations of *This World* and Blits's abstract "natural rights" interpretation of a contemporary American social problem would make his application of second-generation Straussianism seem to be the act of an initiate.

70. See Guy Sorman, *La révolution conservatrice américaine* (Paris, 1983), and the revealing essay by the French anti-Communist social thinker and Collège de France professor, Jean-Marie Benoist, "Généalogie d'une rupture," *Le monde*, 25 August 1983, 2–3. Benoist deals here and in his book *La révolution structurale* (Paris, 1975) with the growing split between Marxist thinking and Marxist political loyalties and the post-1950s French intelligentsia. Benoist identifies *"la cité démocratique,"* in its struggle against Communism, with "the rejection of statism, a liberal constitution, and the vindication of free trade and pluralism."

71. See Alain de Benoist, *Orientations pour des années décisives* (Paris, 1982), 56.

72. Ibid., 69.

73. Ibid., 73.

74. See Alain de Benoist, *Les idées à l'endroit* (Paris, 1979), 115, and *Les Indo-Européens* (Paris, 1966).

75. On the problematic nature of America's "liberal" conservatism, see John Lukacs, *Outgrowing Democracy: A History of the United States in the Twentieth Century* (Garden City, N. Y., 1984), 327–67.

76. Russell Kirk, *The Roots of American Order* (LaSalle, Ill., 1974), especially 441–76.

77. See Will, *Statecraft as Soulcraft:* especially 93–96, 127–29.

78. Edmund Burke, *Reflections on the Revolution in France*, ed. C. C. O'Brien (Baltimore, 1969), 194–95.

79. Ibid., 173.

80. See Bradford, *A Better Guide Than Reason*, and Jeffrey Hart's introduction to Bradford's essays, ix–xxi.

81. See Will Herberg, *Judaism and Modern Man* (New York, 1973), 300.

82. Harry V. Jaffa, "Equality as a Conservative Principle," *Loyola of Los Angeles Law Review* 8 (June 1975), 475.

83. Mircea Eliade, *Mythes, rêves et mystères* (Paris, 1957), 21.

84. See my "Mircea Eliade und die Mythen der Moderne," in *Mircea-Eliade Festschrift*, ed. Hans-Joachim Duerr (Heidelberg, 1984).

85. See Strauss, *Natural Right and History*, 253, 320–21; and Paul Norton, "Leo Strauss: His Critique of Historicism," *Modern Age* 25 (Spring 1981), 143–54.

86. See H. Y. Jung, "Two Critics of Scientism: Leo Strauss and Edmund Husserl," *International Journal of Philosophy* 2 (1978), 86–88; and V. Gourevitch, "Philosophy and Politics," *Review of Metaphysics* 22 (1968–1969), 235–37.

87. Eric Voegelin, *From Enlightenment to Revolution*, ed. J. H. Hollowell (Durham, N.C., 1975).

88. An essay that suggests and even defends the historicist origin of American and European conservatism is Vigen Guroian, "Natural Law and Historicity: Burke and Niebuhr," *Modern Age* 25 (Spring 1981), 162–73.

89. See F. A. Hayek, "Our Moral Heritage," *Heritage Lectures* 24 (Washington, D.C., 1983), 4.

90. Kirk made this point about the evolution of his thinking on Burke in the introductory address at a conference on Irving Babbitt at Catholic University of America on 18 November 1983. His remarks on Babbitt and Burke are now part of an anthology, edited by Claes G. Ryn and George A. Panichas, in press with the Catholic University of America.

91. Thomas Copeland, "The Reputation of Edmund Burke," *Journal of British Studies*, May 1962, 89–90; see also Carl B. Cone, "The Burke Revival," *Burke Newsletter* 3 (Winter–Spring 1961–1962), 81.

92. *The Philosophy of Bertrand Russell*, ed. P. A. Schilpp (Evanston, Ill., 1944), 12.

93. See, for example, W. T. Harris, "The Right to Property and the Ownership of Land," *Journal of Social Science* 12 (1886); and "Review of Hegel's *Philosophy of Right,*" *Philosophical Review* 6 (May 1897), 288–93.

94. Although certainly not *all* historiography produced by conservatives is aimed at refuting the Left, almost all significant historical writing done by recognizably conservative authors in recent years has been critical by intent. Much of the work of Forrest McDonald, America's most prominent self-acknowledged conservative historian, is polemical even when it purports to be biographical. The first five issues of *Continuity*, a conservative historical journal, bristle with arguments against "establishment" and leftist historians; and one of the historical works most touted in journals of the Right in 1983 was Thomas B. Silver, *Coolidge and the Historians* (Durham, N.C., 1983), a spirited rebuttal of the denigration of Calvin Coolidge by Arthur Schlesinger and other liberal historians. For conservative historians, the problem of how to move from polemics to alternative interpretations remains. Producing refutations may be a necessary precondition for evacuating intellectual debris, but it is only a point of departure, not even a provisional resting place, for understanding the past.

95. John Lukacs, *Historical Consciousness*, 263.

96. See, for example, Howard Zinn, *A People's History of the United States* (New York, 1980).

97. Sidney Hook, *The Hero in History* (New York, 1943), 65.

98. Karl Löwith, *From Hegel to Nietzsche: The Revolution in Nineteenth Century Thought*, trans. David E. Green (New York, 1965), 21–26, 45–51.

# BIBLIOGRAPHY

THE FOLLOWING IS A LIST OF SOURCES THAT WERE USED IN PREPARING this book. Comments about many of these works can be found in the footnotes.

Because this book deals with contemporary history and because those who represent the movements discussed are also its interpreters, the bibliography does not distinguish between primary and secondary literature.

## BOOKS

Allmayer, Fazio. *Ricerche hegeliane*. Florence, 1959.

Aristotle. *Ars Rhetorica*. Oxford, 1959.

———. *Politica*. Oxford, 1925.

Babbitt, Irving. *The New Laokoon: An Essay on the Confusion of the Arts*. Boston, 1910.

Benoist, Alain de. *Les idées à l'endroit*. Paris, 1979.

———. *Les Indo-Européens*. Paris, 1966.

———. *Orientations pour des années décisives*. Paris, 1982.

Benson, Lee. *Turner and Beard*. Glencoe, Ill., 1960.

Berlin, Isaiah. *Karl Marx*. 3d ed. Oxford, 1963.

Bernstein, Richard. *John Dewey*. New York, 1966.

Bradford, M. E. *A Better Guide than Reason: Studies on the American Revolution*. LaSalle, Ill., 1979.

Buckley, William F., Jr., ed. *Did You Ever See a Dream Walking? American Conservative Thought in the Twentieth Century*. New York, 1970.

Burke, Edmund. *Reflections on the Revolution in France*. Edited by C. C. O'Brien. Baltimore, 1969.

———. *Works of Edmund Burke*. Vol. 4. Boston, 1904

Burnham, James. *The Machiavellians: Defenders of Freedom*. Chicago, 1963.

———. *Suicide of the West: An Essay on the Meaning and Destiny of Liberalism*. New York, 1964.

Coffey, John. *Political Realism in American Thought*. Lewisburg, Pa., 1977.

Colletti, Lucio. *From Rousseau to Lenin: Studies in Ideology and Society*. Translated by John Merrington and Judith White. London, 1972.

Collingwood, R. G. *The Idea of History*. Oxford, 1962.

Croce, Benedetto. *My Philosophy and Other Essays on the Moral and Political Problems of Our Time*. Translated by E. F. Carritt. London, 1949.

Curti, Merle. *Social Ideas of American Education*. New York, 1935.

Dewey, John. *Experience and Nature*. Chicago, 1925.

———. *Psychology*. Chicago, 1887.

Diggins, John. *Up from Communism*. New York, 1975.

Eastman, Max. *Reflections on the Failure of Socialism*. New York, 1955.

Easton, Lloyd D. *Hegel's First American Followers*. Athens, Ohio, 1966.

Eliade, Mircea. *Mythes, rêves et mystères*. Paris, 1957.

Engels, Friedrich, and Karl Marx. *Marx-Engels Studienausgabe*. Edited by Irving Fetscher. Frankfurt, 1975.

Francis, Samuel T. *Power and History: The Political Thought of James Burnham*. Washington, D. C., 1984.

Friedrich, Carl J. *The Philosophy of Law in Historical Perspective*. Chicago, 1958.

Geiger, Rudolf. "Die Entwicklungstendenzen des Kapitalismus bei Keynes, Schumpeter, und Burnham." Diss., Basel, 1959.

Gentile, Giovanni. *Genesis and Structure of Society*. Translated by H. S. Harris. Urbana, Ill., 1966.

Goetzmann, William H. Introductory essay to *The American Hegelians*, edited by William H. Goetzmann. New York, 1973.

Green, T. H. *Lectures in the Principles of Political Obligation*. London, 1895.

Grob, Gerald N. *Workers and Utopia: A Study of Ideological Conflicts in the American Labor Movement, 1865–1900*. New York, 1961.

Harmon, Frances. *The Social Philosophy of St. Louis Hegelians*. New York, 1943.

Harris, H. S. *Social Philosophy of Giovanni Gentile*. Urbana, Ill., 1960.

Hart, Jeffrey. *The American Dissent*. New York, 1966.

———. *When the Going Was Good! American Life in the Fifties*. New York, 1982.

Hayek, F. A. *The Counter-Revolution of Science: Studies on the Abuse of Reason*. London: Free Press Paperback, 1964.

Heer, Friedrich. *Europa: Mutter der Revolutionen*. Stuttgart, 1967.

Hegel, G. W. F. *Frühe politische Systeme*. Edited by Gerhard Gohler. Frankfurt, 1974.

———*Werke in zwanzig Bänden*. Frankfurt, 1970.

Herberg, Will. *Faith Enacted as History: Essays in Biblical Theology*. Edited by Bernhard W. Anderson. Philadelphia, 1976.

———. *Judaism and Modern Man*. New York, 1973.

———. *Protestant, Catholic, Jew*. Garden City, N. Y., 1959.

Herreshoff, David. *American Disciples of Marx: From the Age of Jackson to the Progressive Era*. Detroit, 1967.

Hobhouse, L. T. *The Metaphysical Theory of the State*. London, 1918.

Hook, Sidney. *From Hegel to Marx: Studies in the Intellectual Development of Karl Marx*. 2d ed. New York, 1950.

———. *The Hero in History: A Study in Limitation and Possibility*. New York, 1943.

————. *John Dewey: An Intellectual Portrait.* 2d ed. Westport, Conn., 1971.

————. *Marxism and Beyond.* Totowa, N.J., 1983.

————. *Toward the Understanding of Karl Marx.* New York, 1933.

Jones, M. E. *George Sylvester Morris: His Philosophical Career and Theistic Idealism.* New York, 1948.

Kirk, Russell. *The Conservative Mind.* Chicago, 1953.

————. *The Roots of American Order.* LaSalle, Ill. 1974.

Kraditor, Aileen S. "Jimmy Higgins: An Exploration of the Mental World of the Rank-and-File Communist, 1930–1958." Unpublished manuscript.

Krupskaya, N. K. *Reminiscences of Lenin.* Translated by Bernard Isaacs. New York, 1970.

Lauer, Quentin. *A Reading of Hegel's Phenomenology of the Spirit.* New York, 1976.

Lenin, V. I. *Quaderni filosofici.* Milan, 1958.

Lenski, Gerhard. *The Religious Factor: A Sociological Study of Religion's Impact on Politics, Economics, and Family Life.* Garden City, N.Y., 1963.

Livingston, Donald W. *Hume's Philosophy of German Life.* Chicago, 1984.

Locke, John. *Two Treatises of Government.* New York, 1963.

Löwith, Karl. *From Hegel to Nietzsche: The Revolution in Nineteenth Century Thought.* Translated by David E. Green. New York, 1965.

————. *Meaning in History: The Theological Implications of the Philosophy of History.* Chicago, 1957.

————. *Von Hegel zu Nietzsche.* Stuttgart, 1950.

Lukács, Georg. *György Lukács Werke.* Neuwied am Rhein, 1962.

————. *Historical Consciousness.* New York, 1968.

————. *Outgrowing Democracy: A History of the United States in the Twentieth Century.* Garden City, N.Y., 1984.

————. *The Young Hegel.* Translated by Rodney Livingston. London, 1975.

Marcuse, Herbert. *Reason and Revolution: Hegel and the Rise of Social Theory.* New York, 1941.

Marx, Karl. *Capital: A Critique of Political Economy.* Translated by Ernest Untermann. New York, 1906.

Meyer, Frank S. *The Conservative Mainstream.* New Rochelle, N.Y., 1969.

————. "Freedom, Tradition, Conservatism." In *What Is Conservatism?* edited by Frank S. Meyer. New York, 1964.

————. *In Defense of Freedom: A Conservative Credo.* Chicago, 1962.

————. *The Moulding of Communists: The Training of the Communist Cadre.* New York, 1961.

Meyerhoff, Hans. *The Philosophy of History in Our Time.* Garden City, N.Y., 1959.

Molnar, Thomas. *Christian Humanism.* Chicago, 1978.

————. *Le dieu immanent: La grande tentation de la pensée allemande.* Paris, 1982.

————. *Le socialisme sans visage.* Paris, 1976.

————. *Theists and Atheists: A Typology of Non-Belief.* The Hague, 1980.

————. *Tiers monde, idéologie, et réalité.* Paris, 1982.

Morgenthau, Hans. *Science: Servant or Master?* New York, 1972.

Morris, James O. *Conflict within the A.F.L.: A Study of Craft vs. Industrialism, 1901–1938.* New York, 1958.

Nash, George H. *The Conservative Intellectual Movement in America Since 1945.* New York, 1976.

————. *The Life of Herbert Hoover: The Engineer, 1874–1914*. New York, 1983.

Neusner, Jacob. *Stranger at Home: The Holocaust, Zionism, and American Judaism*. Chicago, 1981.

Niebuhr, Reinhold. *The Irony of American History*. New York, 1952.

————. *Man's Nature and His Communities*. New York, 1959.

————. *The Nature and Destiny of Man*. One-volume ed. New York, 1947.

————. *The Structure of Nations and Empires*. New York, 1959.

Nisbet, Robert. *History of the Idea of Progress*. New York, 1980.

————. *Tradition and Revolt: Historical and Sociological Essays*. New York, 1970.

Oldrini, Guido. *Augusto Vera e la corrente orthodossa*. Milan, 1964.

————. *Primo hegelismo italiano*. Florence, 1969.

O'Sullivan, N. K. *Conservatism*. New York, 1976.

Ottmann, Henning. *Individuum und Gemeinschaft bei Hegel*. Berlin, 1977.

Paolucci, Henry. *A Separate and Equal Station: Hegel, America, and the Nation State System*. New York, 1978.

Pells, Richard H. *The Liberal Mind in a Conservative Age: American Intellectuals in the 1940s and 1950s*. New York, 1985.

Plenge, Johann. *Marx and Hegel*. Tübingen, 1911.

Polybius. *Historiae*. Teubner Edition, Vol. 2. Stuttgart, 1962.

Popper, Karl. *The Open Society and Its Enemies*. Vol. 2. New York: Harper Torchbook Edition, 1962.

Possony, Stefan. *A Century of Conflict: Communist Techniques of World Revolution, 1849–1950*. Chicago, 1953.

Radkau, Joachim. *Die deutsche Emigration in den U.S.A.: Ihr Einfluss auf die amerikanische Europapolitik 1933–1945*. Dusseldorf, 1971.

Riesman, David. *The Lonely Crowd*. 8th ed. New York, 1958.

Ritter, Joachim. "Subjektivität und industrielle Gesellschaft." In *Subjektivität*. Frankfurt, 1974.

Rosenkranz, Karl. *Hegel als deutscher Nationalphilosoph*. Leipzig, 1870.

Rosenstock-Huessy, Eugen. *Out of Revolution: Autobiography of Western Man*. New York, 1938.

Rossiter, Clinton. *Conservatism in America: The Thankless Persuasion*. New York, 1962.

Ryn, Claes G. *Democracy and the Ethical Life*. Baton Rouge, La., 1978.

————. *Will, Imagination, and Reason*. Chicago, 1985.

Sandoz, Ellis, ed. *Eric Voegelin's Thought: A Critical Appraisal*. Durham, N.C., 1982.

————. *The Voegelian Revolution: A Biographical Introduction*. Baton Rouge, La., 1981.

Schlesinger, Arthur. *The Vital Center*. Boston, 1949.

Snider, Denton J. *Abraham Lincoln*. St. Louis, 1908.

————. *The American Ten Years War*. St. Louis, 1906.

————. *The St. Louis Movement in Philosophy, Literature, Education, Psychology, with Chapters of Autobiography*. St. Louis, 1920.

————. *Social Institutions*. St. Louis, 1901.

Sorman, Guy. *La Révolution conservatrice américaine*. Paris, 1983.

Stanlis, Peter J. *Edmund Burke and the Natural Law*. Ann Arbor, 1965.

Strauss, Leo. *Natural Right and History*. Chicago, Phoenix Books, 1965.

————. *Persecution and the Art of Writing*. Glencoe, Ill., 1952.

————. *Six Essays by Leo Strauss*. Edited by Hilail Gildin. Indianapolis, 1975.

———. *What is Political Philosophy?* Glencoe, Ill., 1957.

Strauz-Hupé. *Protracted Conflict.* New York, Harper Colophon Books, 1963.

Trotsky, Leon. *In Defense of Marxism.* New York, 1973.

Ulam, Adam. *The Unfinished Revolution.* Rev. ed. Boulder, 1979.

Ulmen, G. L. *Society and History: Essays in Honor of Karl August Wittfogel.* The Hague, 1978.

Vera, Augusto. *Essais philosophiques.* Paris, 1864.

———. "La souveraineté du peuple." In *Mélanges philosophiques.* Paris, 1862.

Vogel, Paul. *Hegel's Gesellschaftsbegriff und seine geschichtliche Fortbildung durch Lorenz Stein, Marx, Engels, und Lasalle.* Berlin, 1925.

Voegelin, Eric. *Anamnesis. Zur Theorie der Geschichte und Politik.* Munich, 1966.

———. *The New Science of Politics.* Chicago, 1952.

———. *Order and History, I: Israel and Revelation.* Baton Rouge, La., 1956.

———. *Order and History, II: The World of the Polis.* Baton Rouge, La., 1957.

———. *Science, Politics and Gnosticism.* Translated by W. J. Fitzpatrick. Chicago, 1968.

Webb, Eugene. *Eric Voegelin: Philosopher of History.* Seattle, 1981.

Will, George F. *Statecraft as Soulcraft: What Government Does.* New York, 1983.

Wilson, Edmund. *To the Finland Station.* 2d ed. New York, 1956.

Winter, J. A. *Continuities in the Sociology of Religion.* New York, 1977.

Wittfogel, Karl A. *Oriental Despotism: A Comparative Study of Total Power.* New Haven, 1963.

———. *A Short History of Chinese Communism.* Seattle, 1964.

———. "Wasserbau-bürokratische Regierungen" (Hydraulic-bureaucratic regimes). In *Geschichte der bürgerlichen Gesellschaft.* Vienna, 1924.

———. *Wirschaft und Gesellschaft Chinas.* Leipzig, 1931.

———. *Zur Frage einer marxistischen Ästhetik.* Cologne, 1973.

Zinn, Howard. *A People's History of the United States.* New York, 1980.

## ARTICLES

The following periodicals were extensively used for the topics covered in this book.

*Commentary*
*Continuity*
*Modern Age*
*National Review*
*New Leader*
*New Masses*
*Review of Politics*
*This World*
*Unter dem Banner des Marxismus*
*Workers Age*

Articles of particular usefulness are listed below.

Aronld, Matthew. "The Function of Criticism at the Present Time." In *Criticism: The Major Texts*, edited by W. J. Bate. New York, 1952.

Aron, Rayond. Postface to the French translation of *Containment or Liberation?*

*(Contenir ou libérer?)*, by James Burnham. Paris, 1953.

Burnham, James. "Lenin's Heir." *Partisan Review* 12 (Winter 1945), 63–66, 69.

———. "Selective, Yes. Humanism, Maybe." *National Review,* 12 May 1972.

———. "Sighting the Target." *National Review* 2 (29 December 1956).

Canavan, Francis. "Essay on Edmund Burke." In *History of Political Philosophy,* edited by Leo Strauss and Joseph Cropsey. Chicago, 1963.

Chroust, A. H. "Review: The World of the Polis." *The Thomist* 21 (1958).

Cowley, Malcolm. "The Newest Machiavellian." *New Republic* 108 (17 May 1943).

Dewey, John. "From Absolutism to Experimentalism." In *Contemporary American Philosophy,* edited by G. P. Adams and W. P. Montague, vol. 2. New York, 1930.

Eastman, Max. "Am I a Conservative?" *National Review,* 28 January 1964.

Feuer, Lewis S. "The Pragmatic Wisdom of Sidney Hook." *Encounter* 45 (October 1975).

Gottfried, Paul. "The European Roots of American Conservatism." *Modern Age* 26 (Summer/Fall 1982).

———. "Mircea Eliade und die Mythen der Moderne." In *Mircea-Eliade Festschrift,* edited by Hans-Joachim Duerr. Heidelberg, 1984.

———. "On the European Roots of Modern American Conservatism." *Thought* 55 (June 1980), p. 217.

———. "The Scholarship That Failed." *The Alternative: An American Spectator* 9 (April 1976).

———. "On the Social Implications and Context of the Hegelian Dialectic." *Journal of the History of Ideas* 1, no. 3, (Fall 1980).

Guroian, Vigen. "Natural Law and Historicity: Burke and Niebuhr." *Modern Age* 25 (Spring 1981).

Hadas, Moses. "Review of *Order and History,* Vols. I, II, and III." *Journal of the History of Ideas* 19 (June 1958).

Harris, W. T. "The Definition of Social Science and the Classification of the Topics Belonging to Its Several Provinces." *Journal of Social Science* 22 (June 1887).

———. Editor's note. *Journal of Speculative Philosophy* 1, no. 1, 1867.

Hayek, F. A. "Our Moral Heritage." *Heritage Lectures* 24 (Washington, D.C., 1983).

Herberg, Will. "The Basic Dilemma of Socialism." *Workers Age* 9 (8 June 1940), 4; 9 (15 June 1940), 4; 9 (22 June 1940),4.

———. "The Biblical Basis of American Democracy." *Thought* 30 (Spring 1955).

———. "Civil Rights and Violence." *National Review* 17, no. 36 (7 September 1965).

———. "The Crisis of Socialism." *Jewish Frontier* 12 (September 1945), 22–31.

———. "From Marxism to Judaism." *Commentary* 3 (January 1947).

———. "Historicism as Touchstone." *Christian Century,* 16 March 1969.

———. "Limits of Pluralism." *National Review* 23, no. 7, (23 February 1971).

———. "Natural Law and History in Burke's Thought." *Modern Age* 3, (Summer 1959).

———. "Reinhold Niebuhr: Burkean Conservative." *National Review* 11, no. 22, (2 December 1961).

————. "Theory of Relativity and Dialectical Materialism." *Revolutionary Age* 2 (27 December 1930).

————. "Workers' Democracy or Dictatorship." *Workers Age* 3, (15 December 1934).

Hook, Sidney. "Dialectic in Social and Historical Inquiry." *Journal of Philosophy* 36 (6 July 1939).

————. "Marxism, Metaphysics, and Modern Science." *Modern Quarterly* 4 (May–August 1928), 388–94.

Jaffa, Harry V. "Equality as a Conservative Principle." *Loyola of Los Angeles Law Review* 8 (June 1975).

Kirk, Russell. "Burke and the Principle of Order." *Sewanee Review,* April 1952.

Kuhn, Helmut. "Periodizität und Teleologie in der Geschichte." In *The Philosophy of Order: Essays in History, Consciousness, and Politics,* edited by Peter J. Opitz and Gregor Sebba. Stuttgart, 1981.

Levy, David. "Karl Popper: His Philosophy of Politics." *Modern Age* 23, no. 2, (Spring 1978).

————. "On Being Right: Reality, Utopia, and Tradition." *Continuity* 4/5 (Spring/Fall 1982).

————. "Tribute to Thomas Molnar." *Modern Age* 26, no. 3/4 (Summer/Fall 1982).

McDonald, W. Wesley. "Reason, Natural Law and Moral Imagination in the Thought of Russell Kirk." *Modern Age* 27 (Winter 1983).

Meyer, Frank S. "The Twisted Tree of Liberty." *National Review, 16 January 1962.*

————. "Why Freedom?" *National Review,* 25 September 1962.

Miller, Eugene. "On Rules of Philosophic Interpretation: A Critique of Ryn's 'Knowledge and History'." *Journal of Politics* 44 (1982).

Molnar, Thomas. "Au Coeur du Marxisme: La Dialectique." *La Pensée Catholique,* November 1978.

————. "Une Théorie des rapports internationaux: Est-elle formulable?" *Revue européene des sciences sociales et Cahiers Vilfredo Pareto* 19 (1981).

Morgenthau, Hans. "The Evil of Politics and the Ethics of Evil." *Ethics* 156 (October 1945).

Muller, H. J. "Review of *Order and History,* Vol. I." *New Republic,* 29 October 1956.

Niebuhr, Reinhold. "Study in Cynicism." *Nation* 56 (1 May 1943).

Niemeyer, Gerhart. "The Order of History and the History of Order." *Review of Politics* 19 (1957).

Nuechterlein, James. "George Will and American Conservatism." *Commentary* 76 (October 1983).

Rosen, Stanley. "Review of *Order and History,* Vols. II and III." *Review of Metaphysics* 12 (December 1958).

Ryn, Claes G. "Knowledge and History." *Journal of Politics* 44 (1982).

Schlesinger, Arthur, Jr. "Review of James Burnham's *Struggle for the World.*" *Nation,* April 5, 1947, 398–99.

Stanmeyer, William A. "Walter Berns: Philosopher of the First Amendment." *Modern Age* 21 (Fall 1977).

Tonsor, Stephen J. "Myth, History and Desacralized Time." *Continuity* 45

(Summer/Fall 1982).

Voegelin, Eric. "Das Sollen im System Kants." In *Untersuchungen zur reinen Rechts-lehre: Festschrift für Hans Kelsen zum 50 sten Geburtstag,* edited by Alfred Verdress. Vienna, 1931.

———. "Immortality: Experience and Symbol." *Harvard Theological Review* 60 (July 1967).

———. "On Hegel: A Study in Sorcery." *Studium Generale* 24 (1971).

Wilson, Clyde. "American Historians and Their History." *Continuity* 6 (Spring 1983).

Wittfogel, Karl A. "Karl Marx über China und Indien." *U.B.M.* 1, no. 2 (1927).

———. "Marxism, Anarchism, and the New Left." *Modern Age* 14, no. 2 (Spring 1970).

———. "A Stronger Oriental Despotism." *China Quarterly* 1, (1960).

## OTHER SOURCES

I have made ample use of Will Herberg's letters to me between 1971 and 1974 and of the correspondence between Will Herberg and Peter Stanlis for the years 1964–1974. I also cite letters recieved from Elsie Meyer, Russell Kirk, John Lukacs, and Thomas Molnar and material drawn from meetings with James Burnham, Karl Wittfogel, and Will Herberg.

# INDEX